THE PATH OF

OUTRAGEOUS

LOVE

THE PATH OF OUTRAGEOUS LOVE

THE EMERGENCE OF
HOMO AMOR

. . .

*Towards A Planetary Awakening
In Love Through
Unique Self Symphonies*

One Mountain, Many Paths: Oral Essays

Volume 20

DR. MARC GAFNI AND
BARBARA MARX HUBBARD

Author: Marc Gafni and Barbara Marx Hubbard
Title: The Path of Outrageous Love
Identifiers: ISBN 979-8-88834-027-1 (electronic)
ISBN 979-8-88834–030–1 (paperback)

© 2025 Marc Gafni

Edited by Elena Maslova-Levin, Talya Bloom, and Kathy Brownback

World Philosophy and Religion Press,
St. Johnsbury, VT

in conjunction with

IP Integral Publishers

https://worldphilosophyandreligion.org

JOIN THE REVOLUTION!

CONTENTS

CHAPTER 3 WE ARE THE TIPPING POINT OF THE DIVINE

CHAPTER 4 I AM THE EVOLUTION OF LOVE

CHAPTER 5 ONTOLOGIZING LOVE: LOVE IS REAL

CHAPTER 12   OUTRAGE + LOVE = OUTRAGEOUS LOVE: THE SYNERGY OF SACRED ACTIVISM

CHAPTER 13   THE EMERGENCE OF HOMO AMOR: TRANSFORMING THE WAY WE LOVE

CHAPTER 14   THERE'S NO ULTIMATE DISTINCTION BETWEEN COSMIC LOVE AND PERSONAL LOVE

CHAPTER 17 SYRIA AND TURKEY EARTHQUAKE—THE ONLY RESPONSE TO OUTRAGEOUS PAIN OUTRAGEOUS LOVE, PART 2

CHAPTER 18 OUTRAGEOUS LOVE BEGINS WITH RAGE: THE HOLY OUTRAGE OF THE PROPHET

CHAPTER 19 THERE IS ONLY ONE SIDE, THE SIDE OF LOVE: TEN PRINCIPLES

CHAPTER 20   LOVE DEMANDS TRANSFORMATION: CROSSING OVER TO THE SIDE OF LOVE

CHAPTER 21   THE EMERGENCE OF HOMO AMOR: TRANSFORMING THE WAY WE LOVE

EDITORIAL NOTE ABOUT AUTHORSHIP, EDITING, AND THE RADICAL CONTEXT FOR THIS SERIES

ORAL ESSAYS FROM THE ONE MOUNTAIN, MANY PATHS WEEKLY BROADCAST

This volume is part of the Oral Essays library, a series of lightly edited, compiled transcripts of oral teachings given by Dr. Marc Gafni and the late Barbara Marx Hubbard in their weekly online broadcast, *One Mountain, Many Paths,* which they co-founded in 2017. Originally called an "Evolutionary Church," *One Mountain, Many Paths* became a key venue for the articulation of an inspired and deeply grounded new Story of Value in response to the meta-crisis. Marc and Barbara—together with Zak Stein,[1] Kristina Kincaid, Ken Wilber, Sally Kempton, Lori Galperin, Aubrey Marcus and dozens of other thought-leaders over the years—began to articulate what they call a World Philosophy and World Religion[2] as a context for our diversity.

---

1 Zak, together with Ken Wilber, has been Marc's primary intellectual partner and an initiate lineage holder in CosmoErotic Humanism.

2 This project is grounded in four core organizational frameworks: 1) The Center for World Philosophy and Religion, co-founded by Marc Gafni, Zachary Stein, Sally Kempton, and Ken Wilber, and chaired over the years by John P. Mackey, Barbara Marx Hubbard, Aubrey Marcus, Gabrielle Anwar and Shareef Malnik, Carrie Kish and Adam Bellow, and Kathleen J. Brownback. 2) The Office for the Future, chaired by Stephanie Valcke and Ivan Bossyut. 3) The World Philosophy and Religion Press, founded and chaired by Aubrey Marcus, together with Marc Gafni and Zachary Stein. 4) The Foundation for Conscious Evolution, founded by Barbara Marx Hubbard and currently chaired by Peter Fiekowsky. For a complete list of key leadership, see the Office for the Future website, www.officeforthefuture.com.

Until Barbara's passing in 2019, she and Marc transmitted teachings together as evolutionary partners and "whole mates," weaving together insights and transmissions from their decades of practice, study, teaching, and activism into a synergy of wisdom, a grounded vision for future policy across all sectors of society.

Much of the *dharma* material below comes directly from Marc, so it was originally all in quotation marks—but that looked a little odd. So per his suggestion we removed them, and the reader should consider the paragraphs on the next several pages as one extended quote from him. We are joyfully grateful to Marc for the clarity of his *dharma*, the elegance and "second simplicity" of this language, and the mad, Outrageous Love with which he transmits his teachings.

Barbara and Marc called the mission of *One Mountain* "a Planetary Awakening in Evolutionary Love Through Unique Self Symphonies." We are an evolutionary community with a deeply grounded, radically alive, and "post-tragic" revolutionary spirit. We are activating a new humanity and awakening as a new species: *Homo amor*, the fulfillment of *Homo sapiens*.

One Mountain is committed to articulating a Story of Value that can become the ground for the new society that must be birthed in response to the meta-crisis. We recognize that we are living at a pivotal moment in history. In this "time between stories," the great moral imperative is to tell the new Story of Value. It is ours to do, personally and collectively, with great trembling and ecstatic joy.

FROM DOGMA TO DHARMA: ETERNAL AND EVOLVING FIRST PRINCIPLES AND FIRST VALUES

The teachings are grounded in decades of deep study across many wisdom traditions. Over the years, week by week, these teachings were incrementally developed within the framework of the *One Mountain, Many Paths* broadcast. We often refer to these teachings as *dharma*.

This word was originally used in lineage traditions to refer to something like universal law. This is a crucial realization: just as there is universal law in mathematical value, there is also a sense of universal law in ethics and value.

Historically, *dharma* often devolved into unchanging dogma. Evolution was ignored, and the natural process of *dharma* evolution became disconnected from its deep, eternal context. The weakness of the word *dharma* is that too often it did not include the evolving insights of the sciences, it confused local cultural truths with universal truths, and it used words like "eternal," as in "eternal Tao," as opposed to words like "evolution."

Eternal came to mean unchanging, and that kind of thinking often led to overly ethnocentric readings of *dharma*. Local systems would claim their religious and cultural insights as immutable, which stood in the way of the emergence of a genuine world Story of Value that is real, inherent to Cosmos, and backed by the Universe—even as it is also always evolving.

Or, as we often say, "eternal value is evolving value. The eternal Tao is the evolving Tao."

We have shown that, emergent from profound insights in the "interior sciences," eternal does not mean unchanging in time; it means what we call the deeper Field of ErosValue that is beneath culture, geography, and history, which lives beneath all individual and collective values, and beneath time and space itself.

As such, we have gradually transitioned from the term *dharma* to the term *Value*, in the sense of the Field of Value that lives beneath all values. This Field of Value discloses as First Principles and First Values embedded in a Story of Value.

Indeed, as the interior sciences knew and the exterior sciences imply, Reality arises in a Field of ErosValue in which an entire set of mathematical, musical, molecular, moral, and mystical values are the very ground of all being. That Field of Value is eternal—the true ground of the Good, True and Beautiful—even as it is evolving.

But of course, it is equally critical not just to talk about evolving value, but to ground the evolving value in its true nature, the eternal Field of First Principles and First Values, always reaching for ever more life, ever more love, ever more care, ever more depth, ever more uniqueness, ever more intimate communion, and ever more transformation.

As such, when we refer to the word *dharma*, which still appears in these texts together with the word value, we refer to an evolving *dharma* grounded in an *eternal and evolving* Field of Value. Indeed, eternity and evolution are two faces of the whole, opposites joined at the hip, that characterize the nature of our Cosmos in virtually all of its expressions.

It's in these terms that we ground a robust world philosophy that integrates the validated, leading-edge insights of premodern traditional wisdom, modern wisdom, and more recent postmodern insights, weaving them together into a new whole greater than the sum of its parts.

This new whole is a shared Story of Value rooted in First Principles and First Values that are both eternal and evolving.

These First Principles and First Values of Cosmos are woven together into a new Story of Value as a context for our diversity, a new Universe Story. This new story gives us the best possible responses we have to the mystery, and to the great questions:

- Who am I? Who are we?
- Where am I? Where are we?
- What should I do? What should we do?

It is only through such a shared Universe Story—a narrative of identity and ethos as a context for our blessed diversity—that we can realize how what unites is so much greater than what divides us.

Only a new Story of Value will allow us to both respond to the meta-crisis and participate together in birthing the most true, good, and beautiful world that we already know is possible.

THIS ORAL ESSAYS SERIES IS AN ENTRYWAY TO THE GREAT LIBRARY OF COSMOEROTIC HUMANISM

This Oral Essays series is part of the overarching project of the Great Library at the Center for World Philosophy and Religion, led by Dr. Marc Gafni, together with Dr. Zak Stein. The aim of the Great Library project is to articulate a robust and comprehensive new Story of Value, CosmoErotic Humanism, in the form of dozens of well-researched and extensively footnoted academic works.

Our vision is to provide the philosophical framework that will be vital for navigating humanity through this time of immense crisis and transformation.

To begin your journey into CosmoErotic Humanism, we tenderly refer you to the book *First Principles and First Values*, co-authored by Marc Gafni, Zak Stein, and Ken Wilber, under the name David J. Temple. David J. Temple is a pseudonym created for enabling ongoing collaborative authorship at the Center for World Philosophy and Religion. The two primary authors behind David J. Temple are Marc Gafni and Zak Stein, and for different projects, specific writers will be named as part of the collaboration, such as Ken Wilber and others.

Three other volumes complete this introduction: *A Return to Eros*, by Marc Gafni and Kristina Kincaid; *Your Unique Self*, by Marc Gafni; and *Education in a Time between Worlds*, by Zak Stein.

We hope that the Oral Essays in the present volume, with their informal style of transmission, will serve as an allurement and entryway for you into the more formal books of the Great Library that provide the robust intellectual underpinnings of the new Story of Value.

A NOTE ABOUT THE EDITORS

This Oral Essays collection has been edited by students of the new Story of CosmoErotic Humanism. Each of us has actively participated in *One Mountain, Many Paths*, and most of us have been in deep "Holy of Holies" study with Dr. Marc Gafni for many years.

We have been privileged to find ourselves well-versed in the teachings, and even emerging as lineage-holders of CosmoErotic Humanism.[3]

We view this editing project as a privilege and a deep practice of study and clarification. We experience ourselves as a *mystical editing society*, frequently meeting and conversing together about the content—the depth of knowledge and wisdom offered here—as well as the technical intricacies involved with publishing a beautiful and coherent series of books. In so doing, we function as a "Unique Self Symphony," which itself is a Dharmic

---

3 CosmoErotic Humanism is a world philosophical movement aimed at reconstructing the collapse of value at the core of global culture. Much like Romanticism or Existentialism, CosmoErotic Humanism is not merely a theory but a movement that changes the very mood of Reality. It is an invitation to participate in evolving the source code of consciousness and culture towards a cosmocentric *ethos* for a planetary civilization.

The term CosmoErotic Humanism, initially coined by Dr. Gafni and colleagues, points to a complex, multi-faceted, layered, and nuanced evolutionary set of insights that has evolved over decades of intensive research, teaching, and spiritual practice from deep within a wide range of wisdom traditions (including the Wisdom of Solomon lineage tradition, Bodhisattva Buddhism, and Kashmir Shaivism), as well as multiple disciplines including complexity theory, chaos theory, emergence theory, molecular biology, and the more classical disciplines of the humanities.

The seeds of CosmoErotic Humanism were planted with Dr. Marc Gafni's work on a two-volume, 1,000-page opus called *Radical Kabbalah* (Integral Publishers, 2012). This scholarly work, sourced from deep study within the esoteric lineage texts of the Wisdom of Solomon, points to a non-dual, or acosmic, realization which—unlike the prevailing conceptualization of non-duality—does not efface the human being; rather, it is highly humanistic in its nature. The next step in the evolution of CosmoErotic Humanism was the insight that all of Reality is evolving Eros, which lives in, as, and through the human being.

A failure of Eros leads inexorably to the creation of narratives of "pseudo-eros." CosmoErotic Humanism is a response to the modern mental and social breakdown sourced in the proliferation of multiple forms of pseudo-eros and its broken narratives, such as rivalrous conflict governed by win/lose metrics and the dogmatic denial of intrinsic value in Cosmos, which together generate our current "global intimacy disorder."

term that connotes an omni-considerate collaboration between realized Unique Selves synergizing our unique gifts into a new emergence greater than the sum of the parts. Even as we worked diligently to standardize our editing styles, meeting on a weekly basis to debate the nuances of phrasing, we also operated from within a deep appreciation of the unique style that each editor brought to his or her work. As such, the reader might notice some variation in editing style among the books.

Please note that Dr. Marc Gafni has not reviewed these edited Oral Essays, as he is deeply engaged in writing the formal books of the Great Library. But he has been generous in responding to questions and providing overall guidance in the project. Overall, as Marc's students and students of the *dharma*, we have made it a key project at the Center to publish these pieces of work relatively independently.

OUR UNIQUE ORAL-ESSAY EDITING STYLE PRESERVES THE ENERGY OF THE ORIGINAL TRANSMISSION

Dr. Marc Gafni is a uniquely gifted teacher whose oral transmission is imbued with a quality that has proven transformative for his students. Many of us feel mystically transformed by both the content and the underlying energy of the transmission style. Therefore, as we like to say, *trust the magic ways the dharma comes through your unique understanding!*

As Marc's empowered students, colleagues, and beloved friends, we have a deep knowing that these teachings are vital for the survival and thriving of humanity as we know it, and we recognize the importance of publishing his teachings in a written format that will be accessible by future generations. At the same time, we sought to preserve the Eros of the original oral transmission with all of its nuance, power, and depth. Our intention in the editing process, to the greatest extent possible, has been to keep these spoken artifacts intact in order to maintain the flow of the original transmission. We have therefore chosen not to engage in intensive formal editing, as we found that doing so resulted in the loss of the energetic transmission that is so key to fully receiving the *dharma*.

After experimenting with many ways to present these texts, we developed a specific way of laying out the text on the page. Marc, in collaboration with Zak Stein and Russian intellectual/artist Elena Maslova-Levin—and ultimately all of the editors, through many conversations—developed a unique, artistic presentation of the text, using bolding, italics, bullet points, and other stylistic features which together serve to accentuate the immediacy of the oral transmission.

As part of this editing style, intended to preserve the integrity of the original transmission, we have refrained from removing the frequent recapitulations of key themes. We found that each recapitulation contributes something vital to the rhythm and music beneath the words, like the beating drum of our hearts. These recapitulations not only review previous material but also add important new emphases, perspectives, and elements of the new Story of Value. We ask for your patience as a reader to trust the rhythm of these texts, and we trust you as a reader to have the depth and steadiness to find your way through.

KEY COMPONENTS: LINK TO THE ORIGINAL BROADCAST, EVOLUTIONARY LOVE CODES AND PRAYER

To supplement the written word, each episode includes a QR code linking to the original broadcast on YouTube, as well as occasional links to featured songs and video clips.

Each episode also centers around an "Evolutionary Love Code," formulated by Marc. These codes are part of the ongoing articulation and distillation of the *dharma* as it unfolds and emerges, week by week, over the course of many years, through the mystical process we call Outrageous Love or Evolutionary Love.

Another core component of the *One Mountain, Many Paths* episodes is what Marc and Barbara called "Evolutionary Prayer." Prayer is experienced in *One Mountain* not in the old fundamentalist sense of a "cosmic vending-machine god" who is alienated from Cosmos. Marc refers to this as the "god you do not and should not believe in"—and he often adds, "the god you don't believe in does not exist."

GOD IS THE INFINITE INTIMATE

In fact, in the *dharma* of CosmoErotic Humanism, a new name for God has emerged: the "Infinite Intimate," who appears in first-, second-, and third-person expressions. Marc first shared this name as he heard it whispered in 2023, although earlier intimations and formulations of the name appeared as early as 2010.

In first person, God is infinitely alive and as intimate as our own first-person experience.

In second person, God is the infinitely intimate Personhood of Cosmos that knows our name and holds us—the God about whom we say, *whenever we fall, we fall into Her hands.* This is the God who is our Beloved, Father, Mother, Lover, and Evolutionary Partner.

Finally, in third person, God inheres in all of the First Principles and First Values of Cosmos, and in the laws of science (both interior and exterior) that govern manifest Reality.

Therefore, we have a realization of God as not only the Infinity of Power but also the Infinity of Intimacy.

In *One Mountain, Many Paths*, we are reclaiming prayer at a higher level of consciousness. And we are reclaiming prayer as deep, alive, loving, and intimate conversations with God as the Infinite Intimate who knows our name.

THE INVITATION

We invite you to find your way into this revolution. Each one of our Unique Selves and unique gifts are desperately needed as we co-create this new Story of Value together, as part of the covenant between generations, for the sake of the whole.

Let's *play a larger game* and evolve the very source code of consciousness and culture together.

With mad love,

The Editors

LOVE OR DIE

LOCATING OURSELVES: ARTICULATING THE ESSENTIAL CONTEXT FOR THE ONE MOUNTAIN, MANY PATHS ORAL ESSAYS

SETTING OUR INTENTION

Intention setting is everything.

We're here—as da Vinci was with his cohort in the Renaissance—**to play a larger game, to participate in the evolution of love, which is to tell the new Story of Value rooted in First Principles and First Values.**

- ◆ Our intention is to recognize the critical historical juncture in which we find ourselves.
- ◆ Our intention is to take our seat at the table of history and to say, *we take responsibility for this.*
- ◆ Our intention is to participate as revolutionaries for the sake of the whole.

What we're here to do is revolution; revolution for the sake of the evolution of love.

It's a revolution for the sake of the trillions of unborn lives that will not manifest:

- The unborn loves
- The unborn creativity
- The unborn goodness
- The unborn truth
- The unborn beauty

All of it looks to us.

Not because we're engaged in grandiosity. Not at all!

- We're trembling before She.
- We're trembling with joy at the privilege.
- We're trembling with joy at the responsibility.
- We're trembling with joy at the Possibility of Possibility.
- We have to enact a new story in this moment of time. Because it is only a new story that can change the vector of history.

The most revolutionary act that we can do—the greatest moral imperative of this time—**is to articulate a new story at this time between worlds and this time between stories.**

Story is not made up, as postmodernity suggests. **We all live in inescapable frameworks; our framework is the story we live in.** Right now, Reality lives according to win/lose metrics, a story that is generating existential risk. **We need to change that story.**

When we change that story, when we tell a new story—not a made-up story, but a new Story of Value, rooted in First Principles and First Values—**then it all changes.**

We need to participate in the evolution of the source code of consciousness and culture, which is the evolution of love.

It's the most important, exciting, evolutionary, revolutionary act that we can do to alleviate suffering: to be lovers.

Like Rumi, the great poet of Sufism, we have to be "mad lovers," because it's the only sanity.

To be mad lovers is to see around the corner, to not be so obsessed with the details of the contractions of my life.

Let me see bigger.

Let me take complete care of myself in every possible way, let me completely attend to those in my circle of intimacy and influence, and then—*let me expand my circle.*

That's what we're here for.

- Our intention is to participate in the *LoveForce*, the *LoveIntelligence*, the *LoveBeauty*, the *LoveDesire* that literally animates Cosmos all the way up and all the way down.
- Our intention is to participate in the evolution of love.

[In the next few pages we will cover some key concepts which are essential to locating ourselves and setting the context for all the One Mountain, Many Paths Oral Essays. —Eds.]

OVERVIEW: EROS IS NO LONGER A LUXURY—IT'S LOVE OR DIE

Eros is life.

The failure of Eros destroys life.

Our lack of Eros is poised to destroy the world.

All civilizations have fallen because the stories that they lived in were, in some sense, stories based on rivalrous conflict governed by win/lose metrics. Every civilization was weakened by interior polarization caused by the lack of a shared Story of Value.

We now have a global civilization, but we haven't created a shared Story of Value.

We haven't solved the generator functions that caused all civilizations to fall. Our global civilization has exponential technologies and extraction models depleting the Earth of resources that took billions of years to create, which is going to lead to a civilizational collapse.

Existential risk is risk to our very existence.

The choice is clear: love or die.

It's that simple.

Eros is no longer a luxury. It is an absolute necessity for the survival of the individual and the planet.

In the last half a century, modern psychology has documented an age-old truth: a fully nourished baby who is not held in loving arms will die.

So too, our world, both personal and global—even with all the resources of intelligence and technology at our disposal—will die without being held in love, in the embrace of Eros.

We must embrace a personal path of love and a global politics of love.

Not ordinary love. Not love which is "mere human sentiment," but Eros, or what we sometimes call Outrageous Love, which is the heart of existence itself.

We live in a world of outrageous pain.

The only response is Outrageous Love.

WHAT IS EROS?

Eros is the experience of radical aliveness, moving towards, seeking, desiring ever deeper contact and ever greater wholeness.[4] Eros is the core fabric of Reality's being and the motivational architecture of Reality's becoming.

Eros is what animates the evolutionary impulse itself, from the very inception of Cosmos all the way to our very selves, who awaken to the realization that the evolutionary impulse throbs uniquely in each of us.

The realization of human awakening and transformation that lies at the core of the interior sciences is the invitation—or even the urgent and desperate demand—of a madly loving Cosmos animated by infinities of power and infinities of intimacy.

The demand—the desperate invitation, the plea, the tender and fierce command of Cosmos that lives inside every human being—is to awaken: to awaken to our true nature as unique incarnations of Eros and Ethos that are needed and desperately desired by All-That-Is. Said slightly differently: Reality is Eros. Or: God is Eros.

The failure of Eros destroys life. The collapse of Eros is always the hidden (or not so hidden) root cause for the collapse of ethics.

This is true both personally and collectively. We live in a moment of a worldwide and personal collapse of Eros. Our lack of Eros is poised to destroy

---

4 We define Eros through what we refer to as the Eros equation (one of a series of what we call interior science equations):

Eros = Radical Aliveness x *Desiring (Growing + Seeking)* x *Deeper Contact* x *Greater Wholeness* x *Self Actualization/Self Transcendence (Creation [Destruction])*

There are good reasons for the formal language of the interior science equations in these writings, and the reader is invited to explore them on their own, in particular, in our work, David J. Temple, *First Principles and First Values: Forty-Two Propositions on CosmoErotic Humanism, the Meta-Crisis, and the World to Come* (World Philosophy and Religion, 2024).

the world. Humanity is currently experiencing what has come to be known as existential risk, a risk to our very existence, or what I will refer to as the Second Shock of Existence.

EXISTENTIAL RISK: THE SECOND SHOCK OF EXISTENCE

The first shock of existence is the death of the human being—the realization that we will die, which dawns in human consciousness at the beginning of history. We are not talking about the biological fact of death but the *existential* realization of death. Although the interior sciences disclose that death is a portal between two days (there is vast empirical,[5] philosophical,[6] and anthro-ontological evidence[7] for the continuity of consciousness[8]), death is also, in our own direct surface experience, a stark end. And that is obviously not a bug but a feature in the system.

---

5 We refer to evidence gathered by the most serious of researchers, beginning with Henry and Edith Sedgwick at Cambridge University and William James at Harvard University, and continuing in highly rigorous form for the last 150 years, as recapitulated by Whiteheadian scholar David Ray Griffin in multiple volumes. See also, for example, Dean Radin, *Real Magic: Unlocking Your Natural Psychic Abilities to Create Everyday Miracles* (Potter/TenSpeed/Harmony, 2018), *The Conscious Universe: The Scientific Truth of Psychic Phenomena* (HarperCollins, 2010), and other books. Or see the earlier classic by Frederic William Henry Myers, *Human Personality and Its Survival of Bodily Death* (Longmans, Green, 1907).

6 This requires a cogent analysis of materialism and dualism, and the introduction of the far more cogent third possibility which we have called "pan-interiority."

7 We discuss Anthro-Ontology in some depth in *First Principles and First Values*, and see also the fuller conversation in David J. Temple, *First Principles and First Values: Towards an Evolving Perennialism: Introducing the Anthro-Ontological Method*—both published by World Philosophy and Religion Press, in Conjunction with Integral Publishers. For now, we will simply define it as an "innate and clear interior gnosis directly available to the human being."

8 See Dr. Marc Gafni and Dr. Zachary Stein's essay in preparation, "Beyond Death: Anthro-Ontology, Philosophy, and Empiricism." This essay is slated to appear in the book *Towards a World Religion: Homo Amor Essays*. The essay is also the ground for a larger book by the same authors, *Twelve Portals to Life Beyond Death: Responding to the Second Shock of Existence,* in which we discuss three forms of material: the empirical, the philosophical, and the anthro-ontological, and show how each form discredits the notion of death as the end.

Our first-person experience is that death ends this life. It is not the *totality* of our experience if we go deeper inside, but it is obviously intended to be the central, potent, and painful dimension of every human life. Indeed, as Ernest Becker potently reminded us, the denial of death is at our peril.

All the stories and all the plotlines and all the threads of living end at that moment. Whatever happens beyond, we have an actual experience of ending. **Paradoxically, that ending, the experience of the finality of mortality, is what presses us into life.** From the implicit demand of the first shock of existence, human beings were activated and pressed into creative emergence, and what emerged was all of human culture, both interior and exterior.

The second shock of existence is the realization of the potential death of all humanity. After all the stages of human history—matter, life, and mind in all of their stages of evolutionary unfolding—we have come to this place in the evolution of humanity, in which the gap between our exponentially expanding exterior technologies and our stalled (or even regressing) interior technologies of value has created dire catastrophic and existential risks.

This gap generates extraction models and exponential growth curves, rivalrous conflicts based on win/lose metrics, tragedies of the commons, and multipolar traps, in which everyone has to keep producing to the nth degree, including weaponized exponential threats to our very existence because we are afraid that the other parties are going to do it and not be transparent—hide it from us and then dominate us.

GENERATOR FUNCTIONS FOR EXISTENTIAL RISK

Let's outline clearly the main *generator functions for existential risk*.

Rivalrous conflicts governed by zero-sum, win/lose metrics. Rivalrous conflicts generate extraction models at the core of the economic system and exponential growth curves. Both of these drive and are driven by a contrived system of artificially manufactured desires and needs, delivered into culture by ever more precise forms of micro-targeting to individuals and groups through the ever more immersive environment of the internet.

Next, rivalrous conflicts and exponential growth curves animated by win/lose metrics generate **complicated, fragile world systems** highly vulnerable to myriad forms of collapse. Fragile local systems are made exponentially more fragile on a global level by our inability to meet global challenges with social, legal, political, economic, and ethical infrastructures that remain largely local.

All of this is a direct result of the failure to develop more adequate interior technologies that would be sufficiently compelling to displace "rivalrous conflict governed by win/lose metrics" as the motivational architecture for the human life world.

This failure has led to the conditions that will cause the implosion of systems that are already and quite literally on the brink of collapsing themselves. That's what we mean by the *second shock of existence*.

To recapitulate: the second shock of existence is not the death of the human being, but the potential death of humanity.

It is the *Death Star* moment of our species.

THE DECONSTRUCTION OF INTRINSIC VALUE

We stand in this moment poised between utopia and dystopia, at a time between worlds and a time between stories. We need a new Story of Value, eternal yet evolving, rooted in First Principles and First Values, which would become a universal grammar of value and a context for our diversity.

This is exactly what the Renaissance was. It was a time between worlds and a time between stories. In the Renaissance, we had been recently challenged by the Black Death, a pandemic that swept across Europe. The Black Death destroyed between a third to half of Europe and a huge part of

Asia. People died horrifically, brutally, in the streets. They had no idea how to meet this challenge, and so, in response to the Black Death, da Vinci and Ficino and their cohorts understood that they had to tell a new Story of Value.

That story was the story of modernity. Did they get it right?

- They got part of it right, which birthed, to use Jürgen Habermas' phrase, "the dignities of modernity," such as new ways of gathering information and universal human rights.
- But they also deconstructed the source of Value. They lost the basis for the Good, the True, and the Beautiful.

The basis used to be divine revelation: *God told us.* But this claim was owned by religion, and every religion began to overreach and over-claim. The revelation was thus often mediated through cultural categories and wasn't fully accurate.

Modernity threw out revelation, but was unable to establish a new basis for value.

Value was just assumed to be real. As it says in the founding document of the American Revolution: *We hold these truths to be self-evident*—that is, *we don't really have a basis for value; we just take it as a given.*

In other words, modernity took out a loan of social capital from the traditional world. The source of value was never worked out.

And then, gradually, value began to collapse.

- The Universe Story began to collapse.
- The belief that the Good, the True, and the Beautiful are real began to collapse.
- The belief that Love is real began to collapse.

As Bertrand Russell is reported to have said, "I cannot see how to refute the arguments for the subjectivity of ethical values, but I find myself incapable of believing that all that is wrong with wanton cruelty is that I do not like it."

What do you do if you grew up in a world in which value is not real? A world without a source of value, without a Universe Story, without a story of human identity, without a story of desire, without a narrative of power?

In the words of W.B. Yeats, *the center does not hold.*

- You have a collapse at the very center of society, because you no longer have Eros.
- You no longer have a Reality in which value is real, and so you have this lingering sense of emptiness.
- You have a complete collapse at the very center.
- We become *the hollow men and the stuffed men*, gesture without form.

And that's the source of our current existential risk.

THE DEEPER ROOT CAUSE OF THE META-CRISIS: A GLOBAL INTIMACY DISORDER

Above, I have outlined the major generator functions of existential risk. But there is a deeper cause for the existential risk that lurks underneath the rivalrous conflict governed by win/lose metrics and the fragile systems they engender.

And we cannot take the Death Star down without discerning and addressing this. We have already alluded to this root cause above, but at this point we need to make it more explicit so that, from this context, the adequate root response will become clear.

Modernity threw out the revelation, but was unable to establish a new basis for value.

This ostensibly surprising statement can be understood in a few simple steps:

1. All of the catastrophic and existential risk challenges we face are global: from climate change to artificial intelligence, pandemics, systems collapse, and exponential arms races.
2. Every global challenge self-evidently requires a global solution.
3. Global solutions can only be implemented with global co-ordination.
4. Global co-ordination is impossible without global coherence.
5. Global coherence is only possible if there is a global resonance between the parts.
6. Global resonance is only possible if we have global intimacy.

ONLY A SHARED STORY OF VALUE CAN GENERATE GLOBAL INTIMACY

Global intimacy—just like intimacy in a couple—is only possible when there is a shared story.

Not just a shared history, but a shared Story of Value.

- It is only a shared global story that can generate a new emergent quality of intimacy: global intimacy.
- A shared Story of Value must be rooted in shared ordinating values, or what we have called evolving First Values and First Principles.
- Intimacy requires a shared grammar of value as a matrix for a shared Story of Value.

The global intimacy disorder is the root cause for existential risk. The global intimacy disorder underlies the core generator functions for existential risk.

The global intimacy disorder is rooted in the failure to experience ourselves in a field of shared intrinsic value. This failure derives from the deconstruction of value.

Indeed, it is wholly accurate to say that **the root cause of the two generator functions of existential risk is the failed story of intrinsic value, or what we might also call the breakdown of Eros.**

1. The first generator function is **the success story**. Our modern success story is rivalrous conflict governed by win/lose metrics, which violates all the terms of the Intimacy Equation: there is no shared identity and no mutuality of recognition, feeling, value or purpose, and instead of *relative* otherness, there is *alienated* otherness. Such a story generates complicated fragile systems with no allurement or intimacy between the parts, systems which optimize for efficiency (as an expression of win/lose metrics) and not for resiliency and life.

2. The second generator function is **the deconstruction of intrinsic value** itself. The deconstruction of value is the sense that human value does not participate in the intrinsic value of the Real, for the Real is dogmatically declared to have no intrinsic value. Thus, there is no shared identity between the interior of the human being and Reality. There is no common participation in a field of shared intrinsic value. Instead of being intimate with value, we are alienated from value. And only intrinsic value can arouse will: political, moral, and social will.

To sum up, without a shared grammar of value there is no global intimacy, and therefore no global coherence, and no global coordination in response to catastrophic and existential risk, which means, put simply, there will be, quite literally, no future.

HEALING THE GLOBAL INTIMACY DISORDER REQUIRES THE EVOLUTION OF INTIMACY

But we are not hopeless. On the contrary, we are filled with great hope. Hope is a memory of the future. That memory of the future *is* the direct hit that takes down the Death Star, the culture of death. **The direct hit must be**—as it has always been in history—**the emergence of a new stage of evolution.**

Crisis is an evolutionary driver, and every crisis is, at its core, a crisis of intimacy: from the oxygen crisis of the single cells dying which generated multicellular life at the dawn of existence, to the existential risk in this very moment.[9]

The direct hit is therefore structurally self-evident: the evolution of intimacy itself.

What is intimacy, as a structure of Cosmos all the way down and all the way up the evolutionary chain? We engage this inquiry in depth in other writings, but for now we will simply adduce what we have called the "Intimacy Equation":

Intimacy = shared identity in the context of [relative] otherness x mutuality of recognition x mutuality of pathos x mutuality of value x mutuality of purpose

Intimacy is about the capacity of parts to generate a *shared identity* while retaining their otherness, or distinct identity. This requires multiple mutualities, including recognition, pathos (or feeling), value, and purpose. The parts must recognize and feel each other, even as they share value and purpose. But all of this must lead to intimate union—and not pathological

---

9 We demonstrate this principle in some depth in the multi-volume series, *The Universe: A Love Story* (forthcoming) (https://worldphilosophyandreligion.org/early-ontologies), *The Intimate Universe: Global Intimacy Disorder as Cause for Global Action Paralysis* (forthcoming), and in other writings of CosmoErotic Humanism.

fusion, where the distinct identity of the parts disappears—like subatomic particles that successfully become an atom, or two people who successfully become a couple.

THE DECONSTRUCTION OF VALUE IS THE DECONSTRUCTION OF INTIMACY

We have identified the global intimacy disorder as the root cause of the existential risk. But the underlying ultimate failure of intimacy is the deconstruction of value itself.

The deconstruction of value means that human value does not participate in any sense of intrinsic value of the Real. This is not about individual *values,* but about *the Field of Value* that underlies all of them. **When the human being**—moved, often sincerely or even nobly, by myriad cultural, historical, and psychological confusions—**claims to have stepped out of the Field of Value, then intimacy itself is deconstructed.**

The deconstruction of value is the deconstruction of intimacy.

In the absence of a shared Story of Value, a story that is an authentic expression of Reality's Eros, a story rooted in *pseudo-Eros* takes center stage and becomes the generator function for existential risk. Our modern pseudo-Eros story is *rivalrous conflict governed by win/lose metrics.* Such a story catalyzes in its wake the second generator function of existential risk: *complicated fragile systems with no allurement or intimacy between the parts.* It is in that sense that we have argued that the first generator function for existential risk is the success story.

- ◆ The failure of intimacy is precisely the impotent experience that there is no shared identity between the interior of the human being and Reality. **There is no shared identity in the sense of any kind of common participation in a field of shared intrinsic value.**
- ◆ **But only a shared Story of Value can arouse the global will**

required to engage catastrophic and existential risk. For it is only global political, moral, and social will—and we can even say *erotic* will—that can generate the most Good, True and Beautiful world that we have always known is possible.

THE EVOLUTION OF LOVE IS THE TELLING OF A NEW STORY

Coupled with the Intimacy Equation is the scientifically grounded realization, in both the exterior and interior sciences, that Reality is a progressive deepening of intimacies, or, said slightly differently:

Reality is Evolution. Evolution is the evolution of intimacy.

- The evolution of intimacy requires—both personally and collectively—a deeper, more accurate discernment of the nature of our universe, ourselves, and our beloveds.
- This new discernment generates a new global Story of Value.
- The new global Story of Value generates an emergent, heretofore unseen global intimacy and heals the global intimacy disorder.

The new Story of Value is the direct hit that takes down the Death Star and replaces it with the hope that invokes the memory of our best future.

Global intimacy facilitates global coherence, which facilitates global coordination, which activates the possibility of our creative and effectively coordinated global responses to the global meta-crisis in its entirety and its specific expressions.

To solve Bertrand Russell's challenge—the apparent argument for the subjectivity of ethical values—**we have to reground value theory in eternal yet evolving First Principles and First Values, and articulate a new Story of Value.**

This is what we call CosmoErotic Humanism.

CosmoErotic Humanism—together with other emergent strands—**needs to become the ground of a world religion as a context for our diversity**. We need religion, even as we need science, to articulate a shared global grammar of value.

As we said at the beginning, our choice is simple: love or die.

- To love means to participate in the evolution of love, which is the evolution of the human Story of Value.
- To love means to evolve and activate a new cultural enlightenment—rooted in a new narrative of identity, a new narrative of value, a new narrative of intimate communion, a new narrative of desire, a new narrative of power—all of which will birth new narratives of economics and politics.
- The evolution of love is the telling of a new story.

The new story that must be told is a love story, for in fact that is the deepest truth of Reality, rooted in the best exterior and interior sciences, that we have at this moment in time:

- Reality is not merely a fact. Reality is a story.
- Reality is not an ordinary story. Reality is a love story.
- Reality is not an ordinary love story. Reality is an Outrageous Love Story.

Story doesn't mean it's *made-up*.

It means doing the hard work of integrating the validated insights of the traditional world, the modern world, and the postmodern world.

This is the intention at the heart of telling the new Story of CosmoErotic Humanism.

ABOUT THIS VOLUME

The Path to Outrageous Love calls readers to awaken to a new scientific vision of Reality, one in which the very structure of existence is Eros itself. This book is animated by the realization that, in the formulation of CosmoErotic Humanism, Reality is not merely a fact, but a story. It's not an ordinary story, but a love story. It's not an ordinary love story, but an Outrageous Love Story. And finally, your clarified love story is chapter and verse in the Universe: A Love Story. Ordinary love, despite its potential beauty, is often a structure of the ego, a human contrivance. But it points towards a deeper realization: Outrageous Love, which is not mere human sentiment but the heart of existence itself.

The realization that I am an irreducibly unique and personal incarnation of the current of Eros, the Outrageous Love, that animates and drives the Cosmos, is what it means to cross over from *Homo sapiens* to *Homo amor*. *Homo amor* incarnates the possible human, the new human and new humanity.

In a time when technological systems disassociated from value are dominant, we need what we call in CosmoErotic Humanism the "interior sciences," rooted in valences of value—or what we call the "path of Outrageous Love"—to chart our way forward. Outrageous love is the call to join in radical intimacy with each other, with the planet, with the Divine, and with all of Reality. CosmoErotic Humanism is animated and informed by the synergizing of leading-edge interior and exterior sciences, drawn from across space and time into a new vision of the possible human and humanity. It's from the depths of this new vision that we're invited into what we call the "Amorous Cosmos," or the "Intimate Universe." Indeed, they virtually demand that we step up and play a larger game. We are invited to take our seat at the table of history, each in our unique ways, playing our Unique Self instruments in a Planetary Awakening in Love through Unique Self Symphonies.

Reality is incepted by the Eros of the Divine—what some have called the Real, or even God. CosmoErotic Humanism refers to God as the "Infinite Intimate," animated by Eros and intimacy all the way down and all the way up the evolutionary chain. Reality is disclosed as an Outrageous Love Story—a great Story of Value, distinguished by the scientific method and demarcated by mystery. The plotlines of the love story, animated by allurement, exist in the primary forces of allurement and autonomy that bring together quarks, subatomic particles, atoms, molecules, macromolecules, cells, and multicellular organisms. All are configurations of intimacy animated by Eros, desiring ever deeper contact and ever greater wholeness. The love story has evolved over time, culminating in our awakening as conscious evolution, the knowledge that we are evolution in person, the personal face of evolutionary love. This is what we in CosmoErotic Humanism have termed Conscious Evolution 2.0.

The Path to Outrageous Love ecstatically and soberly urges readers to shift from a life defined by myopic separation and contraction to one of intimacy and mutual evolution. Are you ready to live as *Homo amor*? Are you ready to commit your unique Outrageous Acts of Love and give your gifts in a Unique Self Symphony? Are you ready to cross over to the side of love—the only side? This book is a call to "love Reality open," to recognize yourself as an irreducible and irreplaceable actor in a madly loving Erotic Cosmos. Once you realize your true nature as a unique incarnation of the Outrageous Love at the heart of existence itself, you are ready to take your unique risk in order to play your unique instrument in the Planetary Awakening in Love through Unique Self Symphonies.

Volume 20

These oral essays are edited talks delivered by Marc Gafni and Barbara Marx Hubbard between December 2019 and January 2024.

CHAPTER ONE

EVERYONE IS ALREADY YOUR FRIEND

Episode 165 — December 7, 2019

WE LIVE IN INTER-BEINGNESS WITH EACH OTHER AND WITH ALL OF REALITY ITSELF

What's our intention? Our intention is no less than to play a larger game.

Our intention is to step out of the narrow myopic win/lose metrics that currently define the source code of society.

Our intention is to not merely to remain as *Homo sapiens* but rather to become the *fulfillment* of *Homo sapiens* in *Homo amor*.

What we understand is that, at this moment in history, we stand literally poised before a potential utopia: **paradise, a heaven on earth in which every human being gives their unique gift, we all feel for each other, and we actually begin to realize the true nature of the Intimate Universe.**

Abulafia, a mystic writing in the twelfth and thirteenth centuries, wrote of the nature of the new human and the new humanity. Everyone always understood that in order for us to move forward and evolve, we're going to eventually come to a place where the limitations of our egos will explode us. But they couldn't imagine, 800 years ago, the exponential technology creating the exponential risks we're facing today. They couldn't imagine the interconnected systems we have today—*born of technology, but not governed*

by an interior sense of evolutionary love. They knew well that we're moving in a direction where the unbridled egoic structure will destroy us.

They were painting—even then—visions of *Homo amor.* **Abulafia writes that the defining characteristic of the new human and the new humanity is when you can meet anyone in the world and instantly become best friends.** In a brief conversation, you can become deeply intimate and close with anyone, because we realize that *what unites us is so much greater than what divides us.*

The separations of culture, nationality, and language are all in fact surface features. In the depth structure of our being, we live in inter-beingness with each other as human beings. Then we can extend beyond, with human beings living in inter-beingness with all of Reality itself, with every plant and every animal, and then with all of the world that seems to be inanimate.

We can become friends.

We can love each other.

We can stand for each other's unique gift.

TELLING THE NEW STORY: REALITY IS AN OUTRAGEOUS LOVE STORY

This is a revolutionary church rooted in an evolutionary and revolutionary love. It's rooted in a deep understanding that we're called in this moment to evolve the source code. We're called to tell a new story. It's not a fanciful new story: it's not fanciful conjecture; it's not a New Age declaration; it's not a fundamentalist assertion. We're called to a new da Vinci moment—da Vinci who stood in Florence at the dawn of the Renaissance.

This is a church, a synagogue, mosque, a secular humanist center. We're called to bring together the best of the interior sciences and wisdom traditions with the best of the exterior sciences—the best of the humanities,

2

the best of physics, the best of sociology—and weave it together seamlessly and tell a new story that we can offer in ten sentences.

The story is really simple:

- ◆ "Reality is not a fact, Reality is a Story." That's the new realization of the sciences in the last hundred years. A story has a plotline. It's going somewhere.
- ◆ It's a love story—but it's not an ordinary love story, or a Harlequin romance. It's not just ordinary love between human beings who are using love as a strategy of the ego.
- ◆ It's an Outrageous Love Story. It's an Evolutionary Love Story. It's the realization that love is not a mere human sentiment.

Love is the heart of existence itself. It's the love that moves the sun and other stars. It's the love that animates quarks as they come together in holy triads to create the bases of protons and neutrons, which come together to create atoms, which are allured to each other to create molecules. **This precise dance between allurement and autonomy creates all of Reality.**

So, are we ready to play a larger game? Are we ready to step out of our narrow, contracted egos, out of the contrivance of our lives, out of our victim stories, out of our contractions, out of our myopic worldviews?

We are the Love Story and we can actually create a new model for Reality at this moment in time of what a Unique Self Symphony is. We are a Unique Self Symphony, and everyone is the center.

We believe and we understand in science today, that there are multiple energy centers—your heart beating in this moment as part of the One Love, the One Heart. Your heart beating and pulsing allows my heart to beat and pulse—then our hearts begin to pulse and beat together. When two people are in the same environment and they're interacting, their hearts begin to entrain with each other—when there is genuine love between them—as a physiological phenomenon. Can we entrain our hearts? Let's play this larger game. This is the revolution. This is the hub, the place where we reach deep inside of ourselves and rip our hearts open every week in mad love.

Rumi, the poet, talked about mad love. What he meant by mad love is exactly what we're talking about here. **It's not ordinary love but rather Outrageous Love, when I can literally see with God's eyes.**

Welcome to the revolution. Let's do this. Let's step out. Let's open up all the way. Let's go the whole way in this lifetime for the sake of the whole.

LOVING THE MOMENT OPEN, FROM THE INSIDE OF THE INSIDE

Here's a chant that comes from the Book of Psalms, from David. David is the great lineage master, and the father of Solomon, who built the temple in Jerusalem. Solomon talks about, *Its insides are lined with love.*

The entire Western tradition of Spirit, in the Christian tradition and the Messiah tradition—which has influenced all transformative social movements—notes that *I can stand in history and reject the status quo and desire a new future.*

I can access the desire of God/Goddess, the desire of evolution for transformation—that desire for transformation which is inherent in Reality—*as what we call Messiah.*

---

*Messiah is the strange attractor of the future.
It's the memory of the future.*

This is sourced in David, and it's rooted in this deep love and trust that lives between us.

We're going to do this chant, which is very beautiful and elegant. I'm going to give you the Hebrew words, so you can feel it, followed by the English words.

Mizmor shir leyom haShabbat. Tov lehodot la'Adonai.

Le'hagid ba'boker chas'de'cha ve'emunat'cha ba'leilot.

To sing a song of the Sabbath, it's good to sing with God.

To speak of your love in the morning, and to trust you in the night.

Let your heart blow open, wherever you are. These are the original lineage words from 3,000 years ago, passed down in an unbroken chain from David in Jerusalem, from generation to generation.

It's actually shocking.

Speak it to anyone in your life who is either present or not present. Speak it to yourself, who is the Beloved that is you.

We chant and practice to love the moment open. **Let's love this moment open. Let's find the deepest *Inside of the Inside.*** It's the realization that *its insides are lined with love*—from the Song of Solomon, David's son—and that actually Reality is a Love Story. That's the true nature of Reality Itself. Reality is an Intimate Universe.

OUR REVULSION IN THE FACE OF EVIL IS AN EXPRESSION THAT WE LIVE IN AN INTIMATE UNIVERSE

If you ask me, "Why in an intimate universe do we have such unbearable, outrageous beauty, and also such outrageous pain?" This is the deepest *dharma* in the world.

If it wasn't an Intimate Universe, we'd have no trouble with outrageous pain.

In other words, we'd have no trouble with the world not being fair if the world wasn't supposed to be fair.

The very revulsion that we have deep in our hearts for that which is not fair—for that which is unloving, petty, contracted, evil, and that which causes suffering, the knowing in our hearts that that's not the way it should be—**is a function of the Intimate Universe protesting against that which doesn't fulfill the inherent nature of Reality.**

Evil is a failure of intimacy. If we don't live in an Intimate Universe, then there's no reason to think there should ever be intimacy. There's no reason to think that it should ever be fair. There's no reason to think that it should ever be a world in which every human being's intrinsic dignity is affirmed and loved, in which every human story is told, in which every human being is born knowing, "I have a Unique Self and a unique story to tell."

Every story deserves to be lived, honored, cherished, and nourished.

Every person has a story that should be sung in a song, told in a poem, or written in a novel.

None of that makes sense in a non-intimate universe. Those emergent evolutionary understandings of the intrinsic dignity of every human being as a unique configuration of love are all expressions of the Intimate Universe. Opening my heart and—not knowing in my mind, rather finding my way in and actually feeling—*letting the feeling flow through me, the activation of the Intimate Universe inside of me.*

When I chant, what am I trying to do?

I'm consciously activating the Intimate Universe inside of me.

You go on the journey, step out of that web of delusion, and wake up to your true identity, your true nature:

My true nature is, I'm a unique expression of the Intimate Universe.

PRAYER: INTIMATE COMMUNION WITH THE INFINITY OF INTIMACY

God hears. God hears in every stone, in every drop of water, in every expression exchanged. God is the LoveIntelligence, LoveBeauty, LoveDesire, and LoveEnergy of the Cosmos—that's not *less than* personal; God's not only an abstract force. God is a Force moving through Cosmos, and God is also more personal than you, more personal than the most intimate moment you've ever had with your most intimate beloved.

God is Infinite Personhood.

God knows my name—not in the regressive, fundamentalist way of *a grandfather in the sky.* God is the exponentiated grandfather, grandmother, lover, beloved, brother, sister, father, mother, son, daughter. **God is all personhood integrated seamlessly in one Infinity of Personhood.** That's what we mean when we say God is the Infinity of Intimacy.

Imagine all of God in the third person, which is God as the Infinite Energy of Cosmos:

- The laws of physics
- The laws of chemistry
- The laws of biochemistry
- The four fundamental forces: the strong and the weak nuclear, the electromagnetic, the gravitational

7

Feel all of those laws flowing through Reality: the exponential, dazzling complexity—brilliance beyond that which could be manifested by all brilliance and all supercomputers exponentialized—is manifest and incarnate, again and again and again. All of that couldn't even begin to manifest the chlorophyll molecule and the process of photosynthesis. The self-organizing Universe is gorgeousness beyond imagination.

Now, to sense the second person of the Divine, sense that all of that God in the third person is now sitting in a chair looking at you, knowing your name, more intimate than you, more intimate an intimacy than you can even possibly imagine.

Find your most intimate moment and exponentialize it—that is the feeling of God in the second person, the Infinity of Intimacy sitting in that chair next to your bed, table, or couch looking at you and saying, *Oh my God, I love you madly. I love you beyond imagination. I'm madly in love with you, I love you beyond what you can possibly imagine.*

Then feel that love. It just blows your heart right open.

God says, *I need you. I need you to partner with me. There's something you can do out there that no one else can do, and you're my messenger. But in order to do what you have to do, you must let go of your shadow and your contraction.*

Prayer is intimate communion with the Infinity of Intimacy. We bring before God everything, our holy and our broken *Hallelujah*. Nothing is left out. Prayer affirms the dignity of personal need: the need to grow, transform, pay the rent, to eat, to have surgery go well—the need for all of it.

REALITY AND EVOLUTION *IS* INTIMACY

I prayed to go the whole way in this lifetime. I've imagined what the whole way in this lifetime is since, in this lifetime, it appears that evolution itself is shifting from an evolutionary path, which could destroy life, towards this new path where crisis births the new humanity. **Anybody who wants to go the whole way in this lifetime as part of your unique gift, I believe, has to be prepared for radical newness.**

I've been going over this beautiful code and fathom into it, in some deep way. *If Reality is driven by pleasure, and God drives the Reality, then God is driven by pleasure.* **What is God's highest pleasure? It's the radical transformation of everything, including you, me, and us.**

God is on our side. *Your greatest pleasure is transformation.* It's a very deep thing to say that *Reality and evolution is intimacy. Evolution creates newness through intimacy, through connecting separate parts together to make a new whole.*

If we are really driven by pleasure, and the highest pleasure is transformation, then in order to transform uniquely, we need to be connected more deeply in intimacy with each other. What and how do we connect more deeply in intimacy? Bill Clinton made some mistakes in a very superficial way of connecting in intimacy. **To go deep into connecting in intimacy for radical transformation, which is the highest pleasure, we can't do it without connecting more deeply in intimacy.**

We've talked about joining genius as creating the new human. Joining genius is not just joining intimately with anybody, even though you might like many people. In order to have the full pleasure of Reality, we realize God is driven by pleasure, and pleasure comes through a transformation that happens through increased intimacy.

Let's all take a moment and consider the experience of deep intimacy with the person whose genius is closest to your own. When you are intimately joining genius with that person, you begin to fulfill pleasure, transformation, and your deepest heart's desire. God has given us the plan.

Let's all focus on our deepest drive for Reality that comes through our transformation and our pleasure. Our pleasure and transformation come through increased intimacy to make a whole greater than the sum of its parts. Let's each one of us imagine joining in the pleasure of profound intimacy with others.

When we join genius in this way, each of us is becoming *Homo amor universalis.*

It may well be that the new human cannot emerge without us joining genius, just like new babies can't be born without us joining genes in love.

CHAPTER TWO

POWER OF, POWER FOR, AND POWER OVER ARE HOLY

Episode 166 — December 14, 2019

REALITY IS A DIVINE STORY IN WHICH THERE'S MORE GOD TO COME

Evolutionary Church is about our hearts poured open in mad love. It's the knowing that mad love is not just what lives in us, not just the personal, local love that is who we are—it's actually the Outrageous Love, it's the Evolutionary Love that animates and drives all of Reality itself, awakening uniquely in each of us.

That Love, that Godness, is itself the leading edge of evolution. And as the leading edge of evolution, I have Outrageous Acts of Love to commit. I'm an irreducibly unique expression of the LoveIntelligence of Reality. **We are Unique Selves in an evolutionary context, hands joined around the world, in a bottom-up, self-organizing Universe—each of us a unique expression of a self-actualizing Cosmos that's moving towards the evolution of love.**

There are three major views in the world. One view is of the mainstream dogmas of science, which says there is no story; there are *just random, chance facts*. That's not based on scientific evidence but on a dogmatic notion of science that rebelled against the old religion. That's what I'm going to call the "physicalist, materialist" view: "Love is not real, loyalties are not real, values are not real.

There are just random facts; there's no story at all." **That's the physicalist, materialist, no-story view of the Universe which dominates as a de facto wrong assumption and fundamentalist dogma in the secular world.**

The second view is what I'm going to call the "symbolic metaphor view" held by most religions. Most religions have a symbolic metaphor view, meaning: **This world is not where the real action is. There's the world to come, or there's pure consciousness underneath this world, or there's eternity,** *but this world is where you're judged. It's a place where you're formed. You might even be ethically informed, and your soul is refined. But this world is not the real world. It's just a made-up stage. Nothing ever new happens in this world. It's a place where you get to develop in order to get your reward: you get to move beyond your story, get to pure consciousness or get to heaven— whatever the move is. That's religion.* **That's the symbolic metaphor view of the world that people like Jung pick up as their major view.**

Neither of those views reflect the best information of the interior and exterior sciences. There's a new, emergent understanding: what we're going to call the "narrative view" of Reality. *Reality is a story*—that's the new realization.

Reality is not just a set of chance facts that we aggregate. It's not just a symbolic metaphor.

Reality itself is a divine Story.

It's a story in which there's more God to come.

There's a cosmic story, a narrative:

- Reality coalesces: atoms becomes molecules, *in love,* and there is allurement to ever greater and ever-larger wholes.
- We get to biological evolution in which there's a deepening and intensification of intimacy when we come to the emergence of life. Cells aggregate and coalesce to form larger wholes—*and all along there's more and more love, more and*

more consciousness, more and more creativity.

- We get to cultural evolution where hominids are walking on the savanna, awakened. They create larger circles of love and empathy and shared felt care and concern. That's cultural, social, spiritual evolution on the human level.
- Then consciousness as evolution moves in a long arc towards a deeper evolution of love. We move from egocentric to ethnocentric to worldcentric to cosmocentric intimacy.

We just told a story that we take as a given here in church. It's part of our field and language.

We've got to tell that story. Reality is not a fact, it's a story. It's not an ordinary story; it's a love story. It's not an ordinary love story; it's an Outrageous Love Story. And the plotline of the story is the evolution of love. The sub-plotlines of the story are more and more uniqueness, more and more creativity, more and more pathos, more and more wholeness, and more and more aliveness.

The Planetary Awakening in Love through Unique Self Symphonies is a billion deepest hearts' desires, clarified.

There's a book called *A Billion Wicked Thoughts* about sexuality in the internet age. Let's transform the pornographic universe into the CosmoErotic Universe, where there's a billion gorgeously wicked holy thoughts of deepest heart's desire. That desire is burning, that desire is pulsing, that desire is tumescent, that desire is alive.

It's the desire to love it open—to love Reality open as a Unique Self—knowing that my unique gift is desperately needed; knowing that I was intended by All-That-Is; I was chosen by All-That-Is; I am needed by All-That-Is; I am recognized by All-That-Is; I am desired, LoveAdored by All-That-Is. That's the truth of my reality.

We're not making this as an arrogant claim, but approaching with mad humility. **Humility means we're transparent to the Divine Force.**

- We're audacious and fierce, and we're trembling before Goddess.
- We're gentle and tender, and we're claiming for She a new possibility.

The alternative is dystopia. The alternative is *Blade Runner* or *Hunger Games*. The alternative is a widening gap between the haves and the have-nots. The alternative is the nearly million annual suicides, the four million attempted suicides, the 100 million people thinking about suicide, and the billion people who are madly devastated and broken. And the seven billion people searching desperately for happiness in all the wrong places.

- We are creating a new leading edge.
- We are together the new Christ.
- We are together the new Buddha.
- We are together the new God-ness.
- We are together the new human and the new humanity. The new human and the new humanity is the fulfillment of the evolution of love: *Homo sapiens* fulfills herself in *Homo amor*. We are *Homo amor* rising in the evolution of love.

EVOLUTIONARY LOVE CODE: POWER IS HOLY

Power is holy.

Our narrative of power is directly emergent from our narrative of identity which is directly emergent from our Universe Story.

Power is a divine elixir; nectar and not poison.

There are three forms of power. The first two forms of power are *power over* and *power for*. Contrary to the popular understanding which deifies power for and demonizes power over, both forms of power are holy.

14

The third form of power is the power of transformation.

All three forms of power are inextricable from each other: three faces of the one.

I'm going to talk about the place of power. We're so afraid of power, aren't we? We're going to turn to *Amor*, who says "its insides are lined with love." That's a verse from the Song of Solomon, and new information from the sciences is validating this: **Eros drives the Cosmos.**

Have you watched Jimi Hendrix play guitar? Star Spangled Banner, Woodstock, perhaps? We can be Conservatives or Liberals, but Jimi Hendrix transcends all worlds. It's a tragedy that you died at age twenty-seven, Jimi, because you had this explosion of love, but you didn't have a vessel, you didn't have a container to hold the love—so it was too much. He had this love pouring through him, but he didn't have a *dharma* of Love.

One of the things that Hendrix said was, "When the power of love is greater than the love of power, we will have peace." So, Jimi, I love you madly man, and your guitar is part of my God, but you got this one wrong.

Jimi Hendrix set up a false opposition between love and power. However:

- Love and power are inter-included.
- We actually have to love power.
- Power is part of the quality of love.

Homo amor has to be power-hungry. It's not the abuse of power. Let's talk about what it means for *Homo amor* to be power-hungry in the most gorgeous, sacred, and stunning way.

The inside of *Amor* is power. Love is not weak. The first thing my dear friend John Mackey—the Chairman of Whole Foods, and the Chairman of the Center for a number of years—said to me when we fell in love was: "Marc, I get what you're saying because love is not weak. Love is strong."

Love is the most powerful force in the world. *Amor*.

15

PRAYER: WE TURN TO GOD WHO IS THE INFINITY OF PERSONHOOD

We head into prayer, friends. What is prayer? Prayer is the realization that God is not only the third-person force of Cosmos that the New Age folks like to talk about.

It's beautiful—God *is* the force of Cosmos. It started with Spinoza: God is this force of Cosmos, everywhere and everything and inherent *in* everything. Nothing is not God. The great mystics understood that every stone and every tree is literally divine. *Eitzim v'avanim elohut mamash* means that it's held together by the power of divine allurement: Eros, electromagnetism, gravity, the strong and the weak nuclear forces, that which creates matter: all of it is allurement, which *is* God-Love.

It's a huge leap in the *dharma*. **What we're saying is that the bonds that hold Reality together are the bonds of Outrageous Love. That is the Godforce inherent in everything. That's God in the third person.**

Then we have *Thou art that*, the sense that God lives in me, that love is alive in me. That's the first person of God.

We talk here about what the great traditions call *Atah*, You: the second person. That's the God who knows my name and loves me madly. That's not Santa Claus in the sky. It's the Infinity of Personhood. That's what we call it here. **God is the Infinity of Personhood.**

God is supra-personal. God is personal, but not before the impersonal. The Buddhists say *move beyond the personal to the impersonal*, which is a beautiful expression of the third person of the divine. Instead: **You have to move beyond the impersonal to the supra-personal, to the intensification of the personal, to the personal exponentialized.**

Take the most personal moment that you ever experienced in the world: the most beautiful, gorgeous, stunning, personal moment, in which goodness, truth, and beauty were alive, and intimacy, ecstasy, and Eros were all happening. Take that moment and realize that when you exponentialize it, that moment participates in the larger Personhood of Cosmos that knows your name.

That's God, the Infinity of Intimacy that holds us in every second, that hears every word we speak.

What allows me to hear others isn't just my physical ears. Rather, it's the quality of intelligence, consciousness, and intimacy—because:

My quality of intelligence, consciousness, and intimacy participates in the wider field of intelligence, consciousness, and intimacy.

Just like I have a quality of personhood, the field has a quality of personhood, and hears every word I say. That's the most personal and the most intimate; that's God who's our lover, our mad Beloved, our Outrageous Lover who cares desperately about every jot and tittle, every dimension, every detail.

When we pray, we come before the Infinity of Intimacy who knows our name, and we say:

> *Lover, can I share with you everything?*
> *Can I please tell you everything?*
> *Can I share with you my holy and my broken Hallelujah?*

POWER FOR THE SAKE OF, AND POWER OVER

Let's return to power. We know what it feels like to be powerless. To be powerless means, *I feel disconnected from the Field, and I'm alone.* To be broken means, *I'm disconnected from the Field.* To be powerful means, *I'm in the Field.* Power means, *I'm accessing, in my body, the unique expression of the Field's power yearning to emerge through me.*

First, there's *power for the sake of:*

- Power for the sake of the Evolution of Love.
- Power for the sake of creating this One Church—One Mountain, Many Paths—to bring this new story at this time when we're poised between dystopia and utopia.

But it's more than that. We also have *power over*. I have power over you, and you have power over me, and we have power over each other. When we realize that, and we can realize we're actually deepest friends already, we can trust each other. **We have to recognize that so we can trust each other to wield power over each other.**

To be in a relationship is to have power over each other, and to hold our power tenderly, to tremble with our power. But we must be aware of it. A person who's not aware of their power is not trustable.

We all have power over each other. *I want to speak of your love in the morning, and I want to trust you in the night.* There is no power without trust, and there's no love without trust.

I trust you to allow me to surrender to you.

Do you know what true intimacy is? **True intimacy is when I allow my beloved to witness my surrender.** To surrender takes the greatest power of all; to have enough power that I can give up surface power and give up ego power and just live in the true authenticity of my genuine power.

My genuine power is the power of transformation.

- I have the power to transform myself.
- I have the power to be a unique incarnation of *more God to come*.
- I have the power to realize my power, to realize that I'm in the

18

Field of Power, and to realize that Reality needs my power.

This is one of the areas in which the sexual models the erotic. In sexuality, with our Beloved we can play with power, and we completely surrender our power. **We give up all control—and yet we're also fully claiming our power, the power of desire, directed gorgeously, moving through us.**

LOVING THE MOMENT OPEN AND ALLOWING THE MOMENT TO LOVE ME OPEN

But the sexual only *models* Eros. We want to be in Eros; we want to be in our power in every dimension of Reality. In every moment there's a choice:

Do I love the moment open?

Do I allow the moment to love me open?

To allow the moment to love me open is to open up—literally to spread my heart—and receive the full thrust of the power of the moment in me, as it blows my heart open.

As the moment blows my heart open, then power courses through me, and I return that power back to the moment.

I love the moment open.

I Fuck the moment open.[1]

I fiercely, tenderly, kiss the moment open.

I caress the moment open. I pour my mind into the moment, as well as my heart, my body, my soul.

---

1 By "Fuck," we mean our radical aliveness and the core nature of Reality. For a deeper dive, see "A Word on the Word 'Fuck,'" in *The Phenomenology of Eros, Volume One: From the Crisis of Desire to Sex Beyond Shame* (World Philosophy and Religion, 2025).

And then the moment is loved open and gives birth to a newness, to an intimacy, to a goodness, to a desire that's unmatched in Reality.

- I might love the moment open by giving $50 a month to the church.
- I might love the moment open by adopting a child.
- I might love the moment open by asking for forgiveness where I was afraid to.
- I might love the moment open by claiming and giving my unique gift.
- I might love the moment open by stepping up and giving my blessing in the world, and realizing that *the power of blessing moves through me.*

I do it in ways that are not always easy. I do it by standing in places where it's hard to stand. I do it by bringing in split-off parts of myself, by taking the people that I've placed outside of the circle and bringing them back into the circle.

I claim my power by giving up being right. When I give up being right, then I stand in the integrity of my beliefs, in my trust, and in my knowing in an entirely different way. Power moves through me. We have to get over this liberal rejection of power, beyond the failure to distinguish between the abuse of power and the elixir of power. I am power hungry. I am power hungry for holy power. I'm desperate for power. I don't want to feel powerless.

I want to access the full glory. *Mine eyes have seen the glory of the coming of Homo amor.*

HOMO AMOR IS POWER

Homo amor is the fullness of power.

Homo amor is political power.

Homo amor is financial power.

20

But more than anything, *Homo amor* is the power of integrity; unshakable integrity, unshakable love.

It's the power of Outrageous Love. Love is not weak—love is strong.

Jimi Hendrix, holy brother, the power of love does not contradict the love of power. Power and love are the same; they're the inside and the outside of the same thing.

So I claim my power, but I don't abuse my power.

When I claim power *for me only*, then it becomes a form of power over; I've hijacked the power of the wider field and narcissistically tried to claim it as my own. I'm always then crushed by my own power.

When I let the power of the field move through me, when I'm transparent to the power of the field, then the power awakens uniquely in me in a joy that's unparalleled, in a love that surpasseth understanding. The Word moves in me, and power moves in me, and people are allured to me, and I give my gifts, and the world opens, and there's no desperation, and there's a flow of power. **The Infinity of Power, which is divinity, moves intimately and gorgeously in me.**

REALITY NEEDS OUR POWER

We're claiming our power. We're saying we're not going to wait for somebody else to evolve the source code; it's ours to do. We're going to contribute funds, time, creativity, and the radical presence of our flaming hearts. **The biggest contribution in life is the radical presence of your flaming heart.**

I want to give you the radical presence of my flaming heart. I want to receive the radical presence of your flaming heart. Our hearts are aflame. They're aflame with the power to love open Reality in a way that each of us can only do uniquely.

We are the new chapter and verse in the Love Story of Reality. Unparalleled we look at each other's eyes and we say,

How deep is your love?

Be my air, let your power be my air.

Let me roam the body of your heart. No inhibition. No fear.

Let's love it open like we never have before. Reality needs our power.

CHAPTER THREE

WE ARE THE TIPPING POINT
OF THE DIVINE

Episode 167 — December 21, 2019

EVOLUTIONARY, REVOLUTIONARY LOVE IS SUBVERSIVE TO THE NOTION THAT WE'RE CONTRACTED AND SMALL

We are here to love each other, and we are here to love the moment open. **We are here to love the moment open not only for ourselves but for all of Reality**. We experience and understand that the entire process of evolution—the great flaring forth at the moment of the Big Bang bursting forth—brought all of the laws of physics and mathematics into being. But it didn't burst forth randomly; it wasn't a chaotic mess.

- There was elegant order in the first moment of Reality. But if that wasn't strange and beautiful enough, what then happened was even deeper.
- Reality sought to evolve. **Reality yearned to form ever greater and fuller, more complete wholes.**
- And if that wasn't strange enough, these wholes—these new realities, these greater, more coherent, gorgeous, and elegant structures of matter-energy—at some point awakened ever more deeply, and **they had the ability to reproduce themselves**. We went from cosmological to biological evolution. Then Reality kept reaching, kept yearning for more life, for more

contact, for more intimacy, until we burst forth and not only could we reproduce ourselves, but **evolution came to a point where we could represent ourselves.**

- The human being became conscious, and we began to make figures of ourselves. We began to self-reflect and to think *about* ourselves. **So began cultural evolution.**
- If that wasn't strange enough, a few hundred years ago, on a little planet, near one of the many suns, on a planet among hundreds and hundreds of billions, in this grand and gorgeous and inexplicable unfolding of Divinity, **evolution *itself* became conscious, awakening to itself through us**.

The conscious process of evolution awakened as us. We became, in that great phrase coined by Julian Huxley, "conscious evolution in person." We are evolution become conscious of itself.

- We became conscious evolution in person
- We became the Intimate Universe in person.
- We became the CosmoErotic Universe in person.

Our personal stories awakened to the truth that *we are chapter and verse in the Universe: A Love Story.* That's shocking beyond imagination. And actually, it's not just true about the species; it is true about you and me, and about every single one of us.

We're here to come together in this revolution. We understand that **what drives the entire process is not just Evolutionary Love; it's revolutionary love.**

It's completely subversive to the notion that *we're small and contracted and petty.*

It's subversive to the notion, suggested by Heidegger and others, that *we can never find each other, and we'll always be alone.* It's not true!

God looks through my eyes uniquely and sees you, and God looks uniquely through your eyes and sees me.

- We see each other.
- We can find each other.
- We can transcend loneliness.
- We can become evolution awakened to itself, but *only when we make this radical commitment to realize the true nature of our identity.*

So that's our intention.

TO KNOW MY IDENTITY IS TO STEP INTO MY ENLIGHTENMENT

What is our identity? *Who are we? Who am I?*

- I am an irreducibly unique configuration of evolutionary love.
- I have gifts to give and joys to laugh and tears to shed.
- The story of my own being and becoming is infinitely important and contributes something unimaginable to the greater Cosmos.
- The Cosmos not only knows me, and not only intended me, but the Cosmos chose me. The Cosmos desires me and adores me. The Cosmos needs me.

That's my very identity; that's who I am. To know that is to step into my enlightenment.

- I am evolution.
- I am a unique configuration of Evolutionary Love.
- I have particular gifts to give; a poem to write; a song to sing that's unimaginably beautiful and that's utterly necessary for existence itself.

25

When we awaken to that realization, we begin to heal suffering. We begin to speak and reach our hand towards every human being whose heart is broken, whose body is shattered, who lives alone and is desperate—sometimes in the most abject conditions, and sometimes even in a mansion.

This is our intention. We make the following commitment:

Until every being is living the full dignity, divinity, gorgeousness, beauty, and truth of their existence, we will not rest; we will not retreat into our narcissistic ego; we will not contract into our limited separate self.

Instead, we will awaken; we will rouse ourselves up; we will commit all of our energy, all our love, and all our resources towards embracing every human being on the planet until we produce a vision of goodness, truth, and beauty that's unimaginable.

That is the purpose and the intention of all of Reality itself, because we understand that the more we are together, the more God becomes; that we are divinity incarnate; that we are divine miniatures.

That is our sacred and humble and most audacious intention.

We are overflowing with delight and we are privileged to be here. All obstacles are melted away. Our intention is set, and the word is good. So thank you. Every one of us is so radically, wildly important—everyone, every part of you, every part of me, every part of everyone! All of us are the pillars of this One Church, which is a synagogue and a mosque and a secular humanist center. Every one of us is radically needed; if one of us shifts our attention, the entire pyramid falls.

We love each other so madly. We're not embarrassed to love madly. We're delighted to love madly, and we rip our hearts open every week, again and again, in mad ecstasy and mad love, which is the only sane way for us to live. This is our intention. We are—all together—evolution aware of itself. Amen!

EVOLUTIONARY LOVE CODE: THE QUESTION IS EVERYTHING

> Are you ready to be evolution?
>
> Are you ready to participate in the evolution of consciousness and culture?
>
> Are you ready to participate in the evolution of love?
>
> Are you ready to love deeper and wider than you ever have before?
>
> Are you ready to include someone inside of your circle of love that has always been on the outside?
>
> Are you ready to change, to grow and transform in the way that you have long given up on?
>
> Are you ready to be a dreamer?
>
> Are you ready to activate evolutionary love in you, as you, and through you?
>
> Are you ready to be and become more than you ever thought possible?
>
> Are you ready to awaken as conscious evolution?

This Code is a series of questions, and the question is the "quest I'm on." The question is everything; the answer—that's easy!

Remember in *The Matrix* when Neo meets Trinity? There is this incredible scene and Neo asks, "Why did we meet?" And Trinity responds, "Because we are asking the same questions."

We're here in One Church: Many Paths, One Mountain, and we're asking the same questions. *Are we ready to be mad, evolutionary lovers?*

That's the only sane way to be; to own our power.

To know that I am Evolutionary Love is not a social construction; it is not ordinary, it is not even mere human sentiment.

Love is the heart of existence itself.

WE ARE DIVINE MINIATURES BUT ARE SYSTEMATICALLY MISRECOGNIZED ON SO MANY LEVELS

Someone I know felt hurt by me, by something I hadn't done, someone close to my heart. I felt it deeply, and I felt the fragility of human beings. We so want to love and be loved, and it's so easy for us to be hurt by each other; to feel dishonored; to feel disrespected. It's so easy for us to feel insulted—and that's not just a contraction of the ego. It's actually a little more than that; it's that *we experience on the inside that we are divine miniatures, that we are Unique Selves, that we are stunning configurations of Evolutionary Love.*

Beneath the egoic contraction, beneath the narcissistic part of our contractions, there's an authentic and real yearning that is legitimate, beautiful, authentic, and holy that we want to be recognized. **And we're systematically misrecognized on so many levels.**

We want to be seen and heard and held. To be lonely means that I'm not seen. To be lonely means that I can't share the core and the essence of who I am.

Heidegger says that human beings are doomed to perpetual loneliness because human beings can never transcend their ultimate egocentric separateness, and they can never meet each other. Heidegger was wrong. He didn't understand that love is the core of Reality; he didn't understand *Amor.* He thought love was a social construction, but that came much later.

We have to intend love; we have to open our hearts again and again; we have to feel each other.

We don't have to agree with each other; we have to feel each other.

WE REDEEM EACH OTHER IN FELLOWSHIP FROM THE PAIN OF OUR LONELINESS

There's something called the "Tenets of Intimacy," which my friend Zak and I will be writing about later this year. We are referring to the principles of intimacy that govern the Universe. This has been a core of our teaching the last couple of years.

I'm intimate with you. The more I feel you and the more you enter me, the more I can open my heart, and I feel what you feel like.

- I can take your perspective.
- I can let go of being defensive.
- I can feel your joy and rejoice in your joy.
- I can feel your pain and let my heart break in your pain.

When we meet each other in that way, when we recognize each other, then *something happens that is magical beyond imagination.*

Imagine God. Imagine how lonely God feels:

God who both lives in us and God who is also the Source of all the laws of physics and all the laws of mathematics.

God who is beyond all time and space, and God who's the consciousness that's underneath the space-time continuum, the animating self-organizing force who is the Self of Divinity who steps back and loves us so madly that He/She/It says:

I'm going to allow you to choose even when you choose against Me.

I'm going to allow you to fall asleep and not see Me even when I desperately need and want you to be awake and need you to see and recognize Me.

I want to make this world so beautiful, yet you do things sometimes to make it so ugly. It breaks My heart. And My pain is not finite—My pain is infinite.

Do you get that God's not just the Infinity of Power? God is the Infinity of Feeling.

Just like God's joy is infinite, and God's ecstasy is infinite, imagine what it feels like to experience infinite pain.

The infinity of God's pain.

God wants to be met by us; God wants to be recognized by us. The lonely God, said Plotinus, seeks the lonely human being.[2] And we meet and we redeem each other in fellowship from the pain of our loneliness.

That's what prayer is. Prayer and prophecy are two sides of the same coin. **In prophecy, God initiates and invokes the conversation. In prayer, the human being initiates and invokes the conversation. The Divine and the human being meet in both prayer and prophecy.**

The mystics in the lineage of erotic, evolutionary mysticism in the third century said that not only does God initiate prophecy, but God also prays.

God prays: *See Me; share with Me; tell Me everything; hold My hand.*

We turn to God in prayer, and with Leonard Cohen we bring before God the holy and the broken Hallelujah, which is sung by people all over the world, in every language, in every dialect.

We all can hold God's hand and God can hold our hand and we bring before God—our outrageous, intimate Lover—everything.

We bring our holy and our broken Hallelujah. This is not a metaphor or myth; it's not mythopoetic. This is ontology.

Because our intelligence is not isolated; it's not separate. Our intelligence participates in the Field of LoveIntelligence, of Divine Intelligence. Just like

---

2 Plotinus described prayer as "from the alone to the alone."

when we hear, God hears; just like you're hearing me now, God's hearing me. Just like I hear your voice, so my hearing participates in God's hearing. Nothing is left out. We can hear each other; we can listen to each other.

So we turn to you, God, the Infinity of Intimacy that knows our name. All the laws of physics are sitting in a chair looking at us, desperately yearning for us, wanting to know everything about us in a way that is shared by us— receiving us, holding us. *Every place we fall, God, we fall into Your hands.*

So in this moment, we bring before you, God, the ultimate intimacy of prayer; we bring before you our holy and our broken Hallelujah.

EVOLUTION TOWARDS GREATER CONSCIOUSNESS AND LOVE

As I was contemplating this Code, I realized we might as well go the whole way and see that it's really an expression of the cosmic Love Story. In other words, we take all of these original ideas and we see them applying to us, such as:

- Are you ready to play a larger game?
- Are you ready to be evolution?
- Are you ready to participate in the evolution of the culture?

This is the evolutionary impulse itself. **The evolutionary impulse running through the billions of years of evolution is God in action.** If you really love God, you're going to feel ever more deeply God in action *as* you.

When God is in action as you, just for a moment realize what that actually means. Because that God in action, as you and me right now with our prayers, is the God that took us from nothing at all to everything that is. It's the awesome genius of God.

If you realize an illusionary perspective and you're not seeing that it *just happens like that*, what you're actually discovering is the genius of God. In the genius of God, when you're asking, *Am I willing to play a larger game?* who are you asking? What larger game are you getting ready to play?

If what you are calling into action is *the God in you unfolding as you,* and the God in you is always at the threshold, you will see this incredible process of evolution from billions and billions of years.

In my body right now I feel the threshold of our unfolding The great thing about the evolutionary church is that **it's unfolding consciously to us collectively as the evolution of love.**

Now you put all of that together, and you can see that God is really pleased. In fact, you could say **God's been waiting for us for a long time.**

The Universe itself is a Love Story, from quarks to us. And what is the nature of that Love Story? It's totally reinforcing everything we're doing in the church. For all the five mass extinctions and for all the entities that didn't work, the purpose of this evolutionary love story is always going towards three things.

1. It is going toward higher consciousness, from single cells to us.
2. It's going toward greater love and complexity.
3. It's going toward greater freedom of choice.

This is the value system that has been placed in the core of evolution, which is in every one of us now—in you and me—exactly where we are.

God's Code is playing the larger game, and my consciousness in this moment is the consciousness of the Universe evolving.

When I say yes to it, it's an awesome power. It's not just my personal consciousness.

And then when I say yes to the second great thing that nature has been working on for billions of years—from quarks to us, from rocks to Internet—that is true freedom.

It's really interesting to ask yourself, *What is the greatest freedom that this Love Code of evolution is offering to you?*

You probably have many different choices in your life. You could do this, or you could do that. So here's the way I think it's best to do it. **Out of whatever freedom you have, you go toward greater consciousness as a source of evolution, and toward greater love through greater complexity, which is to say you add more love to your system.**

You bring more people in; you go to the person outside and bring that person in.

In other words, if I say yes to myself, I'm saying yes to consciousness, freedom, and more complexity as an expression of the thing itself praying.

Who's praying here? Who's asking? I am; you are. Who are we asking but the thing itself? Isn't that interesting? **We are the thing itself asking.**

Let's just ask ourselves in this moment, *How do we, as the Church of Evolutionary Love, fit into the building of the multi-millennial story of evolution?* Why did a Church of Evolutionary love just crop up? As far as I know, there is no other Church of Evolutionary Love.

There are many churches that are speaking for love, and certainly the earliest Church of Jesus said, "Love me as I have loved you."

Jesus was the personification of love, a loving human form and that formed the original church, but then so many other things came into the church. I'd like to declare that the development of the Church of Evolutionary Love in some respects has a new kind of significance like the very first church did.

People died for that; people lived for that; people then totally transformed culture—until it got taken over politically.

We're not taking over politically. We can totally transform culture by doing exactly what we say we are going to do. I'm holding a vision that this evolutionary church grows and grows.

We now have a YouTube channel, and we're going to replicate. There will be churches in different parts of the world. I see the Church of Evolutionary Love, at the very moment of quantum breakdown and quantum breakthrough of Mother Earth, as promoting the protective mothering-fathering love that is going to carry us through the quantum shift.

CHAPTER FOUR

I AM THE EVOLUTION OF LOVE

Episode 169 — January 4, 2020

AFTER THE POSTMODERN DECONSTRUCTION OF MEANING, WE'RE HERE TO BEGIN THE GREAT RECONSTRUCTIVE PROJECT

We are here for a revolution! We are here to set our intention. We are at this moment poised between utopia and dystopia. We're at a moment in which the entire process of evolution could literally stall, regress, break down, and self-terminate. We live in a world in which there's a fantasy of perpetual growth, a widening gap between the haves and the have-nots, and the ongoing extraction of resources that took billions of years to create. And, **at the core, the failure of a shared story, a shared narrative in which we understand ourselves, could mean we easily devolve into dystopia.**

In place of that narrative, we have a win/lose matrix success story where *I win and you lose*:

- Which drives the perpetual growth
- Which drives the resource extraction
- Which drives the gap between haves and have-nots
- Which drives the suicide rates to almost a million a year in the world now, with four million people attempting suicide, and a hundred million contemplating suicide
- Which drives depression

Depression is the leading malaise in the world. And depression comes from a sense of futility: "What am I here for? I can't make a difference." The old stories of meaning, the fundamentalist stories, don't resonate any more. And yet a new story is non-existent. Postmodernism has deconstructed all the grand narratives. So then, *Where are we? What are we here for?*

We're here to reweave the story. After the postmodern deconstruction of meaning, we're here to begin the great reconstructive project. **It's the single most important thing that could happen in the world today: to reconstruct our story of meaning.** We need to reconstruct it in a way in which we combine and integrate all the deepest truths from all the great traditional religions, all the deepest truths from the greatest streams of science and modernity, and all the gorgeous intuitions of postmodernity.

The last time this took place in history was during the Renaissance, when da Vinci and his cohorts in Florence stood before the Black Death in Europe and realized that they couldn't heal every home, or visit every devastated village, so they did the best thing that could be done: they told the new story. **Like them, we know internally that *we need to respond to suffering.***

They took the best of the traditional religions, along with the best intuitions of the time, and then they told a new story. That was the story of modernity: the story of the scientific method. Within a few hundred years, it did what all the great traditions didn't do: abolish slavery, ushered in some degree of feminine equality, and created a sense of universal human rights. It was the great story of modernity.

Now we're in this postmodern moment where we again need a great story; the suffering in the world is unimaginable, and we are facing several extinction-level crises. Yet, at the same time, we have new information, gathered from all the great periods, that we can integrate and weave together because we have access to it in a way that we never have before in history.

WEAVING A NEW STORY IN A BOTTOM-UP GROUNDSWELL TOWARDS THE STRANGE ATTRACTOR OF WHOLENESS

We have new information that tells a new story:

- ◆ A new story of identity
- ◆ A new story of what evolution actually means
- ◆ A new story of why we're here

This story is based on the deepest readings of leading-edge science, ranging from quantum physics to the interior sciences of enlightenment, from systems theory, complexity theory, and chaos theory to the deepest understandings of transpersonal knowledge. We can weave it together in the most elegant, gorgeous way that we can share in ten minutes with anyone in the world.

This new story is the democratization of greatness.

- ◆ It's the story of Unique Self.
- ◆ It's the story of *Homo amor*; *Homo amor* who is the fulfillment of *Homo sapiens*.
- ◆ It's the story of a Planetary Awakening in Love through a Unique Self Symphony in which every human being gives their gift and Reality self-organizes as we come together as unique collectives. We join genius and we become evolution in person.

We actually realize:

> I am evolution in person. I am a unique configuration of Evolutionary Love, and I have an instrument to play in the Unique Self Symphony that's unlike any other. That music needs to be heard. That musical note adds something to Reality without which the symphony couldn't play.

When we all begin in this bottom-up, networked groundswell—not a top-down command-and-control system—reaching towards the strange attractor of the unbearable wholeness of being, **we reach towards the unbearable beauty of the unbearable wholeness of being that lives in us and yearns.**

We each do it in our own personal stories. Then we come together and create a shared story.

We're radically committed to the unfolding of this *dharma*, to weaving it together with great clarity, with simple clear sentences, with massive footnotes—meaning we go deep into all the sciences, both interior and exterior, to tell this new story. That's the da Vinci move of this generation. The single most urgent thing we can do is to evolve and articulate a shared story of the new human and the new humanity: *Homo sapiens* is fulfilled in *Homo amor*, in which each of us expresses and incarnates our irreducible Unique Self. Gorgeously, stunningly, we come together like any Unique Self Symphony, and we catalyze together out of our personal, ecstatic, gorgeous joy and love—while holding all the pain.

We live in a world of outrageous pain and the only response is Outrageous Love. Outrageous Love is the love that animates all of existence.

It's not ordinary love, which is just a strategy of the ego for success or status. **Outrageous Love is the love that animates all of Reality. It's the Eros that's the essence of all of existence, which lives uniquely and gorgeously in me and in you.** We set our intention in this moment:

We are here to catalyze and be a Planetary Awakening in Love through Unique Self Symphonies.

Imagine, friends, that this was the last thing we ever did. We always want to do everything as if it's our last moment. And when we live as if it's our last moment, then we actually birth an entire new set of possibilities. So as if this was our last moment, that's the way we start.

Let's love it open like we never have before.

TOCHO RATZUF AHAVA: ALLUREMENT AT EVERY EVOLUTIONARY STAGE OF COSMOS

Amor is the basic structure of Reality. *Amor* means love. But love is not a cute, pallid, or simply sweet emotion. Love is the heart of existence itself. Now if you're just listening to that, or if I'm just saying that, and it doesn't blow me out of my seat, then I didn't actually hear it!

As Solomon writes in the Song of Solomon, *Tocho ratzuf ahava*: "Its insides are lined with love." That is to say, **the animating force of reality, that which drives everything, is actually love itself.** That's true from the most fundamental level of manifest reality, which is, let's say, quarks. Quarks disappear from reality if three quarks are not allured to each other and create a triad. Without the ability to create that triad, without being allured and loving each other and creating a larger whole greater than the sum of the parts, at the very fundamental level of manifest reality, Reality disappears. *Reality wouldn't exist.*

Alfred North Whitehead, the great process philosopher, understands that even at the level of atoms there's what he calls "prehension," a proto-sense of feeling, of allurement, which is love in its first manifestation in the world, in cosmological evolution, in the world of matter, or what we call the physiosphere. That love then reappears in a completely new way in the biosphere, the world of life.

That love then reappears in the emergence of sexuality, new forms of feeling, emotion, and the limbic system. And then that love reappears again in the noosphere, in the world of mind. This love is self-reflective and writes poetry, gets wounded and gets ecstatic in an entirely different way. It builds hospitals and creates institutions of care.

When love pathologizes, it creates pain beyond imagination because these forms of love are actually driving all of Reality.

To know that *Amor* **is the center of my life, meaning what drives me, what animates me, is to love and to be loved.** It's underneath everything. And to know that, *it's not just me, but I'm an anthro-ontological expression of the very nature of Reality itself.* Here, *anthro* refers to the human being, and ontological refers to what's real.

Here's the sentence to describe this: "The mysteries are within us." It's a huge principle that we're developing here together.

The mysteries are within us. If I go deep inside, I find the mysteries. **The deeper I go, the more I strip away the surface and I get to the very essence of who I am, the more I cultivate a knowing of my essence, the more I know the essence of Reality.** The mysteries are within.

Amor, the love that drives me, my love story which is the very essence of my life, is participating in a larger frame, which is the Universe: a Love Story.

It's all animated and driven by love—and these are not just *pretty words parading in costume*, but this is the actual ontological essence of Reality itself. If you want to understand in one sense what we are doing here, **we're ontologizing love.**

We're saying that love is real. It's not just a subjective emotion. It's not realized as a social construction. Love is the heart of existence itself. From the subatomic level up through all the structures and levels of evolution— all of it is animated by, driven by, and yearns for love. My love story is chapter and verse in the larger love story of Cosmos. When I begin to know that, I have only one question I ever ask myself:

What does my love story require, demand, and invite me to, in the very next moment?

You can throw out all the law books, throw out all the self-help books, and throw out all the traditions, and just have one question, you can guide your life based on this: "My love story is chapter and verse in the Universe: A Love Story, so what does my love story ask from me, demand from me, and invite me towards in the very next second?" It's so beautiful. It's so gorgeous.

If we just know that and nothing else, then everything is good.

WE LIVE IN AN INTIMATE UNIVERSE IN WHICH EVERY EXCHANGE IS A LOVE SONG

There's a third-century text that reads: "If all the wisdom would not have been given, it would be enough to guide all of life through the Song of Solomon" (the Song of Love). So I want to hold this with you for just a second. My love, we look at each other and we say, "My love! My love!" How else could we possibly address each other? "My love! My Beloved!" But we've exiled love in our culture. We've made love into a particular, narrow form of romantic love that we share with only one person—everyone else is on the outside. Of course:

To have a particular form of romantic love with one person is gorgeous, beautiful, and stunning. But that love has to be the door through which we learn to love everyone.

There's no one whom I turn to where I don't say, "My love! My Beloved! How can I serve you? How could I be devoted to you? How can I receive more of your love? I'm yearning to receive more of your love."

Every exchange is a love letter. Every exchange is a love song. There's nothing else. When I know that, I know that my deepest yearning is a yearning for intimacy. I want to be intimate with you. I want you to be intimate with me. Intimacy can be an expression at every dimension, in every stage of life. Intimacy has one expression in sexuality, but we're not talking about sexuality here. **Sexuality is a beautiful expression of one form of intimacy, but we've exiled intimacy only to sexuality, haven't we?**

However, *all* of Reality is about intimacy.

We live in an Intimate Universe, a universe of allurement—and of appropriate boundaries. It's in that balance between allurement and boundary that love is created. In love we don't fuse with each other; we're actually allured. We break every boundary that should be broken, **but we keep the boundary of our integrity, of our individuated essence—because intimacy desires uniqueness.**

We live in an Intimate Universe. What we're actually saying here together in this *dharma*, through this new story, is that *evolution itself is the progressive deepening of intimacies.* Now if you think, "Yeah, well, we already know that." *Really?* I barely know it! Evolution is the evolution of intimacy. That's such a shocking and radical idea.

Every crisis is an evolutionary driver, and every crisis is a crisis of intimacy. That which heals the crisis is a new configuration of intimacy.

Imagine you're a couple—you and a friend, or you and a partner—and there's a crisis between you. It's a crisis of intimacy. So you need to rewire your intimacy. You need to find new configurations of intimacy between you by bringing more of you to the table, by sharing more, by including and integrating split-off parts of you so that you can create a new tapestry, a new configuration of intimacy.

When single-celled organisms were being poisoned by too much oxygen in the atmosphere, they have to evolve and become multicellular in order to create a new configuration of intimacy. That's always how it works. **It's always a new configuration of intimacy that heals a crisis of intimacy.** One Church is a new configuration of intimacy. We're a Unique Self Symphony arising together. Wow!

So, what's God in this whole story? God is the Infinity of Intimacy. And more: God is the Infinity of Intimacy that knows our name, that wants to be intimate with us.

We express our intimacy not just softly, we express it fiercely. We express our intimacy with all of our creativity. Creativity is a form of intimacy. When I put different parts together and I create a new whole greater than the sum of the parts, that's intimacy. I use all of my power to express my intimate penetration of Reality and I let Reality penetrate me. But when we come together, and we create a new relationship, that new relationship's a new quality of intimacy. Each of us is God's unique intimacy. But we have to begin it softly. We have to begin it with quivering tenderness.

PRAYER: HOMO AMOR, A UNIQUE CONFIGURATION OF INTIMACY, TURNING TO THE INFINITY OF INTIMACY

We now enter into prayer as *Homo amor*, the fulfillment of *Homo sapiens*. *Homo amor* is a unique configuration of intimacy. We turn to God:

- ◆ God who animates
- ◆ God who's the glory of all of evolution
- ◆ God as the animating force and energy in every nanosecond of Reality, the allurement, the holding together and the individuating process and gorgeousness of Reality itself

We turn to God who is not only the process of evolution, as Alfred North Whitehead understood, but is also the intimate Personhood of evolution.

God's more personal than you and me. God is the *most* personal, the Infinity of Personhood, that knows our name and that cares radically about every single being.

And God turns to us and says, "Wow! Do you think you guys are personal? Your interpersonal gorgeous intimacy participates in a larger Field of Intimacy. You hear each other but who hears? Not just your ears but your intelligence—your *intimate* intelligence—hears each other. Your intimate intelligence participates in the Field of *LoveIntelligence*—which is Me, knowing you. And I want to know everything about you. I want to know everything."

That realization, which we call God in the second person, is not a dogma. It's a realization about the true nature of Reality.

We turn to God now. We turn to God who's the Infinity of Intimacy.

> *God, we are your unique intimacies.*
>
> *We're loving each other madly.*
>
> *We're holding each other.*
>
> *You are holding us, and we are holding you because that's Your deepest desire.*
>
> *You love finitude, and You want to be held by us even as we hold You.*
>
> *We hold Your hand, and You hold our hand, and we know that You're the larger space which suffuses our very cells, in which we live every moment.*
>
> *You care about us desperately, and we bring before you our holy and our broken Hallelujah.*

Hallelujah! Let's bring it together. Now can we feel the *Hallelujah*? *Hallelujah* which is pristine praise and *Hallelujah* which is broken intoxication. Oh my God! *Hallelujah!* We'll do it with radical intention. Let's turn to the Infinity of Intimacy and ask for everything. *I can't be a revolutionary, I can't create revolutionary love, unless I'm willing to "ping" God.* You're that "ping" on my computer. We're pinging God. We've got to say to God:

I want everything; give me everything.

I want to be here.

I want to be Your partner.

I need You to help me.

I'm on my knees before You, every time on my knees.

I'm on my knees before You, and I ask for *everything*.

We do this because prayer affirms the dignity of personal need. So let's do it—let's pray. And **if I can't pray, if I can't turn to that Infinity of Intimacy and know that I'm held, then I'm actually alone and lost in the world**

But I'm actually never alone. *I'm always held and never not.* Oh my God! *Hallelujah!*

I love you, God! I love you, Goddess!

EVOLUTIONARY LOVE CODE: I AM THE EVOLUTION OF LOVE

Are you ready to be evolution?

Are you ready to participate in the evolution of consciousness and culture?

Are you ready to participate in the evolution of love?

Are you ready to love deeper and wider than you ever have before?

Are you ready to include something or someone in your circle of love that has always been on the outside?

Are you ready to change, grow, and transform in the way that you have long given up on?

Are you ready to be a dreamer?

Are you ready to activate evolutionary love in you, as you and through you?

Are you ready to be and become more than you ever thought possible?

Are you ready to awaken as conscious evolution?

Loving it open all the way and beyond! Oh my God! It's the knowing that I am Evolution, that evolution depends on me and evolution needs me. I imagine myself at the beginning of the entire evolutionary process. I am there at the first moment of the Big Bang because where else could I possibly have been other than there, at that very first moment of the Big Bang?

> *I am evolution: Evolution is moving in me, and all of the potential of future evolution lives in me.*

When I can access that reality of evolution pulsing in me, when that actually happens, then **I realize that evolution needs me, that evolution needs my service, and I begin to live with an evolutionary relationship to all of life.**

I begin to live in an evolutionary context and then something begins to change. I don't live just for the sake of *making America great again*, and I don't live just for the sake of *making Iran great again*. I can make Iran great or American great. I can be madly committed to Iran as an expression and instrument in the Unique Self Symphony, but we realize *we're all playing music*. I don't make America great again isolated from the world, separated, alienated from reality. I make America great to participate as a gorgeous instrument in the Unique Self Symphony.

- The absurdity of killing each other.
- The absurdity of using exponential high tech to create drones to target enemies.
- The absurdity of Iran deploying all of its resources to target enemies.

What's that about, my friends? Oh my God! What's that about? We need to participate in the evolution of Love. We have to realize that we have so much potential. **We are potentiated—we are the potency of evolution.**

When I feel the evolutionary impulse moving in me, which is the unique configuration of Evolutionary Love that is me, when I realize *I am evolution*, then *I am Eros itself*. But when I don't feel that Eros then I need pseudo-eros. Pseudo-eros is when Iran says *everyone else is an outsider and an infidel, so we're going to destroy everyone because we are the only ones who have the true path*. But within Iran, is it the Shiites or is it the Sunnis who have the true path? *We're not sure so we have to now kill each other within Islam.*

Quite similarly:

- Christianity, through its own set of tragedies for a thousand years, says, *There's no redemption outside of the Church.*
- Tibetan Buddhism says, *We have the only true way where true emptiness is only ours.*
- Islam says, *Dar al harb, dar al Islam.*
- Judaism says, *We're the only chosen people.*

No! No! No! Do you get it?

When we don't have the Eros of being evolution—when evolution's not awake in me, when I don't feel the power of the evolutionary impulse calling me, when I don't realize that Reality needs my service and I am truly the leading edge of evolution itself, giving its gift—then my greatest sense of identity is devastated. I feel small. I feel desperate. I feel like I need something large, so I create a false story. I create a story in which:

- I become inside by making you outside.
- I become me by making you an "other."
- I'm in the circle because I've placed you outside the circle.
- I have an illusion of being on the inside because you're an outsider.

But I'm not really an insider. To be an insider means I live inside the evolutionary impulse, and I know the evolutionary impulse lives inside of each of us.

That is the only response to evil in the world. That is the only response to suffering.

It's all man-made suffering, which comes from us not pointing our love towards how to deal with tsunamis for people in the most disempowered and underprivileged places who get wiped out because we haven't created appropriate technologies for protection. Instead, we're creating drones to strike people. All of that is pseudo-eros.

Pseudo-eros means anything less than the genuine identity of I am evolution, I am a unique configuration of Evolutionary Love.

That's the story we're telling. That's our deepest heart's desire.

I AM AN EXPRESSION OF THE IMPULSE OF CREATION

I'd like to say a word about the phrases, "I am evolution" and, "You are evolution." They give us an angle as we go into the Code. "I am evolution, You are evolution" is such an awesome reality. You're starting before the Big Bang, with the origin of creation. We are coded with the entire story of evolution that made you from the quarks, cells, multi-cells, plants, animals—you're all of those things. Here is what I get about "I am evolution," so we can take this seriously. The seriousness of it is that **I am, and you are, coded with the genius that runs throughout the Universe.** That genius shows up uniquely as each one of us, if we activate our deepest heart's desire.

This is really a lovely thought: that the "I am evolution" inside of you responds most deeply to your deepest heart's desire for the fulfillment of that genius, which is each of us uniquely drawing on the full potentiality of the whole system, the universal evolution of which every one of us is a unique part.

So let's take that in as we look at the Code.

I am evolution. I am an expression of the impulse of creation with the genius that created the entire universe, inside me—uniquely. And as I say *Yes* to that, to go into this Code, the question becomes what kind of impulse are we willing to express? How far are we ready to go?

Let's go into this evolutionary impulse that's been emerging for billions and billions of years. It made the trillions of cells in your bodies—your eyes, your ears, everything—that are all now ready to say *Yes* to you—if you say *Yes* to the whole system.

Are you ready to play a larger game? Wow! Now if you are taking it seriously that you are evolution in person being asked, "Hi evolution in person, are you ready to play a larger game? Listen Ms. or Mr. Evolution, are you?" Well, if you say 'No', you know what happens? You put a lid on the impulse that is you because **the impulse in you and me and every one of us is not only ready to play the larger game, but that's all that it ever does. Evolution is *always* evolving into more.**

So are you ready to play a larger game and if so, what does that feel like? What is this larger game? So, I'll just say that for me it's a Planetary Awakening in Love with the Unique Self Symphonies. That's my larger game. That's also the dedication of the Church. And I would say it's a greeting to the Universe, and She's undoubtedly filled with life. Hello! We are now being born!

Second question: Are you ready to be evolution? Are you ready to participate in the evolution of culture and consciousness? Let's look at that clearly. Are we ready to participate in the evolution of modern culture—

which means the surrounding ideas, thoughts, and innovations that we all live in? Wow! Think about that. Think about how much you love, or do not love, modern culture. What's not so good about it? Modern culture is exactly not a culture of love! I'm not ready to participate in the culture of separation. **I'm ready to participate in the evolution towards a culture of co-creation, where each person is given the opportunity to give their gift to the whole.**

I want culture to be an evolution of consciousness. Well! For that, I need to be aware that I am evolution as a member of this culture, to evolve my deepest understanding and also my activation as a member of this culture and consciousness, playing the larger game toward a Planetary Awakening in Love, as evolution.

Do you see the empowerment that comes when we each personally play all of this out?

Lastly, are you ready to participate in the evolution of love?

I am ready to participate in the evolution of love. Are you? And when you do let's just look at it personally in your own intimate life, what it means to say *Yes* to the evolution of love, not only in general but the evolution of love personally. It's not so much how you love your mate or your children, but how you love the evolution of love itself, as you give your gift to the whole.

Well, I'll just end with this. What is the *feeling* of the evolution of love? I go through the whole core of the spiral and **I feel that the inner impulse of evolution is God**. And God's love is clearly for higher consciousness, more freedom, more order, and more loving creativity.

So, as I'm ready to participate fully in the evolution of love, **I'm ready to join my love with God's love as an aspect of the entire process of creation.**

CHAPTER FIVE

ONTOLOGIZING LOVE: LOVE IS REAL

Episode 170 — January 12, 2020

EVOLUTIONARY LOVE CODE: LOVE IS REAL

Let's begin with our Evolutionary Love Code for the week:

> Reality is lined with love.
>
> The inside of Reality is LoveIntelligence.
>
> This is not ordinary love, what is usually referred to as love. It is rather what we call Outrageous Love or Evolutionary Love.
>
> Ordinary love is the exile of love to a merely human experience. That experience is often a strategy of the ego for security or status. Ordinary love is generally a passing emotional state, and most often the emotion of infatuation.
>
> Outrageous or Evolutionary Love is not "mere human sentiment; it is the heart of existence itself." It is what Dante called, "the love that moves the sun and other stars."
>
> When human love participates in the larger quality of Outrageous Love, it is no longer merely a passing emotion. Rather, it becomes the center of gravity of your life.
>
> You are lived as love—a radically alive, joy-filled, and purpose-driven life.

When you awaken as Evolutionary Love, you realize your identity as an Evolutionary Lover. When you awaken as Outrageous Love, you realize your identity as an Outrageous Lover.

You deepen your identity from I am evolution to I am evolutionary love.

I am an Evolutionary Lover.

I am an Outrageous Lover.

Our intention is to ontologize love. What does that mean? Ontology means "for realsies." It means discovering what's real and true.

Love is real. It's not a social construction. It's not made-up. It's not a custom or a way of engaging Reality that just helps us manage or survive.

Ontology means it's the real, true essence of Reality itself. **Our Evolutionary Love Code is about ontologizing love, so that we actually know in our body the deep physics of Cosmos**—bringing together the best of the exterior sciences, the best implications of quantum physics, molecular biology, etc., with the best of all of the interior sciences of enlightenment, weaving together all the strands of premodern, modern, and postmodern knowledge—**which all point to the fact that love is the most real force in the world.**

Love is not weak. **Love is the strongest force in the world.**

Its insides are lined with love, wrote King Solomon. Now we know the truth of that in a way we never have before, and that Reality at its core is driven by Eros; it's driven by love. The four fundamental forces—the strong and weak nuclear, the electromagnetic, and the gravitational—are themselves animated by an interior Eros, an interior quality of love, that actually drives Reality to become more of itself.

Reality is always seeking more love, more depth. And love here moves towards creativity, intimacy, towards Goodness, Truth, and Beauty.

"The strange attractor," "the chaotic attractor" of the entire evolutionary process—in the best understanding of leading-edge sciences—is Outrageous Love.

Outrageous Love is not ordinary love, which is mere human sentiment, a strategy of ego. **Outrageous Love, or what we sometimes call Evolutionary Love, is the heart of existence itself.** That's what Dante meant when he said it's the *love which moves the sun and other stars.*

WE HAVE THE CAPACITY TO CREATE HEAVEN ON EARTH, WHERE EVERY HUMAN BEING KNOWS: I AM A UNIQUE CONFIGURATION OF EVOLUTIONARY LOVE

First we need to realize that:

- Reality is not a fact, it's a story.
- It's not an ordinary story. Reality is a love story.
- Reality is not an ordinary love story. It's an Outrageous Love Story.

And then when you bring it home in your actual lived realization, you realize that your story is not just a fact—it's a love story. It's not an ordinary love story but an Outrageous Love story. Then you bring those two pieces of information together, and you realize:

- My Outrageous Love Story is chapter and verse in the Universe: A Love Story.
- My Outrageous Love Story is intended and desired and chosen and recognized and celebrated and needed by the Universe: A Love Story.
- When I awaken as my Unique Self—in my Outrageous Love

story, as chapter and verse in the Universe: A Love Story—
then I am lived as love.

♦ Then I give my gifts in ways that are beyond imagination.

Our intention is to ontologize love by bringing together every field of Reality—from physics, attachment theory, psychology, anthropology, biology, and epigenetics, as well as the interior sciences and wisdom traditions—**weaving them all together, as da Vinci did, in this time between worlds.**

We're living in a time between worlds. The old world is completing itself, teetering on the edge of extinction and existential threats. We stand with potential dystopia gaping beneath us.

And at the same time we have the ability to draw together the strands of new knowledge and new information to articulate and tell a new story, as da Vinci and friends did in the Renaissance, which was also a time between worlds.

That new story is the chaotic attractor, the evolutionary attractor.

It's the strange attractor that's going to take us from a potential dystopia to the capacity to create heaven on earth where every human being knows, *I am a unique configuration of Evolutionary Love.* That message, that teaching, that delight, that joy—that is our commitment.

Now, you may think this is going to be done somewhere else. No, there's nowhere else—it's us. In this generation, it's ours to do.

Of course we've got friends and initiatives and people all over the world who are doing their expressions of this but, at the core, it's our job here at One Mountain, Many Paths to realize this transition.

It's our job together to be like da Vinci and to usher in this new possibility, in this time between worlds. Wow.

PRAYER: THE INTIMATE FACE OF OUTRAGEOUS LOVE

We're about to go into prayer, where we actually begin to access this quality of Outrageous Love. One of the faces of Outrageous Love is intimacy. **One of the key principles of the *dharma* that we're working on together, one of the fundamental principles of the structure of Cosmos, is that we live in an Intimate Universe and evolution is the evolution of intimacy. Evolution is the progressive deepening of intimacies.**

When we actually realize this, based on the interior and exterior sciences, we begin to understand and can approach God.

The god you don't believe in doesn't exist. God is not a cosmic vending machine in the sky, nor a father or mother in heaven who punishes us when we act out, or who demands our blind obedience. God is actually the source of Reality, the Infinity of Power. We call that God in the third person, which includes:

- All the laws of physics
- All the laws of quantum relativity integrated together in their final, grand unified integration, when that finally arrives
- All the laws of molecular biology
- The entire table of periodic elements, which is the original alphabet of Cosmos

That's just one dimension of God: God in the third person. That's the Infinity of Power, intelligence beyond imagination. It's that which manifests photosynthesis, which all the supercomputers in the world combined could not even begin to imagine—how to manifest a chlorophyll molecule—which is one of the most dazzling, most radically amazing expressions of God in the third person.

But there's a second dimension of God, which actually lives in me. That's God in the first person. That's *Tat Tvam Asi*, or "Thou art That." But it's not just being—*I'm also becoming.*

I am evolution. What we understand is that evolution is not just a process out there, but that evolution lives in me.

I am evolution.

Not just *I am evolution* but, as we've said, *I'm a unique configuration of Evolutionary Love. I'm a unique configuration of Outrageous Love*—and *Reality needs me.*

So that's I AM, *Tat Tvam* Asi, God in the first person.

But there's also God in the second person, an essential part of Reality, which is the actual Personhood of Divinity. And when we say Personhood, we don't mean it in the sense of personality, we mean the Personhood that's beyond the impersonal.

In other words, **God is not only the Infinity of Power, but God is the Infinity of Intimacy.**

Imagine your most intimate moment ever—the most beautiful moment of your life, your most intimate erotic moment, your most intimate tender moment, *feel the raw pulsing Eros of it, the sweet dripping tenderness of it*—and exponentialize it, and then exponentialize it again, and then exponentialize it yet again. *Then you begin to get the fragrance of Divinity.*

- God is the Infinity of Intimacy that knows your name.
- God knows your name.
- God needs you.
- God needs your service.
- God invites and demands our partnership.

It's only when we partner with God that we can create *more God to come.* We become love in action; evolution is love in action as you and me. And that's what it means when Barbara talks about awakening to conscious evolution.

So in this moment we turn to God in prayer. We're reclaiming prayer, and we're reclaiming God at the center of this revolution—God who's the Infinity of Intimacy, God in the third person and the first person, but also God in the second person, God who holds me.

Every place I fall, I fall into Your hands, and I can bring you—God— everything. I can bring you all of me. Nothing's left out. You hold all of me. Every place I fall, I fall into your hands, and I bring you, and we all bring you in this moment, our holy and our broken Hallelujah.

So the first thing we do as we begin, we bring every flower, every wilted flower, every beautiful flower and we place it on the altar. That's the first part of prayer. Then the second part of prayer is, we ask for everything. We ask for everything because prayer affirms the dignity of personal need—*I can't meet the needs of the world, I can't meet the needs of God, until I can meet and dignify my own deepest heart's desire.* Those are my needs, and I ask for myself and for my uncle and for my cousin and for my daughter and my brother and my sister and...

WE LIVE IN A WORLD OF OUTRAGEOUS PAIN AND THE ONLY RESPONSE TO OUTRAGEOUS PAIN IS OUTRAGEOUS LOVE

Are we ready to play a larger game? Are we ready to participate in the evolution of love? Here's the credo; this is what we stand for. This is what we live for. This is where we lay our life down in the most deep, most gorgeous, and most radically alive way, demanding from ourselves in revolution for Reality. Here's the sentence:

We live in a world of outrageous beauty; the only response to outrageous beauty is Outrageous Love. But we also live in a world of outrageous pain, and the only response to outrageous pain is Outrageous Love.

We refuse to deaden our sensitivity to pain through theology, whether it's Buddhist or Jewish or Christian or Taoist.

- ◆ We refuse to say that suffering is just an illusion.
- ◆ We refuse to say that suffering will somehow be taken care of in the next world.
- ◆ We demand a response to suffering now.
- ◆ We demand it from God.
- ◆ We demand it from the God who lives in ourselves.
- ◆ We take full responsibility for the evolution of love.

The only response to outrageous pain is Outrageous Love, and we *are* Outrageous Love. Evil is a failure of intimacy, a violation of the Intimate Universe. So the only response to pain can be the restoration of intimacy. **The restoration of intimacy is Outrageous Love, when I actually awaken as conscious evolution and realize that the interior of evolution is Evolutionary Love.**

Donald Hoffman is talking very beautifully about the notion that consciousness is fundamental. It's underneath the space-time continuum. He's doing an enormous amount of work in evolutionary game theory and in bringing together anomalies between quantum gravity and loop gravity and relativity—and discussing the ways that physics today basically tells us that space-time is doomed and, with that, the objects in space-time. What I mean by that is the notion that consciousness isn't quite enough—the physicalist, materialist understanding of science is now doomed in science itself, doomed by the leading edges of physics.

So what is the Reality that Hoffman is talking about, along with quite a lot of other people, in a very beautiful way? First, it's the understanding that **consciousness is fundamental.** But that's not quite a deep enough understanding. Consciousness is not just awareness. Consciousness—at its deepest interior core, in the deepest realization of the interior sciences—is love.

Love is the inside of the inside.

Or, as our Kashmir Shaivite friends, our Hindu friends, say it so beautifully: *Sat Chit Ananda.* Barbara and I used to study this phrase together all the time. *Sat* means being, *Chit* means consciousness, *Ananda* means bliss-love.

WHO AM I? WHAT DOES REALITY NEED FROM ME IN THIS MOMENT?

Sat is being. The inside of being is consciousness, *Chit*. But the inside of consciousness is *Ananda*, love. In other words, *its inside are lined with love.* It's not ordinary love but Outrageous Love.

Who am I? I'm an Outrageous Lover. That's the true nature of my identity.

That's not a metaphor. That's not a simile or a symbol. It's not a mythopoetic read.

It's my true nature. I am an Outrageous Lover.

What do Outrageous Lovers do? Of course, Outrageous Lovers keep every boundary that should be kept, and they break every boundary that should be broken.

What boundary do we break as Outrageous Lovers? The boundary of contraction, the boundary of smallness, the boundary of limitation, the boundary that caused me to give up my dreams, to forget my greatness, to forget that I'm intended and desired and needed by All-That-Is.

But what does All-That-Is need from me? What does Reality need from me? Reality needs me to do what Outrageous Lovers do.

What do Outrageous Lovers do? Outrageous Lovers commit Outrageous Acts of Love.

But which Outrageous Acts of Love do Outrageous Lovers commit? Outrageous Lovers commit Outrageous Acts of Love that are a function of their Unique Self.

What's my Unique Self? Your Unique Self is the answer to the one great question we're ever asked: *Who are you?*

You are an irreducibly unique expression of the Outrageous LoveIntelligence and LoveBeauty and LoveDesire that is the initiating and animating Outrageous Love and Eros of All-That-Is that lives in you, as you, and through you.

You are the leading edge of Reality, the leading edge of evolution.

That Outrageous LoveIntelligence that lives in you, as you, and through you—that never was, is, or will be ever again, other than through you—has gifts to give that are utterly unique, that can't be given by anyone that ever was, is, or will be ever again in Cosmos.

So you are evolution in action. I am evolution in action. You are love in action. **You are literally the leading edge of evolution.**

There's one practice in One Church, One Mountain, Many Paths, one question we ask: *Who am I?* And we answer: *I am Outrageous Love.*

There's another question we ask. The question that emerges from the first question is: *What does Reality need from me in this moment?* It's so gorgeous! That's it! That's the whole practice.

> *What does Reality need from me in this moment? Reality needs my Outrageous Acts of Love.*

THE PRACTICE OF HOMO AMOR IS WRITING OUTRAGEOUS LOVE LETTERS

I'm going to add one more piece. How do you access the energy to write, to talk about, to commit your Outrageous Acts of Love? How do you get beyond the contraction, the depression, the hardness, the difficulty of the whole thing? How do you do it?

There's a practice that is not quite meditation—which is a really important and beautiful practice. And it's not prayer—which is core to what we do here, as we address the Infinity of Intimacy that knows our name. This is the third great turning of the wheel in this evolutionary moment, which is the emergence of *Homo amor*—the new human, the new humanity—the fulfillment of *Homo sapiens*.

The practice of Homo amor is writing Outrageous Love Letters. An Outrageous Love Letter is when I exaggerate until I'm accurate.

I can write to myself, I can write to God/Goddess, I can write to a friend, I can write to a Beloved. Or in my Outrageous Love Letter, I can write about an Outrageous Act of Love.

I'm writing to myself, to God, to a tree, to a special person—I'm writing to Reality, and I'm saying,

> *Oh my God! I love you madly! You're more beautiful than you can possibly imagine.*
>
> *And I need you!*
>
> *I'm going to dance with you, and we're going to be alive together.*
>
> *We're going to make the world better together.*

61

When you're writing an Outrageous Love Letter to someone, or to yourself, you sing their beauty. You say, *Behold! You're beautiful Beloved. Behold!* And you speak of their beauty outrageously.

- You become Rumi.
- You become Hafiz.
- You become Tagore.
- You become the Poet.
- You become the enlightened master.

You can write an Outrageous Love Letter to another person, to yourself, or you can tell the story of an Outrageous Act of Love that you committed. But you can't be humble—we don't go for false humility. **You have to be audacious** because your Outrageous Love Letter will inspire ten more people to commit Outrageous Acts of Love.

UNIQUE SELF SYMPHONY COMMITTING OUTRAGEOUS ACTS OF LOVE

And then we come together, each of us Unique Selves committing our Outrageous Acts of Love, and we become a Unique Self Symphony. We begin to generate, via the noosphere—which is now expressed via the internet, through the connections where we virtually connect virtue and Reality—a Planetary Awakening in Love through Unique Self Symphonies, which is the intention of this revolution.

We want to have not a top-down corporation or top-down government, but a bottom-up, self-organizing universe. We each self-organize as our Unique Selves.

I self-organize, I awaken, and I know what to do, because I'm called by the strange attractor of my Unique Self. My Unique Self is a unique expression of LoveIntelligence. I have Outrageous Acts of Love to commit that no one other than me can commit and, as such:

- I become love in action.
- I become the leading edge of evolution.
- I become the dream of God.
- I become the mind of God spoken in the adjectives and verbs of my loving, my Outrageous Acts of Love.

We're now going to take the next step in conscious evolution, which is the democratization of greatness.

How do we generate a revolution of bottom-up Unique Self Symphony? You need to see the Unique Self Symphony as the next iteration of the self-organizing Universe, as the next emergence of intimacy—it's Evolutionary Intimacy.

We come together as a Unique Self Symphony, each of us committing our Outrageous Acts of Love as Outrageous Lovers. Which Outrageous Acts of Love? Those that are a function of our Unique Self.

That's huge. We actually become the Evolution of Intimacy. We become *Homo amor*, the Intimate Universe in person.

This is the revolution. This is the time. This is ours to do.

We can awaken Reality, let this cascade like ripples *as we begin to reclaim love as religion towards a politics of love*. It's a politics of Outrageous Love.

At the center of this entire story is you.

It's your next Outrageous Act of Love that literally can tip the balance. Oh my God!

63

EVOLUTIONARY CHAKRA MEDITATION: BREATHING IN THE STORY OF CREATION

I am feeling within myself what it means to be within an Evolutionary Church. Until we co-created this, I didn't realize that I'd been missing it all my life. I've always felt this impulse of creative evolution coming through me, but I had no place to give it, to share it, to know it until very recently. And as I began to find others, I was turned on with joy and realized that each of us has a tremendous role to play in the evolution of the world. I am grateful that we have formed the Evolutionary Church. We are truly pioneering souls. This has not been done before.

Today, I would like to start out with a meditation of resonance to remember who we are as expressions of the process of creation. I call it the Evolutionary Chakra Meditation.

We're going to deeply breathe in the whole story of creation.

> Place your attention now on Source, on the source of evolution in the mind of God. Breathe in from that source all that was, is now, and will be.
>
> From the first seconds of the Big Bang, see the evolutionary spiral unfolding. Energy, matter, life, the biosphere, single-celled life, animal life, human life, and now humans taking around the next turn on the spiral of evolution, as we face the destruction of all life on Earth or the evolution of life to its next stage.
>
> Breathe in this multi-billion year story of creation into your lowest chakra, and feel the security of that core of the spiral of evolution carrying the genius of all that came before us, infusing the lowest chakra of your body. Feel the security.
>
> Now returning once again to the mind of God, feel the power of that process of creation and impulse of creativity entering your regenerative organs, and see yourself shifting from degeneration toward regeneration, from procreation toward co-creation. Feel the awakening of the immense power of the generative organs to the

impulse of evolution.

Now breathe up once again through the mind of God through billions of years of evolution, through your sense of deep security, through your tremendous powers of regeneration and co-creation. Place that power into your mid power center; and feel the power of your presence, the power of your greatness, and the power of your uniqueness. Breathe the entire impulse into that power center and send it out into the world consciously expressing the power of that impulse as you in the world, with all your genius coated in it.

Radiate that creativity and power.

Starting once again in the mind of God, in one deep breath, bring that impulse of evolution up into your heart, carrying the frequency and genius of the whole process into your deep heart-sense of unconditional love. Love of the entire story of creation; love of all that came before you, and love now of everyone on Earth, starting with those you most love—your sister, your brother, your mother, your father, your children, your friends, your community of influence.

Now let that impulse of love extend even further.

Let it reach out into the global communion of pioneering souls everywhere on earth, just like us awakening to their own inner impulse of creativity, your love touching them in the vast domain of universal intelligence.

Now bring that impulse of evolution further up into the heart, and feel it as your gift of love, your vocation, your calling, your intention to create. Feel that mighty story of the spiral of evolution in your upper heart.

Feel your unique gift of love going out, expressing that which you were given to give, with the joy in the giving of it, to all you love and beyond.

Now going once again up from the mind of God, through all the chakras of your being, feel the impulse reach your throat. Let your voice vibrate when you speak with the resonance of creation, the frequency of vibration of the evolutionary impulse as you.

Sound your note when you speak in the Evolutionary Church with this impulse of power and creativity.

Now bring the impulse of evolution all the way up from Source, through all the evolutionary levels of energy, matter, life, animal life, through your own security, generative organs, power, vocation, and heart.

Bring it up through your throat into your third eye.

Activate the supramental genius of the whole process of creation embodied in you.

Now contact your expression of the divine process, as you, at the threshold of your own evolution. At this precise moment when the evolution of the world is shifting from one stage to the next, place the genius and power of your impulse of creation, shifting the scales of history towards more life, more love, more genius, in the great 13.8-billion-year tradition of evolution. We could say, *Hallelujah evolution!*

Breathe the impulse all the way up and all the way down.

You and we are the whole story of creation in person.

Thank you.

CHAPTER SIX

NO ONE AND NOTHING IS OUTSIDE THE CIRCLE

Episode 171 — January 19, 2020

BECOMING HOMO AMOR, THE INTIMATE UNIVERSE IN PERSON

We're trying—with all our hearts, our full intention, our full directionality, in this time between worlds—to make what we are absolutely convinced is the utterly and absolutely necessary, move towards intimacy in Cosmos.

We live in an Intimate Universe. Evolution is core to the *dharma*, the new story based on the best interior and exterior science, that we are unpacking together. Evolution is in fact the evolution of intimacy—and we've unpacked an entire set of Tenets of Intimacy in our deeper teaching.

The Intimate Universe is the structure of Reality. Evolution itself is the progressive deepening of intimacies.

This is not a casual sentence. It's not a fundamentalist sentence. It's not a New Age sentence. It's actually the structure of the Universe mapped across all fields, from physics, to chemistry, to molecular biology, to sociology, to psychology, to political science, to the major schools of economics.

What underlies them all is this movement towards intimacy. **Intimacy is when separate parts come together to create a new whole.**

And importantly, that new whole is a new value.

- It's a new whole that's greater than the sum of the parts.
- It's a new emergent, a new emergent of intimacy.
- It's a new emergent of caring, of kindness, of love, of goodness, of truth, and beauty.

As Whitehead said, it is the Eros or allurement as Reality is drawn towards ever deeper goodness, ever deeper truths, ever deeper beauty, ever deeper love.

Evolution, at its core, is the evolution of love.

Each one of us is a new emergent. The intention of the church is to come together as a new emergent and usher in—to bring down, if you will—the One Church, the synagogue, the mosque, the secular humanist center, whatever we call ourselves, this global communion.

Our intention is to do as da Vinci did after the Black Death had swept through Europe. It was impossible to go to every village and heal individuals at the beginning of the Renaissance, which was itself a time between worlds. The old world was collapsing, the new world wasn't there yet, suffering was everywhere. We're at a moment like that, but the suffering is exponential and the potential for pain and devastation, because we have exponential tech. And exponential tech can create exponential suffering, and with every new dimension of progress we have a new potential pathology. Our progress, our technological progress, is so immense but therefore so is the potential destruction, so is the potential alienation, so is the potential extinction.

So in this time between worlds we have to articulate a new story, which itself is a new iteration of intimacy. Evolution iterates deeper and

deeper configurations of intimacy. It's the realization that I'm not just *Homo sapiens*, but that *Homo sapiens* fulfills herself in *Homo amor*.

I am *Homo amor*. *Homo amor* is the Intimate Universe in person, as you. Wow!

It's our time. We're just in time for a time like this; each of us, here together at One Church, One Mountain, Many Paths is at this leading edge of evolution. All of our lives led us here. Think about it for a second. How did we get here? All of our lives led us to be here at this time and in this place.

Where are we? We live in a world of outrageous beauty. The only response to outrageous beauty is Outrageous Love. And where else are we? We live in a world of outrageous pain. We can't turn away, so the only response to outrageous pain is Outrageous Love. That's where we are.

We live in a world where the only response to outrageous pain is Outrageous Love. But what is Outrageous Love? **Outrageous Love is the realization of love as ontology: what drives evolution is love itself.**

- Eros is the animating force of evolution.
- Eros animates the strong and the weak nuclear forces, the electromagnetic force, and the gravitational force.
- Eros moves Reality forward.
- Eros transforms Reality from *Oops! Something happened!* to a self-organizing Universe moving to deeper and greater and wider and more stunning expressions of Value, of Goodness, Truth, and Beauty.

Evolution is love in action. And **evolution is the evolution of love.** So who am I in that story? I'm an Outrageous Lover. That's who I am. I'm an Evolutionary Lover. Outrageous Love is not ordinary love, but the heart of existence itself. It's ontological, and it's the nature of Reality: *its insides are lined with love.* *Amor* animates everything, all the way up and all the way down. Wow!

The only reason that we can challenge evil in the world is because evil is a failure of intimacy. **Evil is a breakdown of the Intimate Universe, which is why we cry out against it, because we are the Intimate Universe awake in person as Outrageous Lovers.**

WHAT DOES IT MEAN TO COMMIT OUTRAGEOUS ACTS OF LOVE?

When I awaken as an Outrageous Lover, what do I do?

+ When I awaken as an Outrageous Lover, I commit Outrageous Acts of Love.

Which Outrageous Acts of Love do I commit?

+ Those that are a function of my Unique Self.

And what is my Unique Self?

+ Unique Self is the deepest answer to the question: *Who are you?*
+ You are irreducibly unique—it's not just social, psychological, and cultural conditioning that forms you, there's a Self. *There's a Self on the inside and that Self is who you are.* It's a Unique Self.

You're an irreducibly unique expression of the LoveIntelligence and LoveBeauty that is the initiating and animating Eros and energy of All-That-Is that lives in you, as you, and through you that never was, is, or will be ever again other than through you. And, as such:

+ You have a unique perspective.
+ You incarnate a unique quality of intimacy.
+ You're a unique taste.

And all that together fosters your unique gift. Your unique gift addresses a unique need in your unique circle of influence that can be addressed by no one who ever was, is, or will be, other than you. **When you awaken as evolution, as love in action, uniquely as you, the actions you take to address those unique needs in your unique circle of intimacy and influence are your Outrageous Acts of Love.**

EVOLUTIONARY LOVE CODE: OUTRAGEOUS ACTS OF LOVE AT THE LEADING EDGE OF EVOLUTION

Outrageous Acts of Love are a function of Unique Self.

Outrageous Acts of Love are almost always those which we can get away with not doing.

- An Outrageous Act of Love might be smiling when we want to withhold or opening our heart when it's more comfortable to keep our heart closed.
- An Outrageous Act of Love might be just changing your tone of voice and making it more gentle and more tender in a strident argument.
- It might be sending a text with an overflowing heart so people can feel you.
- It might be taking a stand when we can get away with not taking a stand.

Outrageous Acts of Love always mean we give ourselves outrageously, beyond our trauma, beyond our issues, beyond our patterns. With true Outrageous Acts of Love, there's always a way to rationalize to ourselves why we don't have to do it. We can always think of reasons:

- Why they can be done by someone else
- Why they're not ours to do
- Why it's not our responsibility

But my unique risk in life is to actually commit my Outrageous Acts of Love above and beyond what culture demands from me. **It's the small, still**

inner voice of *Amor* that is the leading edge of Evolution, expressing your deepest heart's desire, coming awake inside of you.

Reality is desire. The deepest heart's desire of Divinity awake in you is to commit those Outrageous Acts of Love that are yours and yours alone to commit.

When we live from that place, we live in Eros. That's what Eros means. Eros means that I'm committing the Outrageous Acts of Love that flow naturally from my identity as *Homo amor*, as an Outrageous Lover, as an Evolutionary Lover.

When I'm not living in that Eros then I feel empty. I feel desiccated. That's why I have to take my unique risk and commit my Outrageous Acts of Love.

In fact, the only real risk is *not* to take that unique risk.

The only real danger is *not* to take my unique risk. When I feel empty— when I feel desiccated, when I feel out of sorts with myself, I feel depressed, I feel the utter futility of life, that nothing I do is going to make a difference, or I feel frustration or rage—**I hide. And then I cover it with this low-grade sadness. That's the breakdown of Eros.**

Whenever Eros breaks down, I have a desperate need to feel like I'm "on the inside," but I don't know how to get there; I don't know how to get inside. So I place someone else on the outside; I create a "them." That might be my partner, when I'm in a constant cycle of argument with them. The "them" might be my society. Or it might be some moment where I was wounded, and then I make that wound affect all of my life, because then I have an outside, something split-off.

I create the illusion of being on the inside by placing someone else on the outside; there's an in-group and there's an out-group. That's a violation of Outrageous Love.

There's always been—all through history—an in-group and out-group. What we're doing as we're awakening to the new human and the new humanity is that we're removing the boundary. **We're entering into no-boundary consciousness.** It used to be, "I'm on the inside and you're on the outside." Now everyone's on the inside together.

I don't create the illusion of being on the inside by placing you on the outside. I want to just take it one step further, and it's so beautiful. Here's the way you do it.

BY EMBRACING AND TRANSFORMING OUR SHADOW IN OUTRAGEOUS LOVE, WE NO LONGER PLACE OTHERS OUTSIDE THE CIRCLE

You do it by loving yourself so madly that you can actually recognize your shadow. When you live as Unique Self, when you live as an Outrageous Lover, you have no trouble recognizing, *Oh, that's my shadow! That's why I messed up. That's why I didn't quite do it.* You recognize and embrace your shadow.

By embracing your shadow, you have no need to project it out onto someone else.

When I split off my shadow; when I split off the unfulfilled parts of me; when I split off the negativity, the pain, the depression, the acting out; when I can't actually own it, recognize it, and transform it; when I don't have enough Eros in me as a Unique Self to be able to look; when I'm not held in love by my Self, when I don't feel held by She; when I don't allow the

Infinity of Intimacy to hold me; when I can't be held in love—it all breaks down.

I can only feel held when I realize my true identity as an Outrageous Lover, as a Unique Self, and only then can I actually recognize my shadow.

Shadow is only transformed when it's held in love.

And it can only be held in Outrageous Love—not ordinary love, but the love that is my very identity; that's the heart of existence itself, holding me.

When I don't hold that shadow, when I don't recognize that shadow, which I can only do when I'm held in love, I split the shadow off. It festers, and it can't go anywhere, so I project it onto you. Tragically, I create an enemy out of you, or an enemy out of a part of myself, and I begin to secretly hate a part of myself, something I can't admit or show to anyone else.

Or I'm in a constant fight with you.

Or I create an "other." For example, the other might be Republicans: *They're all bad.* No, they're not because that's a lot of people. Sure, we can fight it out, we can take issue, we can challenge evil any place where it exists, but we must not create an "other."

We take the "other," whether inside or outside, and transform it in the face of fierce, rigorous, and powerful Outrageous Love. We obliterate the boundary. There's no more us/them. We begin to be a Unique Self Symphony of *Homo amor* committing our Outrageous Acts of Love.

Imagine that, friends, imagine that!

CHAPTER SEVEN

THE PATH AND PRACTICE OF HOMO AMOR—OUTRAGEOUS ACTS OF LOVE

Episode 172 — January 26, 2020

THE STORY IS THE EVOLUTION OF DIVINITY—AND IT'S ALWAYS A LOVE STORY

This is the moment where we set our intention. What are we here for? We're here for the realization that *everyone's on the inside*; that no one's outside of the story.

We're here to articulate a new Universe Story. We're at a pivotal moment in culture, a pivotal moment in history. **For the first time in the history of planet Earth we have the capacity to *end the story*.** We're faced with existential risk that can lead to a dystopia that's unimaginable—think *Hunger Games*, think *Blade Runner*, or think the end of the story. And at the same time, we have the capacity to up-level; we have the capacity to bring together everything we've learned from premodern, modern, and postmodern wisdom and actually tell a new story.

When *Homo sapiens* spread onto the savanna 70,000 years ago and emerged out of the world to become human beings, they emerged out of the larger natural world. *Homo sapiens* came into existence some 150,000 years ago, and about 70,000 years ago we woke up. There was a Big Bang, and self-reflection

began, giving rise to art, deep interiority, poetry, music, trade, the multiplication of knowledge. Everything that we understand to be a human being which is fundamentally different than any expression of life on the Cosmos—that explosion of humanity happened 70,000 years ago.

Most people understand that the reason it happened is because of what science calls the emergence of language. Language didn't just tell us how to hunt a little better, as some people suggest; in language, we are able to tell a story. A story that told us who we were, where we are from, and where we are going: a Universe Story, and a story of identity. Now those stories are evolving; this is the evolution of love. It's the evolution of a story. And the stories were always moving towards: *What does it mean to be noble, to be good, to be radically alive, to be aligned with Cosmos*? Those stories are the evolution of Divinity and importantly, **it was always a love story.**

THE PROBLEM: WE PUT THE BOUNDARY IN THE WRONG PLACE

My friend Howard Bloom wrote a famous book called *The Lucifer Principle*, in which he talks about this notion that *there was always us and them.* There was always an in-group killing the out-group. "So Marc," he asked me, "how could you possibly talk about a love story?"

I said to him: "Yes, there was always an in-group and out-group, but Howard, as you yourself wrote in your book, *the in-group always knew that they had to love each other.*"

Does everyone understand that? The in-group always knew *if you're in the in-group, I've got to love you and I have to love all humans*—but then they said, *We're going to take this group of people and we're going to say, you guys aren't included in human beings.*

The problem was the wrong boundary. What we said is *we're going to create our Eros by placing us on the inside, and you on the outside.* That's a pseudo-eros; that's a false boundary.

76

So, we have to realize: It's always a love story.

There's always an in-group. We've known that from the beginning of time. But what we did is *we placed the boundary in the wrong place.*

What we've done is removed the boundary. Of course, all my natural healthy boundaries exist, and all my natural, inner personal boundaries— where I respect your integrity, individuality—those are all in place.

The boundary I remove is: there's no one outside the circle; there's no one whose story doesn't matter.

To remove the boundary means that every human being has a poem to write, a piece of music to play, a way of being, loving, living, and laughing in the world that's uniquely yours alone. It's not your special talent; it's your unique expression of the entire Field.

- ◆ You are an emergence of the entire Field of Existence.
- ◆ You're an emergence of the entire Field of Being and Becoming.
- ◆ You have a poem to write, a song to sing, a story to tell.
- ◆ Your story matters infinitely.

It's my job, my delight, my honor, and my responsibility as a human being to create the conditions for you to live your story, to create the conditions for you to tell your story, to create the conditions for your story to be received.

And no one is outside the circle; not one human being is outside the circle. If you're in pain I feel your pain, and if you're in joy I feel your joy. That's our intention.

Our intention is to know that *everyone's in the circle.* That's the new story of *Homo amor.* It's the story of me being an expression of the self-organizing Universe. Because I matter, because you matter, because your unique, irreducible gorgeousness matters.

> *Part of your story is your Outrageous Acts of Love; it means that Reality needs your service.*

Our intention is to awaken all of humanity with us to be the storytellers. In this da Vinci moment, in this time between worlds, we are standing here and saying: *we're going to tell the new story*; we're going to articulate the new Universe Story, the new story of identity.

The only way you can up-level is to go into the source code. And the source code of being a human being is the story we tell about the universe, and who we are, and who we are to each other. Now we're going to up-level that story.

The Universe is a love story, and **the plotline of this love story is the evolution of love, the evolution of uniqueness, the evolution of creativity, the evolution of kindness.** We *are* that evolution in person—in each one of us, and our practice, and our church. We want to articulate what it means to be a new human and a new humanity. We want to be *Homo amor*, which is the Intimate Universe in person and as us. As *Homo amor*, each of us knows that we have Outrageous Acts of Love to commit.

I'm going to share with Reality one Outrageous Act of Love that I committed and hope to inspire a thousand people to do the same as we come together in Unique Self Symphony. What an intention—beyond imagination. We're going to talk about it more in depth. We're going to show how to do it. I'm so insanely honored to be here with you. Insanely means beyond normal consciousness. It's the true consciousness. Insanity in this case actually means sanity.

We're the magic, telling the new story is our da Vinci moment.

Reality needs us.

AT THE OUTRAGEOUS LEVEL, THE TRINITY
BECOMES ONE

There's one great practice called meditation. When I meditate I find that the inside of Reality is consciousness, and I see I am that consciousness. That's beautiful and a gorgeous practice.

Prayer is another practice where I pray to God who is beyond Reality, who holds me and holds all of Reality, and who infuses all of Reality. And I ask for everything because prayer affirms the dignity of personal need. That's a great practice.

So the first turning of the wheel is meditation, and the second turning of the wheel is prayer. But now, to initiate *Homo amor* as the fulfillment of *Homo sapiens* we need the third turning of the wheel. The third turning of the wheel is to awaken to the truth that *I am a unique configuration of Outrageous Love*. And in this awakening of *Homo amor* we have a practice.

The practice is writing Outrageous Love Letters and committing Outrageous Acts of Love. Before we get to the practice, let's first understand that when we awaken to the truth that *I am a unique configuration of Outrageous Love*, we're seeing the third-person—the Outrageous Love which is a force that moves through all the Cosmos and animates the strong and the weak nuclear, the electromagnetic, and the gravitational forces—all laws are animated by Outrageous Love.

Outrageous Love is also God in the second person who knows me. It's that relational love, that space in between. It's the Infinity of Intimacy that lives between us and that holds us. This is God in the second person.

But it's also God in the first person: *I am a unique configuration.* **At that "Outrageous" level, the Trinity becomes one.** When I awaken to my true identity and I feel the ecstatic urgency—the feeling of being an Outrageous Lover is ecstatic urgency. When I feel the ecstatic urgency awake and alive in me, and I ask one question: *what does Reality need from me in the next moment?*

79

EVOLUTIONARY LOVE CODE: REALITY NEEDS YOUR SERVICE

> Your Unique Gift addresses a unique need within your circle of intimacy and influence that can be addressed by you and you alone.
>
> In that precise sense, your Unique Gift is needed by all that is.
>
> In that precise sense, you are needed by All-That-Is.
>
> Reality—God—needs your service.
>
> Your deed is God's need.

This is not imaginary; that's not a fairy tale. That's the inner physics aligned with the exterior physics. It's one world and one physics; one love, one heart. Reality is lined with love.

Our code is: Reality needs your service. What service is that? **Service is awakening to your true identity as an Outrageous Lover, as a unique configuration of Outrageous Love, and then knowing:** *I have Outrageous Acts of Love to commit that are an expression of my Unique Self that can be committed by me and me alone, unlike no one that ever was, is, or will be.*

I might not commit this act of Outrageous Love just by myself. I might commit my part of an Outrageous Act of Love by joining genius in partnership with someone else, or I may do it in a particular way by responding to the unique needs of my unique circle of intimacy, influenced by a particular act that I do.

Now, here's the practice. This is the third turning of the wheel. Our commitment here is not the same as to our local church. It's a non-local reality. This is One Church—One Mountain, Many Paths—and our commitment is the evolution of love, which is the evolution of culture and consciousness, which is the evolution of the source code. We do that by invoking and bringing down here together the third turning of the wheel. So, let's turn it. Let's feel it.

The third turning of the wheel is *the introduction into Reality of the practice of Outrageous Love Letters and Outrageous Acts of Love.* Now let's make it specific.

WRITING AN OUTRAGEOUS LOVE LETTER

I can write an Outrageous Love Letter to myself.

I can write an Outrageous Love Letter to Reality.

I can write an Outrageous Love Letter to the bank clerk.

I can write it to my father, my son, my daughter, my friend, my colleague, my beloved, the woman that I divorced, the man I divorced thirty years ago.

In that Outrageous Love Letter, *I exaggerate until I'm accurate.*

I love all the way. I become Rumi. I become Hafiz.

I become drunk with the Outrageous Love that lives in me uniquely, the love that appears in all of Reality this very second, taking the billions and trillions of quarks, hadrons, electrons, protons, atoms, molecules in you, alluring them to each other, creating a gorgeous, non-local symphony within you, this very second.

That Outrageous Love holds and animates everything, and I let that flow in and through me as I write the letter.

That's one way of committing an Outrageous Act of Love. It's writing an Outrageous Love Letter to yourself, to someone else, to a stranger, to someone you've broken up with, or to someone who's in your life now.

COMMITTING OUTRAGEOUS ACTS OF LOVE

A second form of Outrageous Love Letter is to tell the story—it can be three lines or ten lines, or more—of an Outrageous Act of Love that you committed this week. We make a commitment: every day, but every week at least once, *I'm going to commit one Outrageous Act of Love.*

It might be in the middle of a difficult argument, finding your inner core, breaking the pattern of negativity, and saying, "I'm sorry. I love you madly."

- ◆ It might be smiling at the bank teller and asking their name.
- ◆ It might be making a decision to become a member of One Church, One Mountain, Many Paths in a serious way.
- ◆ It might be reaching out to someone I haven't talked to in ten years and reaching out in love.
- ◆ It might be adopting a child.
- ◆ It might be beginning a great project that's a gift to Reality.
- ◆ It might be embracing and integrating a part of yourself you've split off or left out.

Whatever it is. There are lots of ways, big and small—there is no big, and there is no small.

Take your unique risk and commit an Outrageous Act of Love. It is outrageous because it's coming from the deepest part of yourself. It's coming from an awareness that I am evolution. This is not my local self; this is evolution awake and living through me. This is Evolutionary Love alive in me.

I write an Outrageous Love Letter just by telling the story of that Outrageous Act of Love.

OUTRAGEOUS LOVE LETTERS AND OUTRAGEOUS ACTS OF LOVE: BEING AND TELLING THE MIRACLE

So there are a few ways to do this:

- I write an Outrageous Love Letter to myself, to a friend, to a stranger. In that Outrageous Love Letter, I sing their beauty:
    - Where I speak of my love
    - Where I exaggerate until I'm accurate
    - Where I become Rumi, Hafiz, Tagore, etc.
- I write an Outrageous Love Letter where I tell the story of my Outrageous Act of Love.
- I write an Outrageous Love Letter where I tell the story of an Outrageous Act of Love committed by my friend, my daughter, someone else I know, or a stranger I read about. I tell the story of someone else's Outrageous Act of Love—and in me telling the story I'm adding and exponentializing and deepening their Outrageous Act of Love.

Someone has to do the miracle, and someone has to tell the story. So, I'm telling that story in my Outrageous Love Letter.

THIS IS THE THIRD TURNING OF THE WHEEL

So again, I can write an Outrageous Love Letter to a friend, to a stranger, to myself, to Nature, to God, to Reality, *with all of my love.* I let it pour through, I take the lid off, I go all the way, I become the great poet. That's the first form.

That's an Outrageous Love Letter, which itself is an Outrageous Act of Love.

Two, I can write an Outrageous Love Letter where I tell the story of an Outrageous Act of Love that I committed this week—and I don't do it modestly. The old modesty does not work here. It's not arrogance. It's divine pride. I'm telling the story because I want to light the world up and I want to inspire ten more people who will inspire ten more people, who will inspire ten more people. **We want to create a cascading wave of Evolutionary Love that lifts all boats, a self-organizing Universe, a Unique Self Symphony committing Outrageous Act of Love all over the world.**

The third form is that I tell the story of an Outrageous Act of Love of someone I know—someone who I know, or a stranger who I don't know.

We're inviting the third turning of the wheel. I spoke to Barbara this morning, and I said, *This week, love, I'm going to spend more time just landing this idea of Outrageous Act of Love and Outrageous Love Letters.* You can feel how deep that is.

Let's turn the wheel together, the third turning of the wheel. We're invoking this new practice. We keep meditating, and we keep praying. But here we actually become the prayer.

- I am the prayer.
- I am evolution.
- I am Evolutionary Love.
- I am the leading edge of evolution—as a unique expression of the entire story—committing Outrageous Acts of Love now.

Imagine that the whole world is on fire because the world actually *is* on fire. We don't have a place that actually values our fire. So we take it inside, and it burns us from the inside, and it often destroys part of our soul.

But **we can use that fire to light up Reality**. And we light up Reality by literally creating an Outrageous Love revolution. We literally invoke the new human and the new humanity. We invoke *Homo amor*, the fulfillment of *Homo sapiens*, and we light up the world. That's what it means to reclaim love as religion. That's what it means to move towards a politics of love.

As Homo amor, we're reclaiming love as religion, moving towards the politics of love.

The politics of love is the synergistic democratization of enlightenment, which is the Unique Self Symphony, the self-organizing Universe, with each of us as unique leading edges of evolution.

Physics speaks of multiple centers. Each of us is the center, and each of us bows in devotion before the other, who is also the center, no less the center than I am.

We explode Reality and impress our Outrageous Act of Love on the lips of the Divine.

Can you imagine that? That is what we want.

That's the whole story—now we got it.

CHAPTER EIGHT

I AM NOT IN THE UNIVERSE— I AM THE UNIVERSE

Episode 173 — February 2, 2020

WE ARE AT THE CROSSROADS

Our intention is to articulate the vision of the new human and the new humanity, the fulfillment of *Homo sapiens* in *Homo amor*. We stand at this particular time between worlds, a time unlike any other we've experienced in history, where we're literally at the border of a potential heaven on earth. **We have the ability to bring into Reality a level of joy, a level of creativity, a level of realization, a level of goodness, and a level of love that Reality has never experienced before.**

And yet, in order to get there, we have critical steps to take. If we don't take those steps, we will naturally devolve into a dystopia—to a level of suffering, a level of pain, in a way that was never a threat ever before in the history of planet Earth.

We have an exponential possibility. We have exponential technology, which can exponentially destroy us if we don't develop the interior spiritual technologies, the vision, the next stage, the next step of evolution. The interior technology is the articulation of a new Universe Story, a new narrative of identity, a new narrative of community, a new understanding of power, a new understanding of who we are, why we're here, how we emerged out of this planet

Earth, and how to make our lives a triumph and **be the heroes of our own stories**.

WE ARE A HOLY BAND OF OUTRAGEOUS LOVERS

In every generation at the crossroads, there's a band of people or bands of people who come together. In the original Aramaic of the Old Testament, they're called *chevraya adisha*, the holy band, a band of lovers, or a band of what we call Outrageous Lovers.

Outrageous Love is not ordinary love, love that is the strategy of the ego seeking some comfort, a little false security to somehow navigate our way through the pain of life. No. That's legitimate, it's important and it's valid, but it ultimately doesn't hold or sustain us. The love dissipates so quickly and so easily; it often turns twisted and ugly and painful—or simply dead.

We're not talking about ordinary love. We're talking about Outrageous Love. We're talking about the ontology arising of love, and by ontology we mean what's real. When we say *the Universe is a Love Story*, we're talking not about ordinary love. We're talking about the love that moves the sun and other stars.

- It's in that love I trust.
- It's the love that animates everything.
- It's the love that animates me in this second, and breathes me every second into existence—not metaphorically, not mythopoetically, but literally.
- It's the love that moves the atoms and the molecules in the computer that I'm looking into.
- It's the love that drives all of Reality incessantly forward with its own inherent, stunning creativity.
- It's the love that moves the irreducibly unique, gorgeous expression of every being in Reality.

Every human being sitting here today around the world, each of us with our thirty-seven trillion cells, is utterly dazzling, unique, and animated every second by Outrageous Love.

It's Outrageous Love that moves Reality from mud to Mozart, from bacteria to Bach. It drives forward, always seeking more value, more God.

It's Outrageous Love that catalyzes Reality into this exploding, pulsing, yearning, thriving, ecstatically gorgeous movement towards more Goodness, Truth, and Beauty.

WE COME TOGETHER TO ARTICULATE THE BEST STORY OF HUMANITY EVER TOLD

We're coming together to write a Great Library, to articulate a new story, to tell the best story of humanity and the emergent human that's ever been told. **This story is so compelling, so True, so Good, so Beautiful, so potent, so poignant, and so powerful that it will become the evolutionary attractor to draw together the leading edge of humanity all over the world to begin to live, to be, that new story—so that we can become the tipping point.**

We will tip not into dystopia but into a utopia in which every child knows:

- I'm gorgeous.
- I've got a unique gift to give, a life to live, a poem to write, a song to sing.
- My note in the symphony is necessary beyond imagination.
- Reality needs my service.

We can come together as a Unique Self Symphony, as a self-organizing universe, a bottom-up, thriving, yearning, pulsing symphony of Outrageous Love with each of us playing our unique instruments, committing Outrageous Acts of Love and transforming humanity from a top-down, command-and-control structure to an organismic explosion of love in which each of us is alive, each of us is a hero, and each of us is giving a gift that all of Reality needs. **Each of us knows that Reality literally needs our service.** We are being da Vinci together in this new Renaissance, which is so urgently needed. I tremble with joy and tremble with trepidation before the Divine that somehow this is ours to do. Wow!

EVOLUTIONARY LOVE CODE: EVOLUTION IS LOVE IN ACTION AND I AM EVOLUTION

> Your Unique Gift addresses a unique need within your circle of intimacy and influence that can be addressed by you and you alone.
>
> In that precise sense your Unique Gift is needed by all that is. In this precise sense you are needed by All-That-Is. Reality—God—needs your service.
>
> Your deed is God's need.

What a gorgeous sentence. *Your deed is God's need.* Your deed is Reality's need. Evolution is love in action. And I am evolution. We are evolution.

To get this is everything. We think we live in the world, and that evolution is the origin story of the world. That's actually not true. One of the great revelations where science and spirit meet—particularly a revelation of science today, in the last hundred years—is that **we can have faith in the curvature of space-time.** What that means is that in some profound sense—and it's mind-blowing, Earth-shattering, and I feel the Earth move under my feet, literally—is that I'm not *in* a Universe which has evolution as a story. *We are the story—we are evolution in person.*

We're not in a Universe which has evolution as a story. We are the story!
We are evolution in person!

Space-time is not something that Reality *happens inside of*. **The Big Bang manifests space-time.** Space-time emerges out of this great flaring forth, this moment of singularity which explodes into all the laws of math and physics. Space-time emerges, and we—you and me—are emergent from space-time at the very moment of the Big Bang.

Where were you at the moment of the Big Bang? Who did the Big Bang? Who did the whole thing? You did! Where were you at the moment of the Big Bang? You were there. Where else could you have been? You were literally there. That's actually the truth of Reality.

The truth of Reality is you—literally, you—you did the great flaring forth, you caused it all. You are inherent in, an emergent from, an expression of. You're not *in* evolution, you're not *in* the universe.

You are the universe. The entire memory of the entire universe—from the hydrogen, the helium, the nitrogen, and later the heavier elements like carbon and oxygen—**is all literally in you!** All of the structures of your body and all of your interior, all of the Eros that drives the whole thing, the Outrageous Love that literally manifested Reality—all of it is in you.

In other words, we can say that *rocks have Mozart in them*. Do you get what I mean by that? Out of rocks, there's a natural emergence—one piece of the story leads to the next piece of the story, and we move from the first elements, and then we moved to stars, and then second-generation stars, then we moved to galaxies, and then more elements. We ultimately get to life, and then life moves through all of its stages. This emerges into hominids and then into human beings and ultimately manifests utterly irreducibly, uniquely as you.

You are the emergence of the whole thing. You embodied the whole thing. Literally. You caused the Big Bang—it was you. *So you get to take responsibility for the whole thing*.

WE ARE EVOLUTIONARY LOVE: OUR ACTS OF OUTRAGEOUS LOVE ARE LOVE IN ACTION

What is evolution? **Evolution is *love in action*.**

Who am I? **I'm a unique configuration of Evolutionary Love.** Evolutionary Love is the same as Outrageous Love.

When I commit my next Outrageous Act of Love… What is an Outrageous Act of Love? It can be a very simple thing that I do, and we're going to talk about how to land this in the world together as a revolutionary community. But the Outrageous Acts of Love that I commit—that is *love in action*.

 *   I am evolution.
 *   I am Evolutionary Love.
 *   I am *Amor*.

My *Amor* caused the Big Bang. Can we get that? That's a big sentence. My *Amor* caused the Big Bang? My *Amor* is the Outrageous Love that lives in me—and that *Amor* caused the Big Bang.

And when I commit my Outrageous Act of Love, what's happening is *evolution is in action at its leading edge through me.* Wow. Oh my God. *Amor. Its insides are lined with love.*

I am that love. I am Evolutionary Love, and I am uniquely needed by All-That-Is.

Reality needs my service.

GOD IN THE THIRD PERSON—COSMIC MAGNIFICENCE—IS ALSO GOD IN THE SECOND PERSON, THE INFINITY OF INTIMACY WHO KNOWS OUR NAME

We have this realization that all of the physics in the world, all of the laws of mathematics, and all of the billions of light years—we call that, "God in the

91

third person." The laws, the Outrageous Love as the Eros that animates the laws of physics, the strong and the weak nuclear forces, the electromagnetic, the gravitational, all the forces and all the fields of Reality. This is God in the third person, all of God in the third person.

I want to give you, in a way that we perhaps never quite have, **a sense of God in the third person.**

Shut your eyes for a second. Feel this with me:

- We're on Earth. Here we are on Earth.
- The Earth goes around the Sun. And the Sun is eight light-minutes away from us. (Thomas Berry and Brian Swimme do a great description of this—a light-minute is a unit of distance; it's how far light travels in a minute.)
- When we move out from the planet Earth, we come across planets like Jupiter, which is about thirty light-minutes away. And we get to Pluto, which is like five light-hours away, which is just how far light travels in an hour.
- Then you get outside the Solar System and then the next sizable object, the nearest star, is four light-years away, about twenty-six trillion miles away.
- But that's nothing. Because in our galaxy we're surrounded by 200 billion stars that form the Milky Way galaxy. That's pretty crowded! And the stars are about twenty-six trillion miles apart, and we're about 30,000 light-years away from the center of the Milky Way galaxy.
- And right at the center you've got a black hole. Our galaxy is approximately a hundred thousand light-years across.
- Once you move outside the galaxy, you move into deep space. You've got to go 150,000 light-years before you come across another sizable object, which is called the Magellanic Clouds, which are smaller galaxies that circle around the Milky Way galaxy. There are several dozen galaxies circling the Milky

Way.

- ◆ Then as you move further out, you have to go 2.1 million light-years before we get to the next sizable object, the Andromeda Galaxy, which is bigger than the Milky Way. It has 300 billion stars and several dozen galaxies rotating around it.
- ◆ You have this picture of the Milky Way with galaxies around it, and the Andromeda Galaxy with galaxies around it. And all of this is rotating like this wild pinwheel. We call this the local group of galaxies.
- ◆ Moving past the local group, the next object is about 70 million light-years away. That's the huge Virgo Cluster, which about 1,200 galaxies.
- ◆ So just imagine: another 1,200 galaxies—*each* with *100 billion stars*. And our local group is moving around the Virgo cluster.
- ◆ As you move out from there, you get into the large scale, full structure of the universe, which is 15 billion light-years across.

All of this is driven by desire—the desire to explode and impact. **It's not empty space. It's molecules and atoms, alive, attracted to each other in unique configurations of intimacy and desire aggregating into larger and gorgeous units.** Wow!

This is all us. The same desire that moves everything ultimately through all of the stages of evolution on planet Earth—all of that desire is moving.

All of that—and that's just one way of looking at it, just for a second—is God in the third person.

Now take all of that God in the third person, and put it in a chair, looking at you. Feel the personal desire of that person looking at you:

- ◆ Wanting your goodness
- ◆ Desiring to know everything about you
- ◆ Being fully, madly, passionately in love with you

- Tenderly wanting to nourish you in every way
- Wanting to give you the greatest gift possible: the gift of a Unique Self life in which your gift itself matters to the entire Cosmos

That's God in the second person. That's the Infinity of Intimacy, looking at you, knowing your name.

You realize you literally are an expression of the same desire, the same life force, the same God in the third person who looks at you, knows you, intended you, desires you, and needs you. So we come before this God, who's not only the Infinity of Power but what we're calling here the Infinity of Intimacy.

All of that Infinity in the third person is also the Infinity of Intimacy.

Your most tender, your most beautiful, your most poignant, your most sexually alive moment, in the most beautiful and sacred way— *exponentialized infinitely*—that is that second-person God, sitting in that chair, wrapping you up, closer than close. There's no distance. More naked than naked. Naked heart loving you madly beyond imagination.

That's the realization of the enlightenment of God in the second person. So we come before that God, before our most intimate lover, our most potent, powerful Infinite Lover, our most Intimate Lover who wants to make us potentiated and powerful beyond measure, the God who says:

- I love you so much that I need you.
- You're powerful beyond your wildest dreams.
- What you do, what you think, what you feel matters beyond your wildest imagination.

Before that God, before that Infinity of Intimacy, we bring our holy and our broken *Hallelujah*.

This is what it means to pray. This isn't individuals praying. This is a band of Outrageous Lovers. But it's even more than that, this is the deepest prayer of Reality. This is Reality praying. This is evolution yearning to fulfill itself.

This is evolution yearning to fulfill *Homo sapiens* as *Homo amor*.

TO BE THE HERO OF MY STORY IS TO COMMIT MY OUTRAGEOUS ACTS OF LOVE

The only way to change the basic structure of Reality is through story. Story is the source code structure of Reality, and I don't mean that metaphorically. We know today that Reality's not a fact. It's a story. That's what evolution teaches us. Reality's going somewhere, and one piece of the plotline leads to the next piece. We used to think Reality was eternal. It's not.

The manifest Universe is not a fact. It's a story we know even more deeply through the sciences, both the interior and the exterior sciences. It's not an ordinary story but a love story. And we know that each of us are unique configurations of that love.

We want to be heroes of our own story. And to be the hero of my own story is to commit my Outrageous Act of Love. **The way I become the hero of my own story is I become larger than a separate self.**

My story is no longer just my story. My story is actually chapter and verse in the Universe: A Love Story.

And then you realize:

> Your unique gift addresses a unique need within your unique circle of intimacy and influence that can be addressed by you alone. When you commit the Outrageous Act of Love that addresses that unique need and your unique circle, that's your love story. And your love story is chapter and verse—literally—in the Universe: A Love Story.
>
> So when you commit your Outrageous Act of Love, you are actually evolution committing its Outrageous Act of Love.

You're the fulfillment of the purpose of Reality—not figuratively. It's the experience of Rumi, of Hafiz, of the Buddha, of Lao Tzu. It's the experience of Christ. It's the experience of you.

This is the democratization of greatness. It's the democratization of enlightenment.

OUTRAGEOUS ACTS OF LOVE; OUTRAGEOUS LOVE LETTERS

You can write an Outrageous Love Letter and that will be your Outrageous Act of Love, and it can just be an Outrageous Love letter to someone, saying how gorgeous and beautiful and stunning they are and how much you love them, where **you exaggerate until you're accurate**.

Or a second possibility is that you tell the story of an Outrageous Act of Love that you committed. You tell that story and then we read it and others are wildly inspired.

We're going to iterate this. We're going to model this. Then we're going to together take it to the world. We create this Outrageous Love project in the center of Reality, together—we're the revolutionaries. This is like the Marxist revolution, but it's much deeper than Marxism and actually understands, *you can't just change the means of production.* **You have to become the creator.**

You're the creator, we're the creator—we manifested the Big Bang itself.

- We become the creator.
- We manifest through Outrageous Act of Love.
- We become the Planetary Awakening in Love through Unique Self Symphonies.

We're going to bring it into Reality the same way that meditation was brought into Reality. There was a certain point where a band of people brought meditation to the world. Another band of people brought prayer.

The third turning of the wheel is when we become the Unique Self Symphony. We become Outrageous Love. We become evolution. We actually model that.

We become the Planetary Awakening in Love through Unique Self Symphony.

THE MESSIAH LIVES IN THE MONASTERY

I wanted to tell you a story. It's one of my favorite stories. It's about a Hasidic master, a rabbi, and he meets an abbot at a monastery. And the monastery is not going so well; it's breaking down, and it's falling apart. There are only five monks left in the monastery. So the abbot, the head of the monastery, says to the rabbi in this inter-religious dialogue, *what can I do? Let's talk.* So I guess the abbot spoke some Yiddish. He says, *what can I do? At my monastery everyone's leaving. There's just no excitement anymore. I've got to shut it down. Can you help me?*

The rabbi thinks for a second, and he strokes his beard, as rabbis do. And he says, *I'm really sorry but I can't help you.* And then as the rabbi is starting to leave, he looks back and says, *There is one thing. I did hear in a dream that the Messiah lives in your monastery.*

Really?

The rabbi says *yes.* And then he walks away.

So the abbot goes back to the monastery, to the five monks who are left, and they say to him, *did the rabbi give you any advice to help us heal the monastery and to fix it and to grow it and have people come and for it to thrive?*

97

No, he says. *He had no advice at all, but he did say the strangest thing. He said that the Messiah lives in the monastery.*

So everyone thinks to themselves, *well, who's the Messiah?* They think, *well, it must be the Abbot. The Abbot's guided us through these hard times and he's so deep and profound, and he meditates and prays so beautifully. It must be the Abbot.* They treat the Abbott with this extra measure of love and reverence and beauty and delight.

But then like a week goes by and they think, *well, the Abbott's wonderful, but maybe it's Thomas. I mean Thomas laughs so wonderfully, he's always so filled with energy, he's just so positive, and he's held each of us in our hard times. You know, it must be Thomas.*

Then another week goes by and they think, *well, maybe it's sister Claire. Sister Claire is so radiant, so filled with the radiance of the Goddess. And whenever she walks in, you just feel her radiance inviting you to open. And each of us has been so closed at a particular moment, and then sister Claire would come in with her radiant heart. You know, the Messiah must be sister Claire. Yeah, for sure. It's sister Claire.*

Another week goes by, and they would think, *but maybe it's Lucas, the gardener. He takes care of the grounds and he does it with such love…* And you can imagine what began to happen.

Everyone started treating each other so gorgeously, so beautifully that this new radiance, this new aura of beautiful, Outrageous Love emerged.

People started coming because they heard about this place, which was so stunning, and you would feel alive when you walked in. More and more people started visiting and staying at the monastery.

More people came until it became the largest monastery—bustling, thriving, awake, alive—committing Outrageous Acts of Love all over Poland.

I'M THE MESSIAH, RESPONSIBLE FOR MY UNIQUE OUTRAGEOUS ACTS OF LOVE

That's what it means to be the heroes. To know that *you're actually the Messiah. You are the Messiah.* The word Messiah in Hebrew is *Mashiach. Siach* means conversation, which refers to your conversation with Reality, your Outrageous Love Letter, your Outrageous Act of Love.

Literally, you're the hero of the story.

There's something really beautiful one of my teachers once said: *You know why there's atheism in the world? The reason that exists,* he said, *is because you have to know there's no one but you, you've got to do it yourself. And then afterwards you realize you're completely held by the Infinity of Intimacy and filled with Outrageous Love.*

But you've got to have that little bit of atheism so that you think, *oh, it's just me. The whole thing depends on me. I've got to take that on. I initiated the Big Bang. It was me. I was there.*

Once you take that on, once you feel that full power, however, it doesn't mean you've got to heal the whole thing. You don't have to heal the whole thing. You're not responsible for the whole thing.

You're responsible for one thing: **What are the wild, gorgeous Outrageous Acts of Love that are yours to commit every day?**

They don't come from your narrow ego. They don't come from self-interest. They don't come from a "reciprocal altruism" that they talk about in evolutionary theory.

- It's actual love.
- I'm thinking about you.
- I'm feeling you.
- I'm intimate with you.
- I'm committed to you.
- I'm going to commit Outrageous Acts of Love.

- I am listening to you by helping you, by gifting you, by opening to whenever that might be.
- I'm going to outrageously love myself, and I'm going to love you.
- I'm going to outrageously love the world.
- I am the hero of the story. I'm the Messiah.

That is a Planetary Awakening in Love through a Unique Self Symphony.

CHAPTER NINE

JUST IN TIME FOR A TIME LIKE THIS: YOU ARE THE ONE YOU'VE BEEN WAITING FOR

Episode 175 — February 16, 2020

THE BIG YES OF THE BIG BANG

Here's the question: *Are we ready to play a larger game with our lives?*

Do we have a *Yes* on that? Because that's really where it's at. It's the *Yes* we have to find. It's not automatic. It's not a given.

This is what we know about evolutionary spiritual practice: we know that we can go inside ourselves and we can say *Yes*. **It's both the inner physics of Cosmos and it's the actual physics, the exterior physics of Cosmos.**

Where is the *Yes* sourced? When was the first *Yes* that resounded in Reality? It was at the moment of the great flaring forth. Literally, who started the Big Bang? It was you. To really understand that is to know that rocks have Mozart in them; when rocks appear, there's Mozart in them; *Mozart is implicit in the rocks.*

But Reality is not a fact; it's an unfolding story. And the manifest Universe that we understand and know and are beginning to dance with its mysteries—**that manifest Universe screamed its Yes at the moment of the Big Bang.**

The Big Bang is this unrelenting positivity.

Infinity says YESSSSSS to finitude. If you thought my *Yes* was a bit too resounding, like *let's keep it down here*, just think about the Big Bang. There's nothing we know in physics and recorded history that holds anything even vaguely approximating the energy of the Big Bang. So I want you to get that.

What's the Big Bang? Wherever you are in the world, let's just scream it. YESSSSS! Loudly! That's the Big Bang. YES! YES! Barbara and I would talk about this all the time. This is not a metaphor; this is not a mythopoetic reading.

My *Yes* is the same *Yes* that literally initiated the whole thing. In terms of physics, when I breathe in a breath of air, because of wind patterns in the planet I breathe in all the other molecules. **I'm breathing in all of Reality.**

In my body right now, all of the elementary particles that were present at the Big Bang literally constitute me right now. The radiation from the Big Bang reaches us, affects us, and impacts us in multitudinous ways. All of everything: all of the energy, allurement, force, and literally the particles—molecules, muons, leptons, and hadrons, which are proteins—are all there. They're all there and in all of the levels of evolution, one Yes after another, and each Yes leads to the next Yes.

Here's the second question. *Are we ready to participate in the evolution of love?*

Do we have a *YES* on that? Are we ready to participate in the evolution of love and to know that that Yes is not only the same *Yes* as the Big Bang but it is *required* for us to say this *Yes* now?

What are we doing? We are evolution awakening to itself. Humanity is unaware that there's this *Yes* being spoken. **In the incessant creativity of evolution, at every stage of evolution, there's this cry of Yes.** Now we awaken to conscious evolution! We're aware that evolution is living in us. Evolution is awakening to itself in and through us. We move from unconscious to conscious evolution. And conscious evolution is the great cry of *YES*!

What happened when Barbara and I met with each other is that we joined not genes, but genius—and we're joining genius here together. In my joining of genius with Barbara, I brought a meme, an understanding of the physics of the Cosmos which I call the evolution of intimacy in the Intimate Universe, the Universe as a Love Story and the evolution of love. Barbara brought conscious evolution, and we put those together.

Together we realized that that *Yes* is a *Yes* to the evolution of love.

The story of Reality is not the story that Yuval Harari tells in his book *Sapiens* which is a story of "fictions," a story of a random walk of the Cosmos.

At the very center of the Cosmos is non-randomness. It's true that the Cosmos occasionally deploys random structures, but it deploys them in the context of intention, in the context of directionality.

There is non-randomness at the very heart of the Cosmos, with the patterns of vibrating waves, which are all inherently intelligent, specific, alive, and unique. Evolution moves to deeper levels of complexity—which is to say, more and more uniqueness, more and more interiority, more and more consciousness, more and more caring, and more and more love.

Evolution is the evolution of love. We're now in this moment in time awakening to that realization. And just in time. As the great mystic, Abraham Kook, writes: *We are just in time for a time for this.* It's a great evolutionary phrase by one of the great evolutionary mystics.

We are just in time for a time like this.

We are awakening to the realization of who we are, an irreducibly unique configuration of Evolutionary Love and Eros. The throbbing, awake, undulating Eros of your YES is the YES of the great flaring forth. It's the YES of the Big Bang.

But it's more than that because the level of YES at the Big Bang was *implicit*. We didn't yet have evolution awakening to itself.

Now is the moment of the YES.

It's just in time for a time like this. Because it's only that YES that speaks to the very intention of One Church: Many Paths, One Mountain. It is the church of *Homo amor*, which is the fulfillment of *Homo sapiens*, as we tell the new story.

WE NEED A GLOBAL ETHIC FOR A GLOBAL CIVILIZATION

We understand that we are at this moment of existential risk, where there's risk to the very existence of the planet itself at this moment of unbearable joy and unbearable suffering on the planet.

I'm moving in two days. I'm moving from Portland, Oregon to Miami Beach. All boxes are packed up. Kristina and I haven't had a chance to rent an apartment yet because we've been so busy with the Center. So I have this feeling of being between places. Imagine if I was a refugee with no idea of where I was going, and I was uprooting my entire world with no place to go, and I didn't know if I'd have food in two weeks.

There are seventy million refugees in the world right now. What does that mean? It means that our YES is a YES to the evolution of love in this world of globalism.

There is no more local. We're living in this unbearable and beautiful intimacy, where a group of terrorists who feel devastated and can't figure out how to have a conversation between premodernity and modernity, take a plane and crash into the World Trade Center, where some of us lost friends.

There is no local world. Different levels of consciousness are colliding with each other. We are in the unbearable intimacy of a global world. And in a global world, for us not just to survive, but to *thrive*, in this world between utopia and dystopia, we need to usher in a heaven on earth unlike anything that's ever been seen.

But to do that, we have to tell a new story. We have to articulate a global ethos, a global ethic for a global civilization.

We've been at this for a few years, and we're getting close. My hope is in the next five years we'll have put out this Great Library of a global ethic for a global civilization, which is not made up, not New Age or fundamentalist, but based on integrating the best of sciences, both interior and exterior.

This library will become a cogent Story of Meaning that you can tell to a seven-year-old, to thirty nuclear physicists, and to seventy truck drivers—a universal language. That's the da Vinci project of this generation.

We're in the moment of the Renaissance after the Black Death of the medieval period, which decimated almost half of Europe. We're feeling the possibility of disease entering the world again today. We're feeling vulnerability in that way, but we're also feeling vulnerability in the face of enormous existential threat. We know that we're all connected on Facebook, but none of us are face-to-face. **We have to meet face-to-face by finding each other and creating an intimacy—because we're part of a shared story.**

What does it mean to become a couple? It could be a good friend or a wife or husband or a brother and sister or a colleague. That's a couple or a dyad. In the great new *Rise of Skywalker* movie, the movie is about Kylo Ren—

who's actually Han Solo's son, if you know your Star Wars—and Rey—who turns out to be Palpatine's granddaughter, if you know your Star Wars—and they're a dyad in the Force. And there's great power in that.

So what does it mean to create a dyad in the Force? It means that we have a shared story. When we come together as One Church: One Mountain, Many Paths, the Church of *Homo amor*, the fulfillment of *Homo sapiens*, we're here to tell the new story—between each other and in this larger da Vinci move, for Reality itself.

What is Reality? It's a Universe Story. It's a narrative of identity, a narrative of power, a narrative of community, and a narrative of sexuality. And out of these come understandings of education, economics, and medicine.

This is the revolution, and what's our intention? What would Barbara say now? It's a phrase that Barbara and I created together. **Our intention is a Planetary Awakening in Love through Unique Self Symphonies.**

When cultures collide and there's no shared language, it explodes. All you need is one rogue terrorist who is not part of a larger story and who's supported by a network who can't find their place in the larger story. **Telling this larger story has to include the best of premodern, modern, and postmodern wisdom, integrated in a story of nobility and honor and dignity and mission.** It's a Planetary Awakening in Love through Unique Self Symphonies, in which every human being knows:

* I matter. I am Gloria.

I AM GLORIA, I AM LITERALLY A DIVINE MINIATURE

The word glory in Hebrew is *kavod*. The related word *kaved* literally means heavy, but also alludes to gravitas, and thereby to honor and dignity.

Honor, dignity, gravitas. What it means is: I have gravitas. I matter. I am Gloria.

You are Gloria. We are Gloria. Together our Unique Self Symphony is Gloria. So we're going to reclaim Gloria.

Notice what we're doing here, in One Church: One Mountain, Many Paths. We're taking from Hinduism, from Judaism, and from Christianity, to reclaim this vision of religion. Religion is important, so let's not get stuck in our New Age bubble: *Religion: aaaah!* Sixty to seventy percent of the world lives in an organized religion, and we cannot ignore that. So we need to up-level religion.

I am Gloria! It is literally true; I am literally a divine miniature. That is God in the first person, *In Excelsis Deo*.

- ◆ You can say this in Christian terms.
- ◆ You can say it in Buddhist terms.
- ◆ You can say it in secular humanist terms.
- ◆ You can talk about the Planetary Awakening of Unique Self Symphony, which Teilhard de Chardin called the "Christification of the Earth."

Use whatever terms you want, but know you are Gloria. You matter. Your story matters. And your individuated expression of *Amor* matters.

Amor means *its insides are lined with love*. It means that Gloria is not just Christian love. That's where Christianity made its great mistake. That's why we're not a Christian Church. We're not a Jewish Church, and we're not a Buddhist church, and we're not a Native American church. The Native tribes in America made a great mistake: the tribes slaughtered one another. Christianity made a great mistake: they said, *Love only applies to the in-group*. No! *Amor —its insides are lined with love*, writes Solomon.

The very fabric of Reality is Evolutionary Love.

CHAPTER TEN

BEYOND EROS & AGAPE: ONE LOVE

Episode 176 — February 23, 2020

REALITY: ITS INSIDES ARE LINED WITH LOVE

What's my greatness? It's my deepest heart's desire.

We're going to talk about that, but first let's get this clear: Love is at the center of Cosmos; *its insides are lined with love.* This is not ordinary love. It's not pallid love. It's not what the Christians called *agape*, which is this kind of *obligation to virtue.* No. **It's all Eros, and Eros means it's all desire.** But desire is not only expressed sexually; that's only one of the great appetites of Cosmos.

Cosmos is filled by what Alfred North Whitehead, the great English mathematician and philosopher called "appetition." It's filled with appetite. Reality is desire. **Reality shimmers with desire—the desire for the goodness, truth, and beauty.**

The Eros of Cosmos moves towards the *strange attractors* of the Good, the True, and the Beautiful.

Evolution is not a random walk of Cosmos. It's not designed by a God in the sky who looks like Santa Claus. **Evolution is moved by inherent Eros, the ceaseless creativity of Cosmos, which is the eminent expression of the Divine that suffuses and holds and is all.** And in the Eros of Cosmos,

108

movement has direction: the evolution of love, and the evolution of Goodness, Truth, and Beauty.

Reality: its insides are lined with love.

Again, this not love as a mere strategy of the ego, not love which is a social construction, but love which is the *heart of existence* itself.

GOD IS THE INFINITY OF INTIMACY

This love is intimate; it's seeking always greater intimacy.

What does intimate mean? Here's a critical equation of the *dharma*:

Intimacy equals shared identity—if we're intimate, we share an identity—in the context of relative otherness—because we don't fuse, we don't become one. It's union, not fusion.

Plus mutuality of recognition. We recognize each other. The subatomic particles that are going to make up an atom recognize each other. All the dimensions of a cell recognize each other.

Plus mutuality of pathos—we feel each other.

Plus mutuality of purpose—we create shared purpose together.

Intimacy is not finite. It is a quality of Cosmos sourced in the Infinite. **The Infinite itself is intimate.** There's a direct, thematic, threaded, narrative line from cosmological to biological to cultural evolution, from bacteria to Bach, from mud to Mozart, from slime to Shakespeare.

In that same way, the Infinite is not autistically locked in itself. The Infinite is intimate. Infinity *desires* intimacy.

How do we know that the Infinite desires intimacy, that the Infinite desires relationship? Because here we are! We are participating in this Field of Intimacy, which is located in the Infinite.

The Infinite is the Infinity of Intimacy. That's what we mean when we say *God is not only the Infinity of Power but the Infinity of Intimacy.* **God desperately yearns for you.**

It's not the god you don't believe in—the small god, the caricatured god, the superstitious god—but the God who is the Infinity of Intimacy, the God who is the Personhood of Cosmos.

Cosmos has a third-person aspect: the laws of physics, all the billions of years of laws, of mathematics unfolding, laws of chemistry and biology. That's the third person of God.

There is also the divine in the first person that lives in me, as me, and through me: *Tat Tvam Asi,* Thou art That. The Outrageous Love that is me, that runs through me, that's the center of the one heart at the center of my being, that lives me as I'm lived as love—that's God in the first person.

But, actually there's *the space in between*, in physics. According to quantum physics, the reality is neither wave nor particle.

The reality always is the space in between, which is intimacy.

The deepest truth of theoretical physics—not in its pop version, not in its kind of adapted New Age version, which is usually woefully inaccurate. As our beloved friend Ken Wilber points out in his great book, *Quantum Questions*, which features the writings of the quantum physicists who reject these New Age interpretations of physics, in good theoretical physics, you realize that *what's real is the relationship between.*

That's the deep truth.

Intimacy is the heart of Cosmos.

PRAYER: MERGING RADICAL TENDERNESS AND WILD DESIRE

We turn to God, who's the Infinity of Intimacy, the personal incarnation of all that is intimate. Imagine your most intimate moment in the entire world, when you were filled with tenderness and desire, when someone was looking at you with radical tenderness and wild desire, and then exponentialize that moment a billion times—you'll feel the interior experience of the Personhood of Cosmos that knows your name, that desires you, and wants to hold you, nourish you, and love you open beyond all and any imagination.

That's the second person of God, the Infinite of Intimacy. We turn to that God, we turn to the God who knows our name, to the Personhood of Cosmos, and we ask for everything. We don't just ask for peace on Earth. We ask for peace on Earth *and* we ask for everything we need and for everything that everyone who's precious to us needs, and everything the world needs.

We take all these prayers and weave them together, and then we lift them to the sky.

REALITY IS EROS, ALL THE WAY UP AND ALL THE WAY DOWN

We want to see how this *dharma* of deepest heart's desire operates, and why we so desperately need our confessions of greatness and *Homo amor* in culture.

This one-minute Super Bowl clip is a reading of public culture. Let's take a look:

> The ancient Greeks had four words for love.
>
> The first is *philia*. *Philia* is affection that grows from friendship.

111

Next there is *storgē*, the kind you have for a grandparent or brother.

Third, there is *Érōs*, the uncontrollable urge to say *I love you*.

The fourth kind of love is different; it's the most admirable. It's called Agape. Love as an action. It takes courage, sacrifice, strength.

For one hundred and seventy-five years, we've been helping people act on their love, so they can look back or look ahead and say, *We got it right; we did good.*

This is incredible clip, but it actually gets it fundamentally wrong. What does this clip do? It distinguishes between four kinds of love. I'm going to focus on the second two, the classical distinction in Greek and later Christian thought between Eros and Agape.

In this vision of the world, this fundamental split is repeated all over Western culture, it's fundamentally wrong. What's Eros? Just check how that worked. For Eros, you had the woman in the bathing suit in the water—water is always a sign of Eros—walking towards the man, and they come together—it's clearly a sexual moment. What are the words they use? It's an *uncontrollable urge*.

But in our culture, is "uncontrollable" a compliment? Usually not. Is "urge," or a person filled with urges, a compliment? Usually not. *It's an uncontrollable urge.* But then we redeem, we liberate, and we sanitize that uncontrollable urge because we say, *I love you.*

So what it's describing is the sexual moment in a romantic relationship, and they say, *that's what desire is, that's what Eros is.*

We've exiled Eros into desire and romantic love: It's *an uncontrollable urge.*

What do we see in Agape? With Agape, there we see someone washing an elderly man. It's beautiful, noble, fulfilling a virtue—it's your obligation.

That's fundamentally wrong, my friends.

It's actually all Eros. It's all Eros—all the way up, and all the way down.

Eros is the desire of Cosmos, but it's not the desire for sexuality. You get that? The sexual *models* the Erotic. There are twelve billion years of Eros before sexuality. Eros is the experience of being radically alive, desiring ever deeper contact and ever larger wholeness.

Eros is the desire of Cosmos for more and more Goodness, Truth, and Beauty. That desire expresses itself in one channel sexually, but it's actually all Eros, all the way up and all the way down.

Yes, there's an *agapic* face of Eros. I *desire* to wash that old men and to nurture him, to nourish him, but that's also shimmering with Eros. Reality is desire all the way up and all the way down.

- It's the desire to love.
- It's the desire for radical creativity.
- It's the desire for contribution.
- It's the desire to feed people.

It's all desire, the whole thing. We've exiled desire to one narrow expression, and we call it Eros. Reality is desire. Reality is Eros all the way up and all the way down.

Look what happens when we make that false split. So, washing the old man is Agape, not Eros.

Let me ask you a question: Who washes old men in society today? There are orderlies or nurse's assistants who get paid seven dollars an hour. It's the job with the least dignity, and the least amount of money.

You're a woman, you're going out with a guy. You ask him, *what do you do? I'm an orderly and I wash old people in the hospital.* Most people would

113

THE PATH OF OUTRAGEOUS LOVE

stop going out with him; he has no prestige; he's not trading commodities, creating fictitious capital. *No, no, he's washing old people, that's Agape, so we'll pay them seven dollars an hour.* The washing of old people has been demeaned and degraded.

It's actually a sacred art form to wash an old person. It's quivering with Eros, quivering with aliveness, quivering with tenderness. It's all Eros all the way up and all the way down.

Washing an old person is the same Eros as sexuality, the same Eros as Magic Johnson or Kobe Bryant playing basketball, the same Eros as da Vinci creating, the same Eros as Rembrandt, as U2 making music—it's all Eros. One Eros all the way up and all the way down. **But what we've done is we've exiled Eros into one form of desire for which we don't even have a narrative. We don't even have a story about desire. So we split it off.**

Here's the deepest story. You go to the halftime show of the Super Bowl, you see Shakira and Jennifer Lopez, in a huge display of sexual desire and arousal. I'm not in any way saying that's a good display or a bad display.

I'm saying *there's no narrative.* Here's what you have at the Super Bowl:

- Men are killing each other, getting this major trauma which affects NFL players. Men are dying because they're performing.
- They're rewarded by Shakira and Jennifer Lopez who are exploding desire on all the viewers without any narrative of desire. Eros is split off from desire.
- The commercials are saying that *Agape* is the highest form of love, while we're paying orderlies seven dollars an hour.

You get the problem? It doesn't work.

Desire, Eros, is the essence of everything.

My greatness is actually my desire—my deepest heart's desire.

114

CHAPTER ELEVEN

EVOLUTIONARY SURPRISE IS THE QUALITY OF DIVINE LOVE

Episode 178 — March 8, 2020

WE NEED A NEW STORY AT THIS TIME BETWEEN STORIES

We're here at this time between worlds. I want to add a new phrase.

We're not *just* at a time between worlds. The Renaissance was a time between worlds, between premodernity and modernity in which a virus, a plague swept the world.

As we are dealing with this virus [Covid-19] in the world today, this potential pandemic, we have resources available that were unimaginable 500 years ago. Reality has evolved; there's an evolution of goodness, and there's an evolution of human capacity. The Black Death swept and destroyed half of Europe at that time between worlds. In order to confront suffering, in order to confront human yearning back then, and to speak and stand for life, a new story of man and the divine, a new story of woman, a new story of power, a new story of desire, a new story of identity, a new universe story had to be told.

That was the story of modernity.

We, in this moment in time, are actually at the same moment as they were, at a time between worlds, but I want to give it a new name.

We are not only at a time between worlds,
but we are at a time between stories.

And precisely the chinks, cracks, failures of plotline, or failures of integrity in the thread of the story of modernity have generated the potential disasters, the potential ending of the story in this postmodern moment.

Modernity gave us great gifts:

- It gave us the emergence of the individual.
- It gave us the scientific method; it gave us a way to understand and unpack the laws of Cosmos.
- It gave us explosions in human rights.
- It gave us the emergence of the feminine
- It gave us modern medicine.

It gave us the many dignities of modernity.

Modernity also came with its disasters and with its devastation. What we devastated was our ability to locate ourselves in the Universe. We correctly critiqued the cruelties of premodernity—as Voltaire said: *Remember the cruelties.* But we didn't actually find and disclose a new story in which a genuine human nobility was rooted in the very nature of Cosmos. **We didn't locate ourselves in the wider Field of Spirit.**

We differentiated the value spheres. We separated religion from the state. This allowed for democracy to emerge and for scientific investigation to develop independently of the church. That differentiation of value spheres was wildly important. But then because our story of Spirit was a premodern story, we didn't replace it with a genuine, new, and compelling vision of

Spirit. **So we not only differentiated from Spirit, we *dissociated* from Spirit.**

The move of economics—the free hand of the market expressing itself in capitalism and unfettered research—although fantastic in developing progress, created marketplaces of win/lose metrics and the notion that human beings didn't have value unless they were producing.

It dissociated the human from being located in Cosmos itself. It cut us off and alienated us from being able to hear the whispering of the Intimate Universe. The Universe became—in our understanding—mechanistic. **It became a machine; it operated like clockwork according to a fixed order that allowed us to predict and do science. But we actually lost the intimacy of Cosmos:**

- We lost the sense of ourselves being the Intimate Universe in person.
- We lost the sense that we were needed for a central *beingness,* that the relationship between us wasn't just pragmatic and utilitarian.
- We lost an inter-intimacy and inter-beingness with each other.
- We lost a sense of what honor, duty, and obligation means. Because although we correctly critiqued the old notions of honor, duty and obligation, we didn't replace them with a new vision.

In the moment in which we stand—in which for the last hundred years we've extracted resources that took billions of years to create:

- We've dissociated from our need to be held by Mother Earth.
- We've dissociated from larger frames of value that could guide us.
- We've dissociated from the very trajectory of evolution, which moves towards the Good, the True, and the Beautiful.

- We've mistaken evolution as a purposeless, meaningless, random walk.
- We failed to articulate a new evolutionary story.

All of that has left us locked in the pseudo-eros of win/lose metrics in which we have to produce something in order to be valuable, in which we have to place someone else outside of the circle for us to feel the Eros of being in the circle. We've tragically moved towards our own potential destruction. Through the freeing of technology, we've developed exponential power—but that exponential power creates exponential danger and existential risk—a risk to our very existence.

WEAVING A NEW STORY: THE LEADING EDGE OF EVOLUTION LIVES IN THE SURPRISE THAT I BRING TO COSMOS

What can we do, friends? There's only one thing to do at a time between stories. We gather the best truths, the deepest knowledge, in every field that lives separately from each other; we step above and beyond to see the whole picture and to weave together a new story:

- A new story of honor
- A new story of duty
- A new story of joy
- A new story of creativity
- A new story of Unique Self
- A new vision of community
- A new vision of Planetary Awakening in Love through Unique Self Symphonies

We weave together a new story of power where I understand that the evolutionary impulse beats uniquely in me, as me, and through me, in which I understand that I am the surprise of Cosmos—beyond *order*. I'm not just a cog in the order of Cosmos; I am beyond the order of Cosmos;

118

I am Cosmos's great surprise. **The leading edge of evolution lives in the surprise that I bring to Cosmos. It's through that surprise that I can love the moment open!**

SABBATH: FALL IN LOVE IN THE MORNING, TRUST AND BE TRUSTED THROUGH THE NIGHT

Before we go to Amor, I want to do this chant for you, because it's what it's all about, the essence of who we are together. The key word of this chant in the English is: *to speak of your love in the morning and to trust you in the night.*

This chant is 3,000 years old. It comes from David, who was the father of Solomon. Solomon, as in Solomon's wisdom. Solomon is the source of the lineage of Reality as Eros, of the Intimate Universe. He's the source of novels in modernity like *The Da Vinci Codes* and the Mary Magdalene tradition. It's the tradition of Eros, the tradition of the Intimate Universe. It's the lineage that births modern science.

> *Mizmor shir leyom hashabbat*
> *Tov lehodot Ladonai*
> *Lehagid baboker chasdecha*
> *ve-emunatcha baleylot*
>
> *To sing a song of the Sabbath*
> *I's good to sing with God.*
> *To speak of your love in the morning*
> *and trust you through the night*

The Sabbath is anytime we stop the routine and allow ourselves to be surprised by the pulsing newness of this moment—we love it open not with the routine of yesterday, but with the radical newness of today.

To do that we have to Sabbath. I Sabbath on the seventh day of the classical week, which is Saturday. This means I take twenty-four hours to just be in meditation. I did this for many years, and then I lost it for a few years. We switched the Church services to Sunday from Saturday because in the laws of the Sabbath and the tradition that I keep it, one is completely offline.

But you can do Sabbath on Sunday, or you can do Sabbath for an hour on Wednesday. You turn everything off and you go inside, and you feel the Intimate Universe alive in you. **You feel your unique expression, your very *beingness* and how it connects you to everything else.**

You feel how you're needed by everything else to love a moment open that is yours to love open. You're surprised anew and you step out of the routine. That's what this chant is about. When you do that then you fall madly in love in the morning. **You can trust yourself.**

You can trust the Universe; the Universe can trust you.

And your beloveds can trust you through the night.

ARE YOU WILLING TO BE SURPRISED BY REALITY?

We can speak of each other's love in the morning.

We're a band of outrageous lovers. We're here to be the revolution.

We're here to reject the status quo, to allow *the surprise*—to allow *Homo amor*, to allow the next stage of evolution, which is always novelty—to emerge. It only emerges when we become the surprise, when we surprise ourselves, when we become someone that we never thought we could be. We find a dimension of goodness, truth, and beauty that lives inside of us and that takes us over and seduces us to our own greatness.

We confess our greatness, and we're surprised by our greatness.

Are you willing to be surprised by Reality? That's not an easy question. Almost everyone in the world sees things through the prism of yesterday. You can have a person read a sentence with an extra word in it. They won't see the extra word, because they're reading the sentence the way they think it should be. There's an entire literature on this. We construct Reality based on the way we think it was, and on the way it should be. And then yesterday becomes the tyrannical slave master of today.

To step into this moment is to step into the new possibility. God is not just the past or the present; **God is the Possibility of Possibility.**

In science, God is the past. In dogmatic materialism—scientism, not real science—*there's only yesterday.* Daniel Dennett or Richard Dawkins, through huge dogmatic mistakes, talk about the present being fully generated by yesterday: *Physics fully explains biology; biology fully explains human life.* Not true. Science is now waking up to the fact that that's not true.

There's actually a call from the future. Science is about the causation of the past. Most classical religion is about the being of eternity that resides in the present: you get underneath Reality, and you find the eternity of the present. But actually, we are saying something else. We fully receive, and we trust the goodness of the past, and we trust our ability to transform it. We actually feel the being of eternity underneath the present, that's the "be here now," it's the eternal now.

But there's more. **There's the call of the future; there's the memory of the future. And that's what hope is. Hope is a memory of the future.** Wow.

It's the call of evolution itself. It's the understanding that biology emerges from physics because biology lives in the future. Biology is a great surprise. It's a new Big Bang. Then out of biology emerges the human being, the self-reflective mind. There are four Big Bangs, and Reality is a huge surprise out of nothing, out of no-thing.

Why should the Infinite birth the finite? Matter appears and all the laws, are completely in place in the first nanoseconds of the Big Bang. Then matter surprises us and gives birth to life, and then life surprises us and gives birth to self-reflective, self-representing Mind: the human being. **Then we got tired and forgot that there was another surprise coming: the climax of humanity into a new possibility, a new way of being. That's what we call** *Homo amor.*

So here's the question. Are you willing to surprise yourself? Or even better: are you willing to *be* a surprise? Are you willing to be Reality's surprise? Or are you stuck in yesterday?

- ◆ I'm willing to be Reality's surprise.
- ◆ I'm willing to be more than I ever thought I could be.
- ◆ I'm willing to be deeper than I ever thought I could be.
- ◆ I'm willing to be more beautiful than I ever thought possible.
- ◆ I'm willing to be more true than I ever imagined was even vaguely in the cards.
- ◆ I'm willing to be more good, more stunning.
- ◆ I'm willing to be more powerful.

Love generates surprises. That's what love is.

Intimacy generates emergence. Separate parts come together—surprise! Carbon, hydrogen, and oxygen come together in a particular sequence of carbohydrates and you get sugar, even though none of the previous chemical elements were sweet. Sugar is sweet—it's a surprise. When you bring together disparate elements of yourself into a new whole, you become the surprise of Cosmos.

And it's from that place of surprise that you love the moment open.

ELEGANT ORDER AND RADICAL SURPRISE—GOD THE KING/QUEEN AND GOD THE LOVER

Surprise God with your prayer.

Prayer turns to God who is not just the Infinity of Power, but also the Infinity of Intimacy. The Taoists called it *the non-being that generates every moment*. It's the non-being in Taoism that generates surprise. The Taoists called *non-being* what we would call intimacy.

There's this wonderful verse in the Book of Isaiah. The great prophet Isaiah says, *Ata El Mis'ta'ter*, translated as "God hides." **God is the intimate**

lover who breathes reality into existence, the Eros that animates the strong and the weak forces, the nuclear, the electromagnetic and the gravitational fields—and yet is hidden.

The Tao that can be spoken is not the Tao. It's the hidden intimacy that is generating newness in every second, that can break beyond the laws of Cosmos and create a new law, and create a new possibility. It's a new invitation.

I want to invite you into prayer. Prayer means we turn to the Infinity of Intimacy that knows our name. Just as you hear me speaking and I hear you speaking, so the Infinity of Intimacy hears every word. We speak it so we'll know it ourselves. When we speak prayer, we impress it into reality.

So we are going to offer our holy and broken *Hallelujah* and then turn and ask God, the Infinity of Intimacy, for *everything*. We're doing this so we can be all that we can and offer the surprise of each of us; the surprise of your Unique Self that Reality desperately needs—not as a metaphor—to be the goodness, truth, and beauty that can alleviate suffering and bring joy.

Folks like Daniel Dennett and Richard Dawkins, what they call the "new atheists" who have had enormous influence on the world, talk about what they call "Darwin's dangerous idea." The way they understand reality today completely throws out Spirit, and throws out any notion of God. Because when we look at evolution, we see that there's this notion of contingency. Contingency means randomness. There's this notion of randomness; surprises happen in evolution.

In other words, we see that evolution and reality are not just comprised of the laws of nature: it's not just symmetry, it's not just the patterns, but there's actually this enormous element of seeming contingency; radical stuff that just happens "randomnly."

Their notion is: *If evolution is driven by this element of randomness, that is the opposite of God. God is order; God is symmetry; God is beauty.* Randomness or contingency means that something happens that we completely and totally didn't expect. It doesn't come from what happened before, and you couldn't have expected it. In their understanding, this radical notion of contingency, randomness, and unpredictability undermines the notion of a patterned and ordered Cosmos.

That is only correct if you have a very limited notion of how (and the *feeling* of how) divinity acts in the world. If God is only the King (or only the Queen) who organizes the world in radical forms of order, then any sense of disorder, any sense of the *random walk of evolution* will show you that this whole story is pointless and going nowhere, that it's not following any kind of symmetry, beauty, order, and plan.

But that's a very limited notion of divinity.

Yes, God/Goddess, as the Infinity of Power, holds the world. Yes, there's regularity in the world. No one, including Dennett and Dawkins, would deny that there's incredible symmetry and incredible regularity in the order of the world and the beauty of the order.

There's a great book by Michael Behe called *The Secrets of the Cell*, which talks about the incredible neural complexity of a cell and the brain of the cell: every piece has to operate with every other piece with such precision, such dazzling symmetry and beauty. Darwin didn't even know this existed. It blows your mind away. So yes, there's order.

But God/Goddess is also the lover of the world. And when I love you madly, what that means is:

- I have to step back.
- I have to allow for your existence.
- I have to allow for your autonomy.
- I have to allow for your choosing, independently of me.

I have, in some sense, as Isaiah says, *El mis'ta'ter*—to hide my annihilating Presence so as to allow you to emerge in order to allow you to choose. I'm the God who is the lover.

Imagine a parent teaching their child to walk. I remember when I taught my son, Eytan, to walk. I'm standing behind him and I'm holding him. He feels me holding him, the order and stability of it. Then there's a moment where I want him to walk, and I want him to feel what it's like to walk. So I take my hands away and I let go. At that moment when I let go, I was more intimate and closer to Eytan than I ever was before. That is the God who empties Herself, as it were, out of Cosmos. The Kabbalists called it *tzimtzum,* the divine withdrawal, allowing the world room for its own emergence.

If I really love you, then I want you to surprise me. It's when you surprise me that I'm blown away.

It's so deep. Yes, God appears as the order of Cosmos. Yes, God appears as the elegant symmetry. As the wonderful Irish poet John O'Donohue writes, beauty is connected to the precise symmetry and order of things that are dazzling and gorgeous.

That's one order of Beauty.

But there's a second order of Beauty: radical surprise. The contingency of evolution is the infinite divine love that's so intimate to Cosmos and is yet so hidden.

The Tao that can be seen is not the true Tao.

The instruments of science can detect and measure that which is the order of Cosmos.

It's only now that we're beginning to realize—through Heisenberg's principle of uncertainty and Goëdel's incompleteness theorem in mathematics—that there's this element of surprise, of unpredictability, of not knowing. **That not knowing emerges from radical love.** *I love you so much I'm willing not to put you in a box.*

125

HOMO AMOR IS A MEMORY OF THE FUTURE

I'm going to love the people around me so much that I'm not going to put them in a box. So often we put our partners, our beloveds, and ourselves in a box. We use psychological rules and psychological principles to explain and order ourselves. We define ourselves based on yesterday.

Psychology's fatal mistake is believing that *if you reorder yesterday's trauma based on the principles of yesterday, you'll be able to emerge into today.*

Yes, exposure therapy is important.

Yes, the new principles of psychology developed in the last hundred years that allow us to reorder the contractions of yesterday are vitally important to be whole and healthy.

But they're not enough. I have to invite the surprise of tomorrow. I can't just be *Homo pastus*—if I can make up a word—based on my past. I have to be *Homo amor*, based on a memory of the future.

Martin Seligman with four other writers just authored a book—and it cost five million dollars to write the one book—called *Homo Prospectus*. It is a very technical book, and what it basically argues is exactly what we've been saying here for the last ten years: you can only heal a person based on tomorrow, based on being *called by the future*, by the Unique Self that is me.

Uniqueness means that I'm not determined by all the previous principles. Unique self means that I'm a surprise.

I'm a surprise. On the one hand, I am the same as everyone else, I'm ordered by the same principles as everyone else. Yet there's a surprise that bursts forth from the order.

THE DANCE OF ORDER AND FREEDOM

Star Wars is the great, mystical epic of our time—even the writers don't quite understand its depth. It's had more viewers than anything else. It's the modern myth.

In *Star Wars*, what's the name of the bad guys? The Empire. There are three empires that run through the three different sets of the nine movies total. These empires are called the First Order at the beginnning, and when Palpatine is revived it's called the Final Order. In one scene, where the evil empire explains its position, it says *we have to impose order on the universe because order is the nature of the universe.* Yes, that's true. But in fact: **evolution is greater freedom and greater order at the same time.**

They both live together. It's more order—more symmetry, more harmony, more elegance—and it's also more freedom.

The pathology of order is dictatorship. The pathology of order is the belief that *the order of my yesterday determines the freedom of my today.* Order removes surprise.

DON'T TRAVEL TO DISTANT PLACES; SEE WITH FRESH EYES

We know now based on neuroscience, that the way the brain works is that *anything routine doesn't give you pleasure.* Whether it's in sexuality, whether it's in the work you do, whether it's scenery outside your door, whether it's in art, whether it's in food: anything that you expect—that you take for granted, that's part of your routine—doesn't surprise you. Even in sexuality: *I've seen a body, I'm not surprised. Give me a new body, I'm surprised.*

Remember bubble gum machines when we were kids? You put a nickel into a bubble gum machine. You get one piece of round bubblegum: *it's okay.* Let's say the machine malfunctions and you get five: you're surprised, you get a hit of dopamine, and pleasure moves through your system. *It's surprise, and it's newness that generates pleasure.*

I don't want to become addicted to pseudo-surprise; that's pseudo-Eros. The reason we look for surprise, for pseudo-eros, the reason we look for the new is because we want to feel that aliveness. But actually:

Greatness—enlightenment—is to find the surprise in what's right in front of you.

There are hidden miracles that live within order. Order seems like constant order, but it's not; it's actually being recreated anew every second.

You can love this moment open right now. And **there's a moment that can be loved open only by you, if you access the surprise that lives in you and the surprise that lives in the moment.** And that new body: you saw it yesterday, but it's a surprise. You saw that belly yesterday, but today you see it with new eyes. *Don't travel to distant places; see with fresh eyes.*

REALITY IS BEING CONSTANTLY GENERATED ANEW

This is the great doctrine deep in the interior sciences that is called "constant creation." Reality seems like it's continuous order. But when we access the depth of the interior sciences—or the depth as it expresses itself in the zero-point field or the quantum vacuum—**we realize that Reality is bursting into existence anew at every second.**

Reality is being constantly generated anew. This moment is not just the continuity of the moment before. I can trust the order—the moment will continue—and yet, at the same time, this moment is radically new; it never existed before. It's the ability to realize the radical newness in the midst of regularity. I transcend routine even as I take all the past moments with me. As we talk to each other now, it's like we never saw each other ever before, and yet the trust of all the moments that came before stay with us and live with us.

Evolutionary science talks about randomness. Dennett and Dawkins think *that's the end of God*, because *God is the King who imposes order*. That's true, but partial. God is the King/Queen, but God is also the lover:

- Who empties herself out
- Who steps back
- Who allows for surprise
- Who can be trusted to maintain the ongoing trustable order of Cosmos
- Who generates that order anew in every second.

And because it's new, there is new possibility, the Possibility of Possibility, the radical surprise.

Intimacy means surprise. **If I'm really intimate with you, I'm willing to let you be today what you never were yesterday. I'm willing to always see you with new eyes.**

So friends, to be an evolutionary is to see ourselves with new eyes, to see God/Goddess with new eyes, to see Reality with new eyes.

CHAPTER TWELVE

OUTRAGE + LOVE = OUTRAGEOUS LOVE: THE SYNERGY OF SACRED ACTIVISM

Episode 211 — October 25, 2020

WE STAND POISED BETWEEN UTOPIA AND DYSTOPIA

Welcome, friends. I want to set our intention with an enormous sense of delight in my heart, with an enormous sense of destiny, the unimpeachable and irreplaceable importance of what's going on here every week at One Mountain, Many Paths, as we are in this moment between dystopia and utopia.

We are literally poised between these two worlds, as we summon the energy of the evolutionary impulse *whose insides are lined with love*, and we respond to what we know to be the Leonardo da Vinci moral imperative, the overriding demand of this time, which is to articulate a new story, to articulate a new ethos for a global civilization.

We understand deeply that the potential, the possibility that awaits us for beauty and goodness and truth is unimaginable. At the same time, we stand poised before a level of catastrophic risk—and not only catastrophic risk but the precipice of true existential risk, as Toby Ord correctly wrote in his book by that name. That is to say, *there is no future*, we actually devastate the basic systems of Reality, and either humanity disappears or is

130

so crippled, so un-flourishing, so devastated, that we never recover.

In this moment, patchwork solutions won't work. Individual nations retreating into their silos won't work. Polarization is poison.

We need to come together in order to create coherence.

Coherence is only based on intimacy.

Coherence means that there's a shared identity between the parts that create a larger whole. That larger whole is intimate.

- There's a shared identity.
- There's mutuality of recognition—we recognize each other.
- There's mutuality of pathos—we feel each other.
- There's mutuality of purpose—we have shared purpose together.

Global coherence based on a an evolutionary intimacy can only be realized through the only thing that creates intimacy: a shared story. This is true in every couple that shares destiny and not only fate—**sharing fate is not enough; we have to share destiny:**

- We have a shared story.
- We're part of a shared plotline.
- We have a shared vision.
- We have a shared *telos*—we're in some sense going to the same place together.

Not that we lose diversity. Diversity is an essential part of union, a gorgeous Unique Self Symphony in which every nation, every people, every group of people stunningly plays their own instrument in the Unique Self Symphony. It's even a jazz symphony.

We step back in adulation and adoration as we hear the notes of particular gorgeous players at particular moments—this nation or that religion or this system of thought.

But it is a symphony.

- ◆ We're part of the same music.
- ◆ We value that music.
- ◆ We share a fundamental musical score.
- ◆ There's a shared story.

A SHARED STORY WEAVING TOGETHER THE DEEPEST VALIDATED INSIGHTS ACROSS TIME

What is a shared story? A shared story is a weaving together of separate parts: the best and deepest wisdom from premodern times until the Renaissance, from modernity, and from postmodernity from, let's say, the mid-1950s or early 1960s until today.

All of the major wisdom streams—the validated, leading-edge insights from all the major insights, premodern, modern, and postmodern—are woven together in a new, coherent, and intimate whole: that is a new story, a new configuration of intimacy. The crisis we currently face, the pandemic in all of its poisons, is but the expression of the deeper fault lines in society. The core is a global intimacy disorder. It's a crisis of intimacy.

We only heal a crisis of intimacy by articulating the next step, the next vision of intimacy. Because Reality itself, evolution itself, *is* the evolution of intimacy.

I'm speaking here not in metaphor or mysticism. I'm speaking science—interior and exterior science. **Reality is evolution, and reality is the evolution of intimacy.** Reality is the progressive deepening of intimacies, from the first three quarks that come together in the first nanoseconds of the Big Bang, until all the separate parts intimately and progressively cohere in larger and more gorgeous wholes, new configurations of intimacy.

BARBARA WAS ANIMATED BY THE EVOLUTION OF INTIMACY

So as we face this crisis of intimacy, this global intimacy disorder, poised between utopia and dystopia—facing catastrophic and existential risk and yet holding the radical positivity and optimism of evolution that's moving towards the weaving together of new wholes from separate parts—the way we respond to the crisis of intimacy is to generate and articulate a new configuration of intimacy. It's only new configurations of intimacy that respond to crisis. **Our crisis is a birth; our crisis is an evolutionary driver**, as my beloved whole mate and evolutionary partner Barbara Marx Hubbard said.

Barbara is here with us today. This was one of the most exciting things in her life. Barbara, it's so gorgeous to be here with you. There are a number of movements in the world today trying—in some very sweet, naïve sense—to place Barbara where they find her comfortable, **but during the last five years of Barbara's life, she was aflame in a new way**.

- ◆ She wasn't just repeating the same old.
- ◆ She was wildly excited, wildly ecstatic.

We spoke or communicated four or five times a day, and this new set of First Principles and First Values, the sense of evolution as the evolution of intimacy and the evolution of love, this movement from what Barbara used to call *Homo universalis* to what Barbara and I together called *Homo amor*—**this emergent new human and new humanity who is a unique configuration of intimacy and Outrageous Love—is what animated her**.

That's why she was on fire.

Barbara, you're with us today, and we're with you. We're all together.

ONLY A SHARED STORY WILL ALLOW US TO BIRTH GORGEOUSNESS AND BEAUTY FOR THE FUTURE

Our intention is to play a larger game. Our intention is to step into the breach and be the revolution, to speak at the abyss of darkness and say, "Let there be light," to cry out against all forms of injustice. More importantly, our intention is to add light, to add intimacy, and to articulate the new story, because **it's only that shared story that in this moment of humanity's eleventh hour will allow us to walk through the breach and birth gorgeousness and beauty for the trillion possible future generations— instead of this generation or one of the next five or ten being the last.**

- We couldn't be more serious, and we couldn't be more delighted.
- We couldn't be more devoted, and we couldn't be more devastated.
- We laugh out of one side of our mouth, and we cry out of the other.

And we set our intention.

EVOLUTIONARY LOVE CODE: OUTRAGEOUS LOVE— THE SYNERGY OF OUTRAGE AND LOVE

What is the character of the Outrageous Lover? And why do we call it Outrageous Love and not unlimited love? Because Outrageous Love is animated by both outrage and love.

Outrage and love come together in a higher synergy of sacred activism.

And yet the Outrageous Lover is filled with pure joy, and yet the purity of the Outrageous Lover is always tinged with a little bit of paradox.

It is joy and paradox that merge outrage and love into a higher union of Outrageous Love.

LEONARD COHEN WAS A LOVER

Friends, let's get a sense of this Code. This Code is taking us in a new direction. It's taking us in an unbelievably important new direction.

Leonard Cohen—who we're about to hear from, and Leonard's with us every week—**was filled with outrage.** He was filled with outrage at corruption, and he wrote song after song, outraged at corruption.

At the same time, Leonard lived for joy. He battled depression his whole life, and he knew that joy and depression were opposites. His whole life was devoted to accessing the portal to joy and love—**he was a lover.**

He has a great song called "I'm Your Man," which is about just serving in devotion the feminine, but if you know anything about Leonard Cohen's songs, they're all love stories.

His whole life was a series of successive love stories. He said, "They call me a womanizer. I'm not a womanizer. I'm just madly in love."

We're not talking about or suggesting how a person should live their life. We just want to honor the fact that Leonard Cohen was a lover.

- He believed he was in devotion to the feminine, and he was in devotion to love.
- He battled depression with joy, and he battled outrage.
- He embraced outrage and yet allowed the outrage to come together with love.

WHAT IS THE QUALITY OF HOMO AMOR, OF THE OUTRAGEOUS LOVER?

We're going to talk about what that means today—in the old traditions they would talk about *what's the nature of a Homo religiosus? What is the quality of the righteous one? What is the quality of the enlightened one?* So let's ask it this way:

- What's the quality of *Homo amor*?
- What's the typology and character of *Homo amor*?

Said differently, who is the Outrageous Lover?

- What does the Outrageous Lover feel like?
- How do they play in the world?
- How are they responsible in the world?
- How do they feel inside?
- What's the interior feeling of the Outrageous Lover?
- What is the mind of the Outrageous Lover?
- What's the heart of the Outrageous Lover?

That's what we're going to be talking about.

It's what we've talk about when we say that **the Outrageous Lover—*Homo amor*—can only make the revolution, can only articulate the new source code, can only transform Reality if we're filled with joy.**

Today we're going to bring that together with Outrageous Love.

OUTRAGEOUS LOVE: OUTRAGE AND LOVE

The words "Outrageous Love" have in them outrage and love. So what is the relationship between joy and Outrageous Love, and particularly between outrage and love?

- How do I prevent that rage from burning me up?
- How do I prevent that rage from turning me into that which is degraded and poisoned and ultimately corrupted by rage?
- How do I allow myself to be madly in love and at the same time hold the holy, explosive quality of outrage?

Because, friends, there is much to be rageful about.

THE THREE FACES OF PRAYER

But let's start with prayer.

You can't access Outrageous Love without prayer. Remember, the god you don't believe in doesn't exist, so prayer doesn't mean we're talking to Santa Claus—and I love Santa Claus—but **we're talking to the Infinity of Intimacy, the quality of intimacy that inheres throughout Cosmos, which has a personal face.**

Cosmos has a third-person dimension—the laws of physics, the laws of chemistry, the laws of mathematics, the third-person qualities of Eros that animate the four fundamental forces: the strong and weak nuclear, the electromagnetic, and the gravitational.

There's also a first-person quality: Reality having a *me experience*. That's the first-person experience of the divine.

But then there's the second person, the personhood of Cosmos that knows my name, the Infinity of Intimacy. We turn to the Infinity of Intimacy, and we say, "Hold me. Sometimes I couldn't feel, so I tried to touch. There's a blaze of light in every word, the holy and the broken *Hallelujah*." And I throw myself as a lover, as a child, as a daughter, as a sister, as a brother before the Infinity of Intimacy, and I say, "Hold me. Let me whisper my secrets into your ear. Hold me, hold me. Promise me you'll never drop me." So we turn to Leonard Cohen, to our weekly hymn, "Hallelujah."

We pray and we ask for everything, because prayer affirms the dignity of personal need.

Prayer has nothing to do with fundamentalism. Prayer has nothing to do with inappropriate magical thinking.

Prayer is validated by the sciences, interior and exterior, and is an expression of a First Principle and First Value of Cosmos, which is the Personhood of Cosmos.

How does it work? Imagine you hear my voice. How do you hear my voice? Your *intelligence* hears my voice. It's not your ears. Your ears are but the physical exterior expression of intelligence. So in the same way your intelligence hears my voice, the larger Field of Intelligence hears our voices. How could the Personhood of Cosmos *not* embrace me? So we pray, and we ask for everything.

We ask for our outrage and our love to come together in sacred activism.

Let's bring it all together, let's raise it up, and let's impress these prayers on the lips of the Infinite Personhood of Cosmos, the Infinity of Intimacy that holds us and lives in us in the very same moment. The word is good, and all obstacles are melted away.

Thank you, thank you, thank you, and thank you.

THE CHARACTER OF THE OUTRAGEOUS LOVER

We have to go deep into this dharma today. Let's try and understand the character of the Outrageous Lover:

- ◆ Who embodies the evolutionary impulse
- ◆ Who articulates the new source code
- ◆ Who stands at the breach
- ◆ Who is evolution

What does it feel like to be evolution in this moment in time?

What does it feel like to articulate the new story?

Why is there outrage and love together?

You can't have Outrageous Love without outrage. But then you have to bring outrage and love together.

138

Outrage has two qualities. One quality is outrageous in the sense of explosive. It's not ordinary. Outrageous love is not ordinary love.

Ordinary love is a particular human expression that we call romance, which lasts for a few weeks or a few months. We've exiled love to the human realm. We've exiled love to the romantic expression of human emotions and to a particular period of infatuation. Ordinary love is often a strategy of the ego or a hormonal expression, which is beautiful but fades away. It's beautiful, and it's even sacred, but it's not yet Outrageous love.

Outrageous Love is the heart of existence itself.

- It's what pulses in every atom.
- It's the song of every beetle.
- It's the yearning of every tree.
- It's the delight of the coral reef.
- It's the cry of the dolphin.
- It is all the macromolecules in their stunning cacophonies.
- It's all of it.
- It all inheres literally with Outrageous Love.

We've talked about the science extensively: the pulsing of allurement and Eros that animates the four fundamental forces of Cosmos.

In their own language in the interior sciences, they had access to the same Reality. In *The Upanishads*, they write:

> *Whenever you dissolve into helpless laughter—*
> *transported by a magic show,*
> *opened by a joke,*
> *your body and belly tickled,*
> *drenched by a sudden shower,*
> *—dive into that source of laughter.*
> *Surrender to the surge of joy, illuminating the essence of Reality.*

So, yes, there is joy that inheres in Reality itself, which is a quality of love, and that love is Outrageous Love. That's one quality of "outrageous."

The second quality of outrageous is rage: *I'm angry.*

So let's get angry.

There was a movie from many years ago about the sense in the world that, *Oh my God, I'm angry. It's corrupt. It shouldn't be this way.* It was called *Network.* There's a particular moment where the protagonist in the movie says to everyone, "Open up the window and just say, 'I'm angry.' *I'm mad as hell and not gonna take it anymore.*"

And people all over the world were shocked.

We're angry. We're outraged.

I am outraged that people are actually willing to put a little calf in a tiny cage and cause the calf to suffer immensely and intensely for three months, bloating the calf in order to get a little piece of meat that you get to eat for ninety seconds, because you think your ninety seconds of joy is worth imposing excruciating pain on that calf for three months.

I could go on.

- ◆ I could start talking about milk farms and chicken farms.
- ◆ I could just talk about the outrageous pain that we inflict frivolously on the animal world.
- ◆ I could talk about the fact that two billion people in the world today don't have access to sanitation, or to clean drinking water.

I could talk about the fact that there are literally tens of thousands of people dying in the country that I live in, because they don't have fundamental health insurance, so they can't afford to get life-threatening conditions treated. So children sit by their mother's bed—their mother who has worked their entire life—and she dies, because she can't afford treatment. Really? Is that possible?

We're angry. We need to get outraged.

I am outraged by the fact that Google is not in fact a company that is organizing the world's information, as they say. Google is a data-mining firm selling advertising based on predictive analysis, turning your personal experience into data that can be the object of manipulation for targeted ads for consumers and voters.

The entire imperative of the entire world of Facebook, Verizon, Google, and the rest is robbing our personal experience in order to manipulate us through the emergence of digital dictatorships. That's outrageous. The new, emergent totalitarianism will actually create a caste system in the world that will make India's caste system look like the most benevolent nursery school in history. **We're outraged.**

But be careful. Those of us who live in the United States tend to focus all of our outrage on a particular person, and we think if that person is removed then it's all going to be solved. But actually *the issues are systemic.* They're part of the fabric, and we have to change them.

We're only going to have the energy to change them if we're willing to open up our window and say, "I'm angry. I'm outraged. I'm mad as hell."

In the great wisdom traditions, and in the Aramaic texts, they called this *reticha d'oraita.*

It's the anger of the prophet. It's the anger of Malcolm X.

Martin Luther King Jr. got it right. He got love right. He got non-violence right. But Malcolm X got something right also: We have to get outraged.

Access outrage:

- Evolution as me is outraged.
- I'm furious.
- I am angry.
- I am beyond angry.
- I am outraged.

Feel the outrage. Let it well up.

- It's impolite.
- It's not New Age kosher.
- It's not fundamentalist kosher.
- It's not neoliberal kosher.
- It's not conservative kosher.
- It's actually the evolutionary impulse itself.

It's the anger and the outrage of the prophet. And outrage is messy.

I have to access that outrage, and that outrage has to turn into activism. Without outrage, you will not get sacred activism.

- Love by itself will not generate sacred activism.
- Love and outrage need to be brought together.

That is the fierce feminine rising. It's the fierce masculine rising. It's the fierce face of the evolutionary impulse itself.

We are outraged. And we must claim our outrage.

WE'VE GOT TO BEWARE OF THE HIJACKING OF OUTRAGE

We also have to beware of the hijacking of outrage. For example, the outrage of the great traditions was hijacked, and was turned against those who were called infidels and unbelievers. **Outrage became a tool for power manipulation**, as Nietzsche pointed out in his *Genealogy of Morals*.

It's not by accident that Voltaire, leading the modern Enlightenment, said, "Remember the cruelties."

Outrage is easily hijacked. Outrage easily goes wrong.

The gorgeous experience of direct, stunning, unimaginably beautiful participation in the Infinity of Intimacy which characterizes the depth of realization is beautiful. But then when you actually take God's name in vain and say, "Okay, I'm going to be outraged for God," what actually gets mixed into that are:

- Egoic agendas
- Old trauma
- Power agendas

As Crosby, Stills, Nash, and Young said, back when I was twelve years old: *How many people died in the name of Christ? I can't believe at all.*

That's taking God's name in vain.

That's hijacking outrage.

The Crusades were a cynical political hijacking of outrage in the name of God. And at the same time, in culture today, we have so many voices hijacking the fierce feminine. There are so many people in different dimensions of culture who are attacking others.

- Demonizing whole groups of people
- Forgetting about the rules of evidence
- Demonizing entire populations

For example, the demonization of the masculine, which is tragic, is sometimes ostensibly done in the name of Kali, the fierce feminine. No. That's a violation of Kali. Kali would never demonize the masculine. **The masculine and the feminine live together**.

- We don't just need more feminine consciousness, and we don't need more masculine consciousness.
- We need more feminine and masculine at a higher level of consciousness.
- We need a feminine that's not only ethnocentric—the mother of the Nazi who sends her children to battle.

- We need more masculine that's not only ethnocentric—which goes and pillages and rapes the Earth.
- We need masculine and the feminine not at ethnocentric shadow consciousness. We need the masculine and feminine at worldcentric and cosmocentric consciousness, animated by Outrageous Love.

We need the masculine and the feminine to come together.

HIJACKING OF THE FIERCE FEMININE

You can hijack the fierce feminine—you can hijack Kali in all of her modern New Age forms—for the sake of every form of evil. You can pretend to be a victim's advocate and be engaged in being a terrible perpetrator. That's called the victim triangle: *I pretend like I'm a rescuer. Or I pretend like I'm a victim. But I'm really the perpetrator.*

That's the hijacking of the name of God.

The name of God includes the name of the Goddess, the fierce feminine. So you've got to be careful.

WE HOLD OUTRAGE WITH TENDER CARE AND LOVE

This doesn't mean we reject outrage. That's the principle of non-rejection, which is core to evolutionary tantric thought.

We don't reject outrage, but we hold outrage with tender care. We bring outrage together with love.

Does everyone begin to get that now? **Outrage and love have to come together.**

- When outrage is split off from love, then outrage becomes evil; it becomes a tool of power.
- When love is split off from outrage, then love becomes pallid, insipid, limpid, and weak.

Outrage and love have to come together.

How do you bring outrage and love together?

FIVE QUALITIES THAT BRING OUTRAGE AND LOVE TOGETHER

There are five qualities that allow us to bring outrage and love together, that allow the marriage of outrage and love. **It's only when outrage and love come together that we feel Outrageous Love.**

- Outrageous love is the shocking joy of the Cosmos awake as love.
- It's also the Cosmos demanding perfection, crying out in rage against that which is un-love.

How do we bring outrage and love together? How do we create Outrageous Love? How do I do it in my own body as *Homo amor*?

There are five qualities, five dimensions, five alchemical qualities that bring it together.

1. The first is that *I have a raging open heart*. When I'm in my fierceness, my heart has to be open. *I'm fierce beyond imagination*. Whenever I access my quality of fierce raging, my heart has to be wildly open. That's true in every dimension in life. For example, in sexuality when you're engaging in a kind of vital sexing, the play of radical vitality in sexing, it's beautiful and sacred if your partner can feel your tender, quivering heart wide open in the same moment. So you never lose touch with your wide, radically open heart.

2. Number two, which is related, is joy. *I'm always in joy. I am always accessing joy.* Here's the key: I don't wait for complete fulfillment to get to joy. One of the great mistakes of revolutionaries is thinking that *we can't be in joy until the revolutionary succeeds.* That's not true. I'm in joy all the time.

Joy and blessing comes from satisfaction—but I can be satisfied a thousand times a day. There are a thousand blessings in the day. **We have the capacity to experience full joy in partial fulfillment.**

There are a thousand portals to joy every day:

- Being together with you for me right now is radical joy.
- Drinking a hot tea is radical joy.
- Actually realizing, *Oh my God, I have a liver, my liver is functioning*—radical joy.
- I see a color, and the color just blows me open—radical joy.
- I hear the wind, and the wind moves me—radical joy.
- I see a face of a child lit up—radical joy.
- I do Outrageous Acts of Love. Every Outrageous Act of Love brings me radical joy.

The revolutionary is animated by full joy from partial fulfilment.

3. Three, the Outrageous Lover has to balance the purity of Outrageous Love with the ability to hold paradox. **If you can't hold paradox you can't do Outrageous Love.** It can't be done.

- It's always both. It's never quite good or evil.
- It's never quite full joy or a broken heart. I've got joy and a broken heart at the same time.
- I'm masculine and feminine at the same time.
- I'm universal and particular at the same time.
- I'm black and white at the same time.

146

In that holding of paradox I reach for a third, higher integration. I reach for a higher union.

This means that I'm laughing all the time, because the quality that allows us to hold paradox is laughter, and if I lose access to laughter and joy then my outrage goes dark, it goes corrupt, it goes evil.

That's what Umberto Eco writes about in his novel *The Name of the Rose*, where the priests are being poisoned and we're not sure who's poisoning them. It turns out that every priest who goes to the library and takes out Aristotle's *Nicomachean Ethics* and turns to a certain page, is poisoned and dies. Which page is poison? The page that talks about laughter, because the assistant rector is against joy and against laughter, because it mocks the outrage he feels against the corruption of God's word. So whenever outrage loses touch with joy and laughter, we try to poison our fellow human beings, we poison the animals, we poison the Earth.

I need to be able to not only *wake up* to Outrageous Love, but I also have to be able to grow up. I need to evolve my consciousness. That means two things.

One, to grow up means psychological maturity:

- I can see my traumas.
- I can hear the voices of my parents.
- I can see how I'm so defensive and so reactive and I get so outraged, because my stepfather or my mother is talking to me.

To actually grow up is to move beyond my early trauma and be fully present in the present. I am not constantly rehashing the circle of trauma. That's the first part of growing up.

Then I need the second part of growing up, where I move from an egocentric circle of intimacy where I have a felt sense of love, care, concern, and joy only for me and my family. Most Westerners are egocentric; their felt sense of love, care, and joy is only for themselves, their family, and their friends. That's the whole deal. Particularly the liberal world is profoundly egocentric.

First, I have to move to ethnocentric intimacy, to have a felt sense of love, care, and joy for my people, my nation—not in the shadow form but in the healthy form.

But I can't stop there. I have to move beyond ethnocentric to worldcentric intimacy. **I have to feel the pulsing joy of every human being on the face of the planet, live in the shared new story, and know that that which unites us is so much greater than that which divides us.** But then I've got to jump to cosmocentric. Every animal, every fish, the oceans, Cosmos itself—I take responsibility for the whole thing. I feel the pulsing of life in the allurement of subatomic particles. I feel the whole biosphere radically alive, pulsing with life, joy, interiority, and meaning. I'm cosmocentric.

4.   Quality four of an Outrageous Lover: In order to hold Outrageous Love I have to grow up—psychological maturity—and, critically, move from egocentric to ethnocentric to worldcentric to cosmocentric consciousness.

So far, we have four dimensions:

- One, I have a radically open heart.
- Two, I can be outraged even if I'm filled with joy.
- Three, I hold paradox.
- Four, I grow up, psychological maturity, and I actually up-level my consciousness to a genuine cosmocentric consciousness.

That's Outrageous Love. Wow!

Then we can look at each other, and we can say, "We live in a world of outrageous pain, and the only response to outrageous pain is Outrageous Love." Wow! The Outrageous Lover commits Outrageous Acts of Love.

AS AN OUTRAGEOUS LOVER I TAKE MY UNIQUE RISK AND PERFORM MY OUTRAGEOUS ACTS OF LOVE

At the core of everything is: *I awaken to my identity as an Outrageous Lover and my heart becomes aflame with fierce sacred activism.*

- ◆ I take my unique risk.
- ◆ I step into the breach.
- ◆ I wake up like I've never awakened before.
- ◆ I'm filled with outrage. I'm angry.
- ◆ And, oh my God, I'm a lover. I'm madly in love at the same time.

My outrage and love come together. That's the quality of Outrageous Acts of Love. That's the transmission of Outrageous Love.

Outrageous Love is not tepid. It's not insipid. It's not a kind of, "Let's get together and do an exercise." *I'm actually filled with the fierce passion of evolution itself awakening uniquely in me as a unique configuration of Outrageous Love.*

And in fact, I become an atheist, meaning: *there's no God to do it, there's only Divinity as me that's going to address a unique need in my unique circle of intimacy and influence that can be addressed by no one who ever was, is, or will be—except for me.*

That's my unique risk, and that's my Outrageous Act of Love.

It's got a quality of outrage, meaning it's outlandish, beyond imagination. All of us, we're Outrageous Lovers, Unique Selves.

My Unique Self means I take my unique risk, and I commit my Outrageous Acts of Love.

THE PATH OF OUTRAGEOUS LOVE

I'M PARTNER WITH THE LARGER FORCE OF COSMOS THAT HOLDS ME

I want to finish with one piece. I want to give you a sense of what it means that *I'm an Outrageous Lover, I am evolution, I am the intimacy of Cosmos, I am the savior.* We are the saviors of God, and in the very same moment— forget about the particular fundamentalist cast of it—I can access that quality of intimacy where I know I'm being held in every second.

I never lose touch with that quality of being held and known by All-That-Is.

This is the fifth quality of Outrageous Love.

The Outrageous Lover has to know, *I'm partner with the larger force of Cosmos that holds me.*

It's not just me. That's what Marx and Lenin lost touch with. You become a demonic monster if you lose touch with the larger field that holds you in every second, tenderly embracing you.

That's the fifth quality.

5. Quality five of an Outrageous Love: I can only be an Outrageous Lover if I know that the personal face of Outrageous Love is holding me all the time; we're partnering, we're holding hands every second.

On the one hand, I am Outrageous Love.

On the other hand, the interior scientists say: *Every person needs to be an atheist when it comes to committing your Outrageous Act of Love.*

- There's no God to do it—it's all you.
- You are the voice of God.
- You're God's hands. You're God's feet.
- We pray with our feet when we go to protest. We pray with our hands when we take into our own hands a particular

situation and destiny that needs engaging and transforming.

♦ We are God's heart.
♦ We are God's verbs.

Atheism was created—according to one master—for just that moment when you turn to the Infinity of Intimacy that's uniquely configured in you, as you, and through you, that never was, is, or will be ever again, other than through you.

♦ You're filled with the explosive outrageous joy.
♦ You're filled with outrage against injustice.
♦ You demand justice and you become justice.

But you never become corrupt because you never lose the joy, you never let it get hijacked. You never let your personal trauma, personal agenda, or personal ambition hijack Outrageous Love when you're actually a perpetrator hiding as a rescuer or hiding as a victim. Beware.

You bring outrage and love together in their most gorgeous reality.

RECAPITULATION OF THE FIVE CHARACTERISTICS OF BRINGING OUTRAGE AND LOVE TOGETHER IN OUTRAGEOUS LOVE

Let's do it one more time:

To bring outrage and love together is what it means to be an Outrageous Lover.

To do that I need:

1. **Outrage and love are married, which means in the midst of my outrage, my heart is wide open.** I'm fierce beyond imagination, and I'm quiveringly tender beyond tender at the very same time.

2. **I'm filled with joy.** You cannot be filled with joy, and you cannot access joy, unless you're living in your Unique Self. There's an electric cord that is all of us, but at the end of the cord there's a plug. That plug is my Unique Self and it's only my Unique Self meeting the unique moment that plugs into the electricity of joy which is Cosmos and allows me to access the surging joy which is the very aliveness of Reality. This joy animates and illuminates, in the language of the *Upanishads*, all of existence. I have to be filled with joy, and *I can only be filled with joy through the mediating prism of my Unique Self*. My Unique Self has to meet the utter uniqueness of that moment.

3. **I can only be present in the uniqueness of that moment if I can move beyond the trauma.** I move beyond the circle of trauma in which I keep repeating old moments that then cause my outrage to be corrupted, and I devolve into a form of pseudo-Eros to cover over my pain—and then I become corrupt. I have to be able to move beyond the trauma to access the unique presence of this moment and merge with my Unique Self, which is my portal to joy. I grow up—I'm not only egocentric or ethnocentric. My love is worldcentric and cosmocentric. This includes my egocentric family and my people, my group, my nation— but it also includes every human being and all life, all of Reality.

4. **I need to know how to hold paradox—not contradiction but paradox.** The Outrageous Lover always holds paradox, and the Outrageous Lover always holds an ability to know that good and evil, righteousness and corruption, are far more ambiguous than we thought. I'm outraged, I stand against it all. I'm an angel of justice, and yet I hold paradox.

5. **Finally, I know I'm held and known by All-That-Is.** I know that it all matters, that there's a purpose, that there's a direction,

that no one's an extra on the set: no life-form, no sentient being, no dimension of my life. Every detour is a destination. Every place I've been I needed to be. It all matters. I'm awash with the nectar of knowing that even though so much of it is mystery, it's all meaningful.

Those are the qualities of the Outrageous Lover, and all of them come to bear when we commit our Outrageous Acts of Love.

CHAPTER THIRTEEN

THE EMERGENCE OF HOMO AMOR: TRANSFORMING THE WAY WE LOVE

Episode 261 — October 10, 2021

THE ARCHIMEDIAN LEVER AT THIS TIME IS TELLING A NEW STORY OF VALUE

The quality of One Mountain, Many Paths is revolution, and the quality of revolution is ecstatic urgency; we're animated by a kind of ecstatic urgency. We're focused, we have a direction, and our direction is: *tell the story.* What story?

We tell the new Story of Value, rooted in First Principles and First Values. We share Evolving First Principles and First Values that are embedded in a Story of Value.

We call that the new story. Why? Because our lives have inescapable frameworks. We live inside of a story, and that story is often invisible to us.

The story is the source code of our personal and our political reality.

The personal and the political meet, and the personal and the archetypal meet. The archetypal story of culture, the political story of culture, and my personal story—it's all

one story. **That story determines who we are, whether humanity flourishes, or humanity self-terminates.**

The tragic and corrupted plotlines in the postmodern and modern story are each a direct cause for the rivalrous conflict and win/lose metrics that dominate Reality all the way up and all the way down—on every level, everywhere in the world, across culture—which in turn generate fragile, complicated systems. These in turn are the two primary generator functions for existential and catastrophic risk, which means massive suffering and pain, the deaths of billions of people, and the possible self-termination of humanity. That is to say, there's no future. **For the first time in history, our exponential technologies have generated a reality in which these two generator functions can cause our own self-termination.**

But we've noticed something wildly joyous, and that's where our ecstatic urgency comes from. We've noticed that underneath these two generator functions, there's an even more primary root cause. **Underneath those two generator functions there's a global intimacy disorder** that is the core of both win/lose metrics and complicated, fragile systems. In both instances, the parts don't talk to each other. They're not just disconnected—they're completely dissociated from each other. They're non-intimate.

So what do we need to do? **We need to create a new structure of intimacy.**

How do we create a new structure of intimacy? What creates intimacy in a couple or an organization? **We tell a new story.**

It's a story emergent from a universal grammar of value that we all share.

- It's not just a new story.
- It's not just a shared story.
- It's not just a global story.
- It's a global Story of Value, based on a shared valuation of Reality. It's a global Story of Value rooted in genuine First Principles and First Values.

That is the one possibility we have—from a human perspective—to heal the global intimacy disorder, and from there, after we've generated global coherence, to look into the face of suffering.

You can't generate global coherence and global coordination without global intimacy, and you can't have global intimacy without a shared story.

That's what we're here to do. From everything that I understand—having spent my life, from Barbara having spent her life, reading thousands of books and analysis and newspapers, at the heart of where we are in this moment of time, this time between worlds, this time between stories— **the Archimedean lever, the fulcrum which can change everything, the change that changes everything, is healing the global intimacy disorder through this new story**.

The new story is not fanciful, and it's not mere conjecture. It's a Story of Value. The story is real, based on the deepest integration of validated premodern, modern, and postmodern insight.

Friends, can you imagine more gravitas than that? Just feel that together— it's unimaginable. We're setting this evolutionary intention. Let's feel it together, and let's feel the Possibility of Possibility, which is the very quality of Divinity itself, awake and alive in us. If you think this is impossible, it means that you're stuck in contraction; you're stuck in a set of limiting beliefs that are not true.

All of the energy of evolution from the moment of the Big Bang literally moves in us. *I am evolution*—which of course is an essential part of the new story.

We have all the capacity of the evolutionary impulse moving in us together as a radical community. We're not willing to do politics in the low sense, not willing to do corruption, and not willing to do ego jousting. We're not doing any of that. We're loving each other madly, like Rumi said. It's not ordinary love—let's love each other madly because *the only sanity is mad love.*

RECLAIMING PRAYER FROM THE POLITICALLY CORRUPT PRISMS OF ETHNOCENTRIC CONSCIOUSNESS

When we do prayer every week, what are we doing? We're not doing premodern prayer, turning to a cosmic vending-machine and putting in a quarter and getting out what the Catholics called an indulgence. It's not that; we're not going to the grandfather in the sky. So what are we doing in prayer?

We're specifically reclaiming prayer. Because one of the problems in liberal communities is that they say things like, *We don't do things like prayer.* No.

If you leave prayer out of the conversation, you've left God out of the conversation. If you've left God out of the conversation, you've left a huge part of Reality out of the conversation.

But even if you don't think that's true, which it is, you've left two-thirds of the world out of the conversation. Two-thirds of the world has this deep relationship to some force, which you might call the Implicate Order, or you might call it *Ma'at*, or *Geist*, or *Atman is Brahman*, or *Shiva*, or *Shakti*, or *Adonai Hu Ha'Elohim*, or the incessant ceaseless creativity of Cosmos. Whatever words you use, there's this quality of presence, this quality of power, this quality of intention, that both lives in us and holds us.

Of course, sometimes the access is corrupt. Sometimes the way we interpret this experience is as *a God of my religion who's ethnocentric and homophobic and doesn't like earrings.* But that's a mediation problem, which means I'm mediating my intuition about this great truth of Reality through an ethnocentric prism or through a psychologically corrupt prism. So we've got to clarify. That's what Blake meant when he said, *you've got to cleanse the doors of perception.*

THE COSMOS IS AMOROUS

One of the core structures of Reality is that it is intimate. It's an Amorous Cosmos. An atom is an amorous aggregation of subatomic particles. A molecule is an amorous aggregation of atoms. *Its insides are lined with love, all the way up and all the way down the evolutionary chain.*

It's not just love as a third-person aggregating force. It's not just the love that lives in me. The love has a quality, and that quality is also second-person; *the love knows me.* It's why we're so hurt sometimes in relationship, and why we're so ecstatic in relationship.

- ◆ The love knows me.
- ◆ The love sees me.
- ◆ The love is intimate with me.
- ◆ The love realizes that *we share identity together in some deep way;* we can come so close we share identity. We share pathos.

We feel each other. *You feel me, and I feel you;* that's intimacy. The second loop of intimacy: *you feel me feeling you, I feel you feeling me.* The third loop of intimacy: *you feel me feeling you feeling me, I feel you feeling me feeling you.* That's intimacy.

It's why we call sexuality intimate relations. Because in sexuality, we can feel each other feeling each other. **But the sexual models Eros—it doesn't exhaust Eros. The sexual models intimacy—doesn't exhaust intimacy.** We've got to feel that resonance and tumescence between us when we talk to each other, when we partner.

Because we're not just role mates doing roles together, and we're not just soul mates looking into each other's eyes, but we're whole mates acting in resonance for the sake of the whole; *we're omni-considerate for the sake of the whole.*

We live in this Intimate Universe as amorous aggregations, all the way up and all the way down. The Force—the intrinsic quality that makes it all real, that animates it, that births it in every second, the quality that inheres in it all—is God-ness. It's Divinity, Infinite Consciousness, Absolute Spirit.

God is not just the Infinity of Power. God is the Infinity of Intimacy who knows our name and receives and holds our holy and broken *Hallelujah.*

WE PRAY TOGETHER IN THIS GLORIOUS AND ECSTATICALLY URGENT MOMENT

When we pray, we're reclaiming prayer at a higher level of consciousness. I'm not sharing information with you. This is like saying *I love you; I love you* is not information. I don't meditate for information; we're meditating now. This is not a lecture—we're meditating together.

We're accessing and entering the Field of the Infinity of Intimacy where everything is held.

Who has experienced a broken *Hallelujah* this week? Those have to be held, because no broken *Hallelujah* is not held. No broken ever cried alone. No holy *Hallelujah* is not ever celebrated. Sh We bring it to Her, to She, and She holds it, and She holds us, a our hands. When we're at the worst times in our lives, She can shoulders. So when we're walking on the beach and we look behind us, we only see one set of footprints, because we're so together, we're so intimate.

We turn to She—to that quality of presence that incepted us, that birthed us, that breathes us, that knows our name—**and**

159

we sing, and we pray, and then we're blown open from that place of prayer. Let's listen to Leonard Cohen's "Hallelujah."

The holy and the broken *Hallelujah*—take us inside.

In prayer, we turn to the Infinity of Intimacy that knows our name, and we ask for everything. Because prayer affirms the dignity of personal need. We ask for ourselves and for our uncle and our cousin and our brother and our sister specifically, and then we ask for everything.

Let's take these prayers, gather them together, and lift them to the sky. Let's press them on the lips of God, on the Infinity of Intimacy.

No one cries alone. **Every time we cry, we cry for all the times we've never cried before, and for all those who have never cried before.**

And as we cry, we laugh out of the other side of our mouths.

Let's not even take it for granted for a moment that:

- We're here, that we're together.
- We can feel each other around the world.
- We're alive. That energy is moving through our body.
- We can hold each other's holy and broken *Hallelujah*.
- We can set this great intention and be a band of Outrageous Lovers.

It could be gone tomorrow. We'll be here as long as we breathe, and we don't know how long we have left to breathe. **This is a glorious and ecstatic moment. It's ecstatically urgent, with gravitas beyond imagination.**

I want to start in three parts today, and here's part one. *I want to know what love is.* For many years, we played that song by Foreigner as a prayer, and we may even play it again today at the end—*I Want to Know What Love Is*.

Part of the new story is a new understanding of love. And a new understanding of love begins by understanding the distinction between ordinary love and Outrageous Love, or between ordinary love and

Evolutionary Love; what some of the mystics in the interior sciences called *love before creation and love after creation*, or relative love and absolute love.

There's this great distinction, and it's very simple. Ordinary love is limited to the human world; it's usually limited to infatuation or romance, whereas **Outrageous Love lives in the human being**—you become clear and awake, and your true identity is clarified as you realize, *I'm a unique configuration of Outrageous Love*—**but Outrageous Love is not limited to the human being.**

Outrageous Love is not mere human sentiment. It's the heart of existence itself. It is Evolutionary Love.

It's the love, as Charles Sanders Peirce noticed, that animates and drives all of evolution. It's the desire that Whitehead understood as the appetite of Cosmos towards ever more value. Outrageous Love is the very quality of Reality itself. As Solomon understood in the Song of Solomon, *its insides are lined with love.*

When we talk in science today about how allurement goes all the way up and all the way down, we're talking about the balance, the dance between attraction and repulsion. We're talking about the vector of autonomy and the vector of allurement, and how those dance together. We're talking about the balance between my allurement to you and my autonomy, which is Eros. That Eros is a quality of Cosmos, all the way down the evolutionary chain.

I was just talking to my dear friend and colleague, Howard Bloom, about the first nanoseconds of the Big Bang, looking at the physics and the mathematics, and we were talking about the quality of allurement and autonomy that is inherent in literally the first nanoseconds of the Big Bang. *That's* Outrageous Love.

161

WRITING OUTRAGEOUS LOVE LETTERS

Every generation has its practice.

- Meditation allows me to realize that *I'm one with the Field of Consciousness.*
- Prayer allows me to access the Infinity of Intimacy, the Personhood of Cosmos that knows my name.

Those are two great turnings of the wheel; two great practices. Then there's a third great practice: the writing of Outrageous Love Letters.

When I write an Outrageous Love Letter, I exaggerate till I'm accurate.

- I can write it to myself.
- I can write it to the Divine.
- I can write it to a tree.
- I can write it to a beloved.

It's not a simple love letter practice; it's not a mere psychological practice. It means I'm letting Outrageous Love live in me awake and alive.

I actually become Rumi, or I become Hafiz. Today when we want to write someone a letter that has Outrageous Love in it, the love of the Cosmos, we get a Hallmark card that quotes someone; we can't find it in ourselves. We've all had that moment where we tried to write a little poetry ourselves. We wrote some bad poetry, and maybe we sent it or maybe you didn't. **That was Outrageous Love, something much bigger than romantic love, something bigger than the personal personality self. It's the Personhood of Cosmos moving in and through you.**

I write ten Outrageous Love Letters every day to different people. They're often one or two words, sometimes half a sentence. At different times, we write Outrageous Love Letters in much greater length; we write two lines, three lines, four lines. But we always exaggerate until we're accurate, until we feel the ecstatic explosion of urgency.

Let me describe you for real. Let politics fall to the wayside. Let my ego contraction, my fear of the ritual of rejection, let that disappear. I'm in this psychoactive expanded self, which is who I really am. I'm an Outrageous Lover.

That's an Outrageous Love Letter.

OUTRAGEOUS ACTS OF LOVE

Then there's what we call Outrageous Acts of Love. **An Outrageous Act of Love is that which I have the capacity, through my irreducible uniqueness, to commit in Reality. I have Outrageous Acts of Love to commit that are a function of my Unique Self.**

Now, my Unique Self is not my Myers-Briggs test. It's not my personality structure. It's not the cultural, social, psychological conditioning of my personality, or separate self.

My Unique Self is the unique quality of Eros and Outrageous Love which is part of the Field of Eros, the Field of Desire, the Field of Cconsciousness, the Field of Outrageous Love, my unique expression of that field, which is seamless but not featureless, and I am its irreducibly unique feature.

Reality is having a *You experience*; you become God's verb.

When I become God's verb—when I become Reality's verb, when I become evolution's eyes and hands, when I wake up and realize that *I am evolution*—**I realize there are unique Outrageous Acts of Love that can be committed by me and me alone,** and that is my unique purpose, obligation, joy, and response-ability; it's my ability to respond to Reality. That's my Outrageous Act of Love.

Now, I might write an Outrageous Love Letter to you about you, which is gorgeous. Or I might write an Outrageous Love Letter sharing with you an Outrageous Act of Love that I committed.

Because we're no longer at a place where we can commit Outrageous Acts of Love in private.

163

We need to generate not just individual Unique Selves, but a Unique Self Symphony; the Universe self-organizes at the human level.

THE SIMPLE PRINCIPLE OF UNIQUENESS, REPEATED INTO GORGEOUS COMPLEXITY WITH ALLUREMENT BETWEEN THE PARTS

As in complexity theory, where we get great and gorgeous complexity through simple rules repeating themselves again and again, when we extend that to interior science, we get a new world which is not complicated and dissociated, but allured together.

In systems theory, we call it *complex* and not *complicated*, because there's allurement between the parts.

We get to that world by **applying a simple principle again and again: your uniqueness**. Your uniqueness is your unique set of allurements that allure you to your particular Outrageous Acts of Love, that no one who ever was, is, or will be, can do—other than you.

When I begin to be lived as love, I write Outrageous Love Letters to access that quality.

I know that I'm not merely a contracted, separate-self *Homo sapiens* in rivalrous conflict governed by win/lose metrics, I'm actually being lived as love. *Homo sapiens* is being fulfilled as *Homo amor*: the new human and new humanity.

I'm asking one question in Reality: What Outrageous Act of Love does Reality need for me in the next second?

It's not ordinary; it's outrageous.

It breaks the boundaries that should be broken even as it always keeps the boundaries that should be kept.

Those are Outrageous Acts of Love.

OUTRAGEOUS LOVE STORY

What's an Outrageous Love Story?

Homo amor knows that their story is an Outrageous Love Story; it's not just a fairy tale. It's not just *my personal romantic story, in which I look to you obsessively to give me an experience of being worthy, and without you, I'm broken and contracted and desperate and filled with anxiety. If you dare to leave me, or not to love me, or not to show up the way I need you to, I'm utterly broken because I've made you into an idol.*

No, it's not that quality.

It's not the separate self doing ordinary love as a desperate bid for comfort. It's a desire not for comfort, but for pleasure, and the opposite of pleasure is not pain; the opposite of pleasure is comfort.

I want pleasure, and pleasure always involves pain; they're always together.

An Outrageous Love Story is more than that.

An Outrageous Love Story is when Outrageous Love awakens in me as a human being. I feel the whole Eros of Cosmos moving through me. I'm in the Field of Outrageous Love. It's living through me uniquely.

I realize that story is the fundamental quality of Reality. That's today's Code.

EVOLUTIONARY LOVE CODE: YOUR STORY AND MY STORY ARE CHAPTER AND VERSE IN THE UNIVERSE: A LOVE STORY

Reality is not merely a fact; Reality is a story.

Reality is not an ordinary story; Reality is a love story.

Reality is not an ordinary love story; Reality is an Evolutionary Love Story, an Outrageous Love Story.

Your story—your Outrageous Love Story—is chapter and verse in The Universe: A Love Story.

Reality is not just an Outrageous Love Story. Reality is an Outrageous Love Story which is a Story of Value rooted in First Principles and First Values.

Existential and catastrophic risk generated by complicated (not complex) systems and exponential technology, cannot be addressed by a new story alone, and cannot be addressed only by First Principles and First Values. Existential risk can only be addressed and transformed by First Principles and First Values embedded in a Story of Value, or, said differently, a Story of Value rooted in First Values and First Principles.

Finally, your Story of Value, rooted in First Principles and First Values, is chapter and verse in The Universe: A Love Story.

Reality is not merely a fact; Reality is a story. Reality is not an ordinary story; Reality is a love story. Reality is not an ordinary love story; Reality is an Evolutionary Love Story, an Outrageous Love Story. Finally, here's the key part of the Code we're going to focus on right now. *Your story and my story are chapter and verse in The Universe: A Love Story.*

So that's an Outrageous Love Story. The realization that my love story—with myself, with my people, with my brother and sister, with my friends, with my beloved(s)—**all those love stories are written in the heart of God. Those love stories are chapter and verse in the Amorous Cosmos, in the love story of Reality**. So that's step one.

Let's take one huge step now, step two. I want to share with you just very briefly—**the six qualities of an Outrageous Love Story.**

Quality one, **I know that story is real.** In Outrageous Love Story, I realize story is not merely a social construction of Reality. It's not as my colleague Maria Popova writes, in a poetic restatement, coming from *the bankruptcy of existentialism.* It's not just that *our stories are chance events that we string together as fictions into a coherent narrative.* It's not quite that. There's a dimension of story that is that. It can be a victim story. It can be an ego story. But the clarified plotline of my life has infinite dignity and participates in the storyline of Cosmos.

So the first realization of *Homo amor,* the new human and the new humanity, is that Reality is an Outrageous Love Story. Story is not a social construction, it's not a fiction. There are stories we need to move beyond, the recursive loops that we get stuck in. That's true, and we've got to work with our traumas that keep us stuck in certain eddies that keep repeating themselves again and again, vortexes that drown us and take us beneath the surface. Yes, that's true. But there's a deeper story, my Unique Self Story, which is real.

Story is real as a quality of Cosmos.
In other words, Reality is a Story.

Reality moves, and it has a storyline, and it has a plotline. Every story has a plotline, and the Universe Story is no exception. **The plotline of the Universe Story is** not just ever more complexity, but **ever more intimate coherence between parts.** Reality is the progressive deepening of intimacy.

- The plotline of Reality is not just simplicity to complexity. It's the progressive deepening of intimacies—plotline one.
- It's the movement towards ever deeper differentiation which is ever more uniqueness, climaxing at the human level in Unique Self—plotline two.

167

- Ever more creativity—plotline three.
- Ever deeper consciousness and ever deeper awareness—plotline four.
- Ever more goodness and ever more love—plotline five.

It's the evolution of love—the expansion of my circles of care and felt concern—from myself to my people, to my larger community, to every human being, to all of Reality. The evolution of love is the intensification, deepening, and widening of all my circles of intimacy.

Those are the five plotlines of the Universe Story. You begin to see that the Universe Story is real. That is the first quality.

THESE SAME PLOTLINES RUN THROUGHOUT ALL THE BIG BANGS

Those plotlines run through all of the Big Bangs:

1. The First Big Bang: explosion of matter. All through levels of matter, there's more and more amorous aggregation, there's more and more mutuality of pathos.

2. Second Big Bang: the emergence of life. Then all through life, the biosphere, there's more and more empathy, more and more love, more and more uniqueness, and more and more creativity.

3. We get to the self-reflective human mind, the Third Big Bang, and we go through all the levels of human emergence. All five plotlines are at play. There's more and more complexity, consciousness, creativity, uniqueness, intimacy, and love.

4. Then we get to the Fourth Big Bang, which is the emergence of the new human and the new humanity: *Homo amor*. For the first time, I'm a new configuration of intimacy—I'm actually lived as love. Evolution becomes conscious of itself in me in a new way because I'm now conscious. I know I am Evolutionary Love. I'm a unique configuration of intimacy

and desire. I am Outrageous Love itself moving awakened and alive through me, and my story is an Outrageous Love Story, and my Outrageous Love Story is chapter and verse in the Outrageous Love Story of the Cosmos.

When my romantic love participates in Outrageous Love—when it's not a narrow contracted, ego self, separate self, moved to cover up the emptiness in a desperate bid for security and comfort with the wrong person—**when I allow my romantic love to access and come from my deepest identity as a Unique Self, as an Outrageous Lover, then the romantic story and Outrageous Love Story become one.** That's an Outrageous Love Story; those are the first qualities in an Outrageous Love Story.

Let me just add a couple more qualities.

I realize that:

1. My personal story is chapter and verse in The Universe: A Love Story.
2. I can be the teller of the new story.
3. Part of my Outrageous Love Story is that I realize that *in my life, I'm telling a new dimension of The Universe: A Love Story that's never been told before.*
4. I realize that the Story of the Universe is not finished; I'm telling a new story.
5. Reality needs my story. Reality needs my service. Reality needs my Outrageous Love Letters. Reality needs my Outrageous Acts of Love. Reality needs the quality of beingness; the Outrageous Love that lives in me, as me, and through me. The story of Reality is unfinished.

To recapitulate our major themes here:

*   I know that story is Real.
*   I know that the story of all of Reality lives in me.
*   I know that the inner quality of Reality that animates

everything is Outrageous Love.

- I know that Outrageous Love moves in me.
- I understand that the configuration of Outrageous Love is story.
- Then I realize, now I'm the storyteller of the Universe; it's my job to tell the Universe Story. One of the ways I tell it is by living a chapter of it in my life.
- I realize that the story is unfinished.
- Finally, I realize that this unfinished story has to be finished in some unique way through me.

I've got a unique contribution to the next stage of that story. My story is needed because it's chapter and verse in The Universe: A Love Story. I am part of this new human and new humanity—the fulfillment of *Homo sapiens* as *Homo amor*—and in that, I become omni-considerate for the sake of the whole. **I'm lived as love and I feel the whole living in me; all of evolution lives in the interiors and exteriors.**

I begin to act in Unique Self Symphonies for the sake of the whole.

That's an Outrageous Love Story.

I'M WILLING TO LET YOU LOVE ME UNCONDITIONALLY

Part of *Homo amor* is that we change the way we love. We look at each other and we say, *I'm willing to let you love me unconditionally.* If you get a sense of it, you understand that these words are unimaginable. What does that mean, *I'm willing to let you love me unconditionally*?

Most of us don't want to be loved unconditionally; we want to be loved conditionally.

- I want to be loved because I'm beautiful.
- I want to be loved because I'm smart.

- ◆ I want to be loved because I'm powerful.
- ◆ I want to be loved because you think I'm cute.

In other words, we want to be loved conditionally, and we're conditioned to believe that only if we fulfill certain conditions are we lovable. So of course we can't say, *I'm willing to let you love me unconditionally*, because to say that means I have to trust that I'm lovable *without conditions*.

What does that mean? It doesn't mean I go become an axe murderer. It means the quality of my selfness—that unique quality of Outrageous Love that is me—is madly lovable and madly sufficient. Now, of course, there are ways I express that quality:

- ◆ I might do it in kindness.
- ◆ I might do it in audacity.
- ◆ I might do it in Outrageous Acts of Love.
- ◆ I might do it by giving my Unique Gift.

But those are not my egoic, contracted, and coiled self, desperate to fulfill a set of conditions so that someone will be willing to love me in ordinary love.

What emerges out of my unique quality of Outrageous Love is this ecstatically urgent explosion of goodness, kindness, truth, and beauty.

But that's an expression of my essential quality: *I'm willing to let you love me unconditionally*.

Now, we often can't access that, and we're not even sure what the words, *I'm willing to let you love me unconditionally*, mean.

Does it mean *I'm unconditionally willing to let you love me*, or *I'm willing to let you love me unconditionally*, or *that you love me without conditions*?

We don't want to wrap our heads around it; it's non-conceptual.

THE PRE-TRAGIC, TRAGIC AND POST-TRAGIC STAGES OF UNCONDITIONAL LOVE

Let's try and find it even deeper. Who do we have an experience of loving unconditionally? We love a baby unconditionally. The poet Wordsworth writes that *the baby is born trailing clouds of glory*. What does that mean? It means that when you look at a baby, we're not looking at the conditions; we're not involved in what Buber called an I-It relationship. We're curious: *Who is this going to become, and who is this quality?* We look at the baby and literally our whole hearts open; our ego defenses fall. There's no instrumentation. I'm right there and present. I want to hold the baby, and as I look down at the baby, love streams from me to the baby. So if the baby would have a voice, the baby would say to us, *I'm willing to let you love me unconditionally.*

The baby is pre-tragic; the baby is coming from the Divine.

However, babies are not "good" because they haven't developed the quality of goodness, but *they are trailing clouds of glory*; they still have this quality of unmediated Divineness, of unmediated Essence, of unmediated Beauty. **We love the baby because the baby participates in a particular quality of Divinity.**

Essentially, what the God voice is saying to the human being is, *I'm willing to let you love me unconditionally.* The God voice in me says to you, *I'm willing to let you love me unconditionally.* Meaning, **the baby is accessing that quality of self that is *actually* me**—my Unique Self, my irreducible and infinitely valuable, gorgeous Reality: Divinity having a me experience.

But the baby is still pre-tragic; the baby is before the conditions of the world have begun to act. It's before the baby has gone through what Margaret Mallory called "separation-individuation," which is necessary, or what Gurdjieff called the great shock of separation. **We call it the tragic. But it's a necessary tragedy.**

172

I move into my separation, and I begin to practice my winning formula in order to get attention. So I may start becoming funny because I noticed I got a certain response by being funny, or I might start becoming kind because I got a certain response by being kind. I feel that I've got to develop a certain kind of false self, so that I'll be able to get something I desperately need. Because I realize that I'm separate, and I'm massively afraid of that separation, trauma, and that shock of separation.

When someone fixates their attention on me in a way that makes me feel that I'm at home, I begin to make that which I did to evoke that kind of attention, my winning formula. Then I keep repeating it again and again. That's the tragic stage.

Now I'm being loved conditionally, and I've lost contact with that sense of, *I'm willing to let you love me unconditionally*. Most human beings can't even begin to say the words, but *Homo amor* can. The movement from *Homo sapiens* to *Homo amor* is the movement from the tragic to the post-tragic. In the post-tragic, we reclaim our second innocence. In the post-tragic, we reclaim the baby, but it's the baby at level three.

Recall our *dharmic* phrase, *she comes in threes*:

1. First, it's the innocence of the baby; pre-tragic.
2. Then all of the complexity, pain, and conditionality of adult living, which is level two, the tragic.
3. Then I move into level three, where I'm an adult and a child at the same time; post-tragic.

Truly great people have a sense of child in them; they're mischievous, they're playing. We're always playing because we realize at some level we are still the baby. We reclaim the innocence of the baby—not from the pre-tragic place, not from level one, but from level three, from the post-tragic place.

So now, as the baby/adult, the child/wise one, I can look at you and I say— because poet Yeats is how we always explain the post-tragic:

When such as I cast out remorse.

173

So great a sweetness fills my breast.
We can dance, and we can sing.

We can play; we can become *Homo ludens* again, human being who plays.

We are blest by everything,
And everything we look upon is blest.

That's the play of the baby the erotic mystics called *sha'ashua*: the Divine erotic play, when the child and the adult merge again.

From that place, I can look at you and I can say *I'm willing to let you love me unconditionally.* Then from that place of unconditionality, I begin to act.

- ◆ From there, I become *Homo amor*.
- ◆ From there, I begin to commit my Outrageous Acts of Love.
- ◆ From there, I write my Outrageous Love Letters.
- ◆ From there, I realize that my story, literally, is chapter and verse in The Universe: A Love Story.

CHAPTER FOURTEEN

THERE IS NO ULTIMATE DISTINCTION BETWEEN COSMIC LOVE AND PERSONAL LOVE

Episode 329 — January 30, 2023

EVOLUTIONARY LOVE CODE: LOVE IS THE HEART OF EXISTENCE ITSELF

Reality is lined with love. The inside of Reality is LoveIntelligence. This is not *ordinary* love, not what is usually referred to as love. It is what we call *Outrageous Love* or *Evolutionary Love*.

Ordinary love is the exile of love to a merely human experience. That experience is often a strategy of the ego for security or status. Ordinary love is generally a passing emotional state and is most often the emotion of infatuation.

Outrageous or Evolutionary Love is not "mere human sentiment, it is the heart of existence itself."

It's what Dante called the love *that moves the sun and other stars.*

When human love participates in the larger quality of Outrageous Love, it is no longer merely a passing emotion. It becomes the center of gravity of your life.

You are *lived as love*—a radically alive, joy-filled, and purpose-driven life.

When you awaken as Evolutionary Love, you realize your identity as an Evolutionary Lover.

When you awaken as Outrageous Love, you realize your identity as an Outrageous Lover.

You deepen your identity from *I am Evolution* to *I am Evolutionary Love*.

I am an Evolutionary Lover.

I am an Outrageous Lover.

This code is an unbelievable code. This is the code that changes everything.

It's the code that re-codes Reality.

We are going to dive into it and reanimate this revolution, because at the very heart of the revolution is Eros:

- ◆ A politics of Eros
- ◆ An economics of Eros
- ◆ Relationships of Eros

We need a response to the meta-crisis, as we are poised between utopia and dystopia, that comes from the heart of Eros. We have to begin with this realization in response to the tragic confusion that modernity and postmodernity brought to the very simple question: *Is love real?*

We saw, a few weeks ago, a response from ChatGPT-3, which of course said: *Well, no, love is just an emotion. People have different understandings of what it is, and it can affect your life, but it's not real.*

But love *is* real, meaning:

- ◆ Love is an ontology.
- ◆ Love is constitutive of Cosmos.
- ◆ Cosmos is constituted by Eros all the way up and all the way down.

- ◆ Every moment is constituted by Eros, constituted by love.

How many people have a sense of what I mean when we say that it's *constituted by love*? It means **love is the core, and that Eros is the primary value of Reality**. It is the primary First Principle and Value of Reality.

The word *love* often connotes something which is smaller:

- ◆ What we might call *ordinary love*
- ◆ What we might call *love which is a strategy of the ego*
- ◆ Love which is *a social construction*
- ◆ The kind of love described by postmodernists

For example, my dear friend Howard Bloom, who I love dearly, in his book *The Lucifer Principle*, challenges the word *love*, I think wrongly (and I've talked to Howard about this). He is expressing the basic postmodern idea, which is tragic and misguided, that love is a social construction, that love is a fiction, that love is a figment of our imagination.

It's not that we don't *experience* love—we have an experience of, or we have an emotion of, love—**but is it a real constitutive structure of Reality, as opposed to an amoral accidental force generated by random Cosmos, which does not have intrinsic value?**

That's the question of the day.

LOVE IS REAL AND IT LIVES IN EVERY MOMENT

We say *I love you*.

I love you is our sacred creed.

But the words have grown tepid, flaccid, and limp. They are not throbbing; they are not tumescent; they are not pulsing. We no longer quite understand what we mean when we say I love you.

We too easily love hamburgers, and love the weather—and what's the relationship between loving hamburgers and loving you, we're not sure.

We use I love you. We know I love you is our sacred creed. We know that's what matters. When the World Trade Center was going down and people have just a few seconds left, we see that:

- People didn't say the *Shema*, the great Hebrew lineage prayer (although some people may have of course).
- People didn't say or recite the Triple Gem of Buddhism or the *Om Mani Padme Hum* mantra.

What everybody said—the universal structure, the constitutive element that needed to be present in that moment—was *I love you*. People phoned home and people said, *I love you*. **I love you, and I've always loved you, and I'll always love you—that's what people said.**

And yet, we don't know what *I love you* means. We have the voices of postmodernity, from ChatGPT-3 to my friend Yuval Harari, saying:

- No, these love stories are fictions—they are figments of our imagination and social constructions.
- They are not anchored in the Real, in ontology, in the ultimately Real.

When you're talking about Outrageous Love, you can be sick, or you can have a fever—because we are fevered with Outrageous Love, and the fever of Outrageous Love—oh my God!—purifies all fevers.

We are going to come back to the code at the end, and Whitney Houston is going to resonate our code for us (and Whitney Houston lived an incredible, tragic, and beautiful love story, and lots of incredible post-tragic moments). But to really resonate our code, we need to create some context.

What are we saying here?

- The first thing we're saying is that **love is real**. Love is absolutely real.
- The second thing we're saying is that **this love lives in every moment**.

178

It's so beautiful, my friends. Solomon writes, *smolo tachat roshi, viymino t'chabkeni*, "your left hand is under my head, and your right hand embraces me."

Solomon who is the source of the wisdom of Solomon, the wisdom of Solomon which suffuses both East and West in the lineage traditions— because remember, friends, it's all one source. All religions come from one source. Whatever we're going to identify that source as, it all comes from one source, it all comes from The One.

- It comes from the one heart.
- It comes from the one love.
- It comes from the one Eros.

There's an entire set of esoteric sources suggesting that Solomon might have been core to that, or maybe there was another deeper, earlier tradition from which everything emerged—but all temples are rooted in the one temple. All loves are sourced in the one love. All Eros. All breath is in the one breath. It's one love. It's one heart. It's one breath. It's one temple.

And it's real.

So Solomon writes, *smolo tachat roshi, viymino t'chabkeni*, "your left hand is under my head, and your right hand embraces me." What Solomon is saying is, wherever you fall, you fall into the hands of She.

Can you feel that, friends?

Wherever you fall, you fall into Her hands.
That's an ontological Reality of Cosmos.

ChatGPT-3, my dear friend, no, love is real. My dear friend, Yuval, *chaver shili matsim shili*, love is real. The love you feel for your partner participates not just in a social construction of Reality, but in the ontology of Cosmos itself.

179

Ontology means it's ultimately real. It's more real than anything else. The actual Reality of every moment is, *smolo tachat roshi, viymino t'chabkeni* "your left hand is under my head, and your right hand embraces me."

People talk about searching for love, about trying to find love. We need to realize that, in the deepest sense, love is never absent.

- Love is not a mountain that needs to be scaled.
- Love is not hard to find—love is impossible to avoid.
- Love is the fundamental quality of every moment.
- Love is the fundamental quality of *this* moment.

THREE FACES OF THE REAL

I had a wonderful conversation with my dear friend Ken Wilber, many years ago. Out of this set of conversations, and conversations with Brother David and Father Thomas, there emerged this notion that we later came to call the three faces of the Divine.

These three faces of the Divine are fundamental in the structure of Reality. In the great lineage of Hebrew wisdom, they are:

- *Ani*: I
- *Ata*: you
- *Hu*: him or her.

These are the first person, the second person, and the third person.

The third person of Reality is the force of love moving through Cosmos. When you look at the third person, you can understand the story of Reality from its exterior perspective. You see that Reality is getting more and more complex. The self-organizing universe that structures more and more complexity. Science often looks at the third person of Reality.

The first person of Reality is my experience: what's moving through me?

180

The second person of Reality is what's in the space between. It's the second person of Reality, and it's the second face of the Real—that's what I want to call it. The second face of the Real is this second-person Eros, this force that, in every moment, is bringing us together, uniting us, creating larger unions, creating deeper mutualities, creating more profound recognitions, creating wider and deeper and more intense embraces.

This is what's happening every second. This is the nature of Reality. **To become the new human, to become _Homo amor_, is to be fully aware that this is the same force of Eros that moves in the third person.** It moves through all the structures of Reality, moving Reality towards ever larger unions (or complexities, in the language of science), or aggregating ever larger, ever wider, and ever deeper aggregations.

This is the force of love that lives in me in the first person (which is the interior quality of my consciousness) and the force of Eros that moves between us—and it is my own essential nature.

These three faces of the Real live in me. I am a unique expression of those qualities of the Real, that never was, is, or will be ever again—other than through me.

As such, I am a new ontology of the Real. I not only, as Buddhism says, participate in the original face of the All, but I am a uniquely original expression of the All that has never existed before.

I am a new dimension or expression of all three faces of Eros.

At no point is it ever true that I am ever un-love. Un-love is an illusion.

What we do when we practice is: we participate in the very movement of evolution itself, which is the movement towards ever deeper love:

- Ever deeper love in the spaces in between (second person).
- Ever deeper love aggregating Reality, moving Reality towards larger, deeper, more intense, more beautiful, more good, and more true unions (third person).

- Ever deeper love literally running through me as I become aware that I am an irreducibly unique expression of that LoveIntelligence and LoveBeauty (first person).

That's actually who I am.

ENLIGHTENMENT IS SANITY

That's the code. It's not just that evolution, the third person of Reality, aggregating to larger wholes, lives in me. That's shocking enough: I'm not just living in an evolutionary context—the evolutionary context, quite literally, lives in me. I am evolution.

But I am not just evolution—I am Evolutionary Love. I am the unique configuration of Eros that never was, is, or ever will be again. And when I practice, when I do—not spiritual practice, I don't like the word spiritual—we're doing practices of the Real. These are sanity practices. These are enlightenment practices, and **enlightenment is sanity**.

That's all enlightenment means.

Enlightenment is not an esoteric luxury of the elite or of the avatars. Not at all. Enlightenment is sanity, and **sanity is to know my true identity**:

- To know *who* I am
- To know *where* I am
- To know *what there is to do*, to know what Reality needs from me

Enlightenment is not clarity. Enlightenment is sanity.

Yes, enlightenment clarifies the nature of Reality. But at its core, Enlightenment is sanity.

Do you understand how that changes everything? What that means is we cannot rely on the elite to be enlightened, we have to stand for the democratization of enlightenment. The democratization of enlightenment is the democratization of great love. Does everyone understand that? In other words, **great love is not just for avatars, saints, whirling dervishes, and great lovers**.

My nature is to be a great lover. Great love moves through me.

That's the nature of enlightenment: it is to realize that this love—in the first, second, and third person—is actually moving through me.

Love is not hard to find. Love is impossible to avoid.

Let's feel into this, and let's understand: *Who are you?* Who am I? I am a great lover.

IN THE PROCESS OF EVOLUTION, SPIRIT BECOMES *MORE*

Let's go deeper. In the great lineage understandings, we talk about involution and evolution. Involution means that Reality throws itself out into the lower and denser realms of Reality. Each of these realms of Reality are the Real. They are Spirit, but they're in *lila*—they are playfully more ignorant versions of Spirit.

Spirit descends into soul, and soul descends into mind, and mind contracts into body, and then the biological living body condenses and contracts into matter—but matter is but disguised love.

Matter is but desire in disguise, which is why matter then explodes at the singularity of the Big Bang, and matter blows Reality into existence. The Big Bang is the moment in which the singularity, the material universe, blows into existence, and then begins.

- ◆ Matter reaches for the Divine.
- ◆ Reality moves and self-actualizes matter—mathematical

183

laws, configurations of intimacy, Eros exponentialized in the first moments, the first nanoseconds of the Big Bang.

- Then, it self-organizes back to Source.

So, there is an involution, in which Spirit condenses itself to a point—and then there is an explosion, in which Spirit unfolds and evolves back to Source. But in that evolution back to Source—and here's where it's beautiful, and it's dramatic, and it's stunning, and it's unimaginable—Spirit becomes more.

If you didn't just faint, then those words didn't make any sense to you, then you didn't get it. It means I didn't say it clearly (so I apologize), and it's impossible to say.

Spirit becomes more by emptying itself out into the singularity of matter, and then going through the entire process of evolution. Spirit, when we return—when evolution returns back to Source—is more than it ever was before. Just think about it. The Big Bang happens, and several billion years go by as matter self-organizes to ever deeper and wider complexities:

- At some point, the first life emerges, the first life forms.
- Then several more billion years go by, and then higher life emerges.
- Then millions of years after that, human beings, as it were, emerge, walking on the savanna.

In each of these cases and each of these expressions, we are getting to higher and deeper levels of consciousness and realization. We increase the number of perspectives we are able to take. We increase our capacity for Eros, for care, for radical aliveness, for pleasure, for compassion.

This is so deep, so beautiful. We need to remember who we are.

Hope is the place where the memory of our past informs the memory of our future.

We know that when Divinity self-contracts and empties Herself into matter, there's a kind of deliberate, divine amnesia, the play of divine forgetfulness. We forget who we are—and the entire process of evolution is the place of remembering.

Open your hearts, friends. Let's open our hearts like we never have before, to actually feel the interior structure of Cosmos.

Evolution is the place in which memories are recovered.

There are two kinds of knowledge:

- There is knowledge that comes from experiment: we experiment and learn something new.
- There's a second kind of knowledge which comes from the recovery of memory, this knowledge in which we recover the memory of who we are. We remember that we have forgotten.

It's okay to forget, but we begin to get clarity when we remember that we've forgotten.

It's okay to forget, my friends—but what happens when we forget that we've forgotten?

When we forget that we've forgotten, then we can't remember. We have to forget that we've forgotten, and then we begin to remember, and when we recover memory—that's when we become whole.

The entire story of evolution is recovering the memory of the Eros that animates and suffuses the entire process and the entire story.

REALITY IS THE MOVEMENT TOWARDS GOD BY THE GENTLE PERSUASION OF LOVE

Reality has direction. Reality is not random. Perry Marshall has written a very good essay on the absurd presentations of randomness. Reality is not random. Reality has inherent direction.

This is not a caricatured, homophobic, anti-body, ethnocentric God imposing order on a dead inert Cosmos, demanding obedience. No, **there is *inherent* Eros.**

Reality is filled with Eros, and that Eros has *telos*. My dear, beloved evolutionary partner, Barbara Marx Hubbard, used to talk about this as a *telerotic* universe. Reality has *telos* and Eros. That's why **Reality is, as Whitehead said, the movement towards God by the persuasion of love.**

Reality is the movement towards realization, towards the recovery of memory. In the recovery of memory, we remember that it's all animated by Eros. That love is not hard to find; that love is impossible to avoid.

But what moves us to the recovery of memory? What moves us to the recovery of Eros?

Reality is the movement towards God by the gentle persuasion of love.

In other words, **the drive of Reality towards self-organization and self-transcendence is animated by the Eros that moves it**. That's why Reality moves from bacteria to Bach, from slime to Shakespeare, from mud to Mozart, from quarks to culture.

The self-organizing process is animated *not* by natural selection. Natural selection is a selection *mechanism*. If you read biology carefully today—people like James Shapiro, a brilliant geneticist at the University of Chicago, on natural genetic engineering, or *The Music of Life* by Denis Noble—you understand that at that leading edge of science, the old notion of random mutation and natural selection as the driver of evolution is dead.

So what's *driving* the whole thing?

It's the Eros that animates the four forces of physics. And that Eros, my friends, lives *in us*. It lives *in* us, *as* us, and *through* us.

- ✦ It's the evolution of love in the spaces between us (the second person).
- ✦ But it's also the evolution of the love which is the interior of consciousness that lives in the first person.

First person and **third person** are two different descriptions of the same Reality. *First person* means what's happening *inside* of me.

Atoms have what Whitehead called *prehension*, which is a kind of proto-awareness. There's a proto-awareness of a dimension of *choice*, even at the atomic level, wrote the interior scientists, as well as the great mathematician Whitehead. That's the first person—an increased proto-consciousness, and then it gets more and more:

- ✦ We get to amphibians, and life forms with neural networks, and then we get to the paleo mammals with limbic systems and the capacity to form images and symbols.
- ✦ We go to chimpanzees and apes and gorillas, with the capacity to form early concepts.
- ✦ We get to the humans, with a triune brain or some version of a triune brain, and the ability to form complex rules and axioms, with the capacity, ultimately, to awaken to **the realization that this entire story is living in me, and that I am actually not separate from Source.**

That's the process of the evolution of love in the first person.

Then there is the evolution of love in the third person. We get to ever greater systems of interconnectivity, complexity, more and more nodes of connection that yield more and more consciousness. **The more complexity there is, the more consciousness there is.** That's the law of complexity and consciousness, and it never fails.

Then we get the evolution of love in the second person, which is **the deepening and widening of the love that exists in the spaces between us.** That's the nature of Reality. Reality is driven by Eros. Love moves Reality to form ever wider identities, ever deeper contact, ever more radical experiences of aliveness. We go from atoms, to molecules, to cells, to organelles in cells, to organisms. And what happens at every level?

- Molecules *include*—they love, they *embrace* atoms. In that embrace, the atoms come together, and they birth something new, and that's called **a molecule**.
- And then molecules, individual molecules are embraced, they're *loved* by **macromolecules**. But then something new emerges, this macromolecule—DNA, for example.
- And then macromolecules, at some point, find each other—they are *allured* to each other. And they say: *Oh my God, let's get married, let's get an apartment, let's form a union*. And a **cell** is born, and a boundary is created, and the cells are wrapped in that boundary.

Thus life comes into being—and that is the movement of Eros. **It's the movement of consciousness, reaching and embracing that which *seems* to be other, which seems to be *alienated*, into a single union.** That's the movement of Reality itself.

EVOLUTION AT ITS VERY CORE IS *YEARNING*

Let's understand this—it's so deep:

- Love is present at every stage, my friends.
- Love is always reaching to create unions—that's what love is always doing.
- Love doesn't emerge out of matter—**matter is an expression of love**.

In other words, from the very beginning, as the Big Bang blows things into existence, the force of union that creates a new identity is *always* Eros, and that's *always* love, and that's **the *same* love that lives in you and lives in me.**

Here's the point, friends, and this is where I wanted to get to today. Here is the big sentence, and here is where it just blows away:

There is absolutely no difference between the cosmic and the personal.

Cosmic love drives Reality, all the way down, and we are always finding what's *there* all the way down?

- Is it atoms, or neutrons, or protons, or electrons?
- Is it quarks?
- Is it strings?

Whatever Spirit's lowest level is, it's animated by the strong nuclear and the weak nuclear, and by the electromagnetic, and by the gravitational force—and all four of those are animated by Eros. **At all levels, you have the transforming *telerotic* drive of Reality, which is Eros.**

Love is present from the beginning. It's inseparable and suffuses the forces that move this matter around. Atoms are brought together to create molecules by Eros, the yearning force of Reality—because **evolution at its very core is *yearning***, my friends.

This cosmic force lives personally in me. It's this cosmic force that awakens in human beings, and the human being is animated and blown open by love, which is why I reach out and find you at night.

- It's why we text each other.
- It's why we love each other.
- It's why we make love.
- It's why we are hurt by each other when we feel unrecognized or unfelt or unneeded or undesired—

What's driving the whole thing is the cosmic love that's personally awake in me, and in all of us. In other words, there is no split between the second person, the first person, and the third person. The second-person space of love in between us *is* Evolutionary Love:

- Yearning for revelation
- Yearning for deeper intensities
- Yearning for deeper unions
- Yearning for deeper mutualities

Love is that which activates us to move out of our alienation, out of our isolation—and into our true nature, which is part of the larger whole, uniquely needed by the larger whole, uniquely and originally *intimated* by the larger whole.

Love not only moves us to become part of a larger union, love moves us to disclose our own irreducible uniqueness.

Because love is a perception of uniqueness, and when I disclose my uniqueness, that uniqueness itself becomes the currency of connection. It's only love that allows the larger union to take place, and it's love which discloses uniqueness, irreducible uniqueness, that then allows for connection—because **uniqueness is the currency of connection**. Uniqueness is not separateness:

- Separateness is the coin of *alienation*.
- Uniqueness is the currency of *connection*.

And so, we begin to understand that the third-person force—the aggregating movement of Cosmos towards ever deeper levels of mutuality, recognition, aliveness, wholeness, embrace—is the *same* force of love that moves me to say to you, and you to say to me, *I love you.*

I love you is the CosmoErotic Universe in person speaking in me, as me, and through me uniquely, in a way that She never could before.

I am an expression of *more* love to come. If we understand that the God Field is the Field of Eros, then if I am more love to come, I am *more God to come.*

Let us get back to clarity—we must *clarify* the doors of perception to the extent that we realize that Infinity is disclosing itself uniquely in us in a way that *She* couldn't in any other.

And what do we say on our deathbeds, my friends? We say, *Oh my God, I wish I would have loved more.*

That's the only thing we say: I wish I would have loved more.

I am born to participate uniquely in the evolution of love, and that's what it means. That's what it means to be *lived as love.*

REALITY IS GOVERNED BY TENETS OF INTIMACY

It's okay to forget, my friends. We all forget once in a while. **But we cannot forget that we've forgotten.** When we forget that we've forgotten, we get lost—so we have to begin, and we have to remember that we've forgotten, and that's the beginning of consciousness.

What am I remembering?

I am remembering that the cosmic love that underlies all and is always present is that love that drenches us in every moment.

We are showered in that love.

We are suffused with that love.

The 37.2 trillion cells, and then the unimaginable number of molecules that live in us, are, quite literally, *patterns of intimacy.* What do you think a molecule is? It's a pattern of intimacy. When we use a word, that word sometimes defines Reality, but then it also alienates us from Reality. **A molecule, an atom—these are *patterns of intimate allurement.*** That's what an atom is. An atom is a pattern of intimate allurement.

I am a pulsating, tumescent, vibrating pattern of intimate allurement that Cosmos uniquely discloses in me *as She*, so that I can reach out and kiss Thee. That's the purpose of existence, that is why we are alive. We are alive for no other reason.

And no one is left out of the circle.

No one gets to be left out of the circle.

My friends, our love lists are way too short. They are way too short. What's the one thing we'll say at the moment of our passing? I want to say it again: *I wish I could have loved more.*

We need to create a world in which no one is left out of the circle, and we need to articulate it clearly. We need to create great literature, not quick bestsellers.

We need to do Darwin-, Freud-, and da Vinci-level work, and realize that Reality is governed by Tenets of Intimacy, tenets that work:

- ◆ Across economics
- ◆ Across physics
- ◆ Across molecular biology
- ◆ Across relational theory
- ◆ Across organizational theory
- ◆ Across governance

Everywhere Reality is governed by Tenets of Intimacy.

Part of the intimacy is: there is mystery. One of the Tenets of Intimacy is, *I honor your mystery.*

We are never going to know everything.

We dance between certainty and uncertainty.

There is a difference between the radical certainty of *Homo amor* and the regressive certainty of fundamentalism.

Part of our certainty is the certainty that there's *always* going to be mystery, and we bow before the mystery—but we also bow before the certainty of what we know.

We know that each of us is uniquely lived as love, and that the world we need to create is a world that works *for everyone*. And if one person is left out of the circle, then there is no circle. Wow!

No one is a stranger.

It's beyond imagination. Can we feel that, my friends?

Now I want to do a prayer with you. Whitney Houston is going to be our prayer, and I want to ask if everyone could be with us. Oh my God, we are fevered with love! Why should I be fevered by myself?

Let us be fevered together. Let us be fevered with love. Oh, my God. Love fever is coming at you, Whitney Houston.

One love lives in us uniquely, and all paths take us home to the one temple.

But what we are saying here is completely different from:

- A fundamentalist message of love, which says that love exists within our own ethnocentric context
- A New Age message of love, which talks about love as a force independent of the very structure of Reality, as a spiritual force *moving through* Reality.

Love is *not* a spiritual force moving through Reality—love *is* Reality. Love is the one breath.

Everything in me moves me towards a union, moves me towards embrace— but not an embrace in which I *disappear*, but an embrace in which I *appear*.

It's the embrace in which I disappear in order to appear, as my unique evolutionary, gorgeous, stunning Self, as *Homo amor*.

BEING LIVED AS LOVE IS POST-TRAGIC

All of the sciences are accurate and necessary, and need to be honored, because they are critical third-person descriptions of Reality—but **science leaves out the first person and the second person.**

In particular, the dogma of scientism engages in sleight of hand and a kind of *politics of the Real*, which causes a disqualification of the universe, in which **the first person and the second person become somehow less real, or unreal, or merely subjective.** That's not the case.

Everything in me yearns for contact, towards aliveness, towards wholeness.

Everything in me *yearns*—yearns towards the realization of my unique gift and giving that unique gift into my unique and gorgeous circle of intimacy and influence.

If we could just do one code, friends, it's about *being lived as love.* Let's read the code again:

> Reality is lined with love. The inside of Reality is LoveIntelligence.
>
> This is not ordinary love, not what is usually referred to as love. No, it's what we call Outrageous Love or Evolutionary Love.
>
> Ordinary love is the exile of love to a merely human experience, and that experience often becomes a strategy of the ego for security or status. Ordinary love is generally a passing emotional state, and more often than not, the emotion of infatuation. That's not Outrageous Love.
>
> Outrageous Love is what Dante called *the love that moves the Sun and other stars.*

Outrageous Love is not mere human sentiment of social construction.

Outrageous Love is the heart of existence itself, and it's my true nature. It is the nature of evolution uniquely alive in me.

When human beings participate in this larger quality of Outrageous Love, it's no longer merely a passing emotion. It becomes the center of gravity of my life.

I am lived as love—a radically alive, joy-filled, and purpose-driven life.

Even if I am in the midst of tragedy, even if my life is hard, even if I've been injured by the multiple injuries of the world, I still am lived as love.

To be lived as love—and this is critical—is not *pre-tragic*.

- It doesn't mean I haven't been hit.
- It doesn't mean I haven't been slammed by life.
- It's not *pre*-tragic.

To be *lived as love* is not some *grasping* for love in the middle of the tragic, where I'm going to love and I'm going to ignore and bypass the tragic. No, **being lived as love is *post-tragic*.**

When I step from the tragic into the post-tragic, *then* I awaken as Outrageous Love.

I realize my identity as an Evolutionary Lover.

When I have realized my identity as an Evolutionary Lover, as an Outrageous Lover, then my heart stays open in *all* circumstances.

When I am crushed, when I break down, I break through.

195

When my heart is broken, my heart breaks open.

Let us break open, my friends.

Let us break open together.

That's the heart of this revolution—the reality of a world in which every human being is *Homo amor*, and every human being is lived as love.

Oh my God, thank you, everyone.

We're feverish with love.

CHAPTER FIFTEEN

THE CREDO OF THE OUTRAGEOUS LOVER: TEN PRINCIPLES OF OUTRAGEOUS LOVE

Episode 330 — February 5, 2023

THERE IS NO OTHER WAY TO RESPOND TO THE META-CRISIS

We are the voice of revolution, and the revolution needs to be, at its core, a revolution in superstructure—a new Story of Value rooted in First Principles and First Values. There is no other way to respond to the meta-crisis.

A Story of Value always needs a credo, so I want to just state ten principles of Outrageous Love.

But before we start: there are no declarative sentences here that are just claims. Every single sentence I'm about to say is based on careful reading of the best validated insights of all wisdom streams—traditional, modern, and postmodern.

So here we go. Are you ready? And then we'll come back and do the code.

1. WE LIVE IN A WORLD OF OUTRAGEOUS PAIN, AND THE ONLY RESPONSE TO OUTRAGEOUS PAIN IS OUTRAGEOUS LOVE

The response to outrageous pain cannot be theology. *Theo-logic*: explaining *why* we suffer:

- We suffer because we are being punished.
- We suffer because we attract it into our lives.

That's a medieval and a popular New Age version of responding to outrageous pain: *You attracted it into your life, either by sinning, or by attracting that energy, or having some personality dynamic that attracted it.*

Yes, there is some *partial* truth in saying that we should take responsibility for any part of the dynamics that we participate in that creates suffering. In that sense, those are two very powerful and good ideas—but **the outrageous pain goes far beyond that**. The experience of 100 million people being killed in the twentieth century, non-combatants brutally murdered in wars, is a level of outrageous pain that's inexplicable through merely *me inviting it into my life*.

Yes, we have to take full responsibility for our own transformation—but we also have to acknowledge that **there is a mystery of outrageous pain which needs to be responded to**. There is only one way to respond to outrageous pain, and that's Outrageous Love.

Outrageous Love doesn't answer the question of *why* there is outrageous pain, it *responds* to the reality of outrageous pain. It responds in two ways.

- One, it responds in *action*. Take responsibility, step in, ask: *how can I help, what can I do?* The question is, **what does Reality need from me in the next moment?**
- Two, the only reason why we have the capacity to protest against outrageous pain is because **we recognize that Reality's intention is Outrageous Love**—because we live in

an Intimate Universe, which is overflowing with value, which is overflowing with what we call *Outrageous Love.*

By *Outrageous Love*, we mean Eros. We mean *the love that moves the Sun and other stars*, in Dante's language. We mean love that's not mere human sentiment or social construction, but love which is the heart of existence itself.

- Reality is Eros.
- Reality is value.
- Reality is standing for intimacy, which means mutuality of pathos and feeling and recognition and value and purpose. It is shared identity, it's quivering tenderness and joy and goodness and truth and beauty.

Because *that's* what Reality is at its core, the suffering, evil, and outrageous pain caused by them are a violation of the very nature of Reality.

When I realize that it's a violation, when I realize that value has been violated, then I am filled with energy, with Eros, with will—with political will, with moral will, with existential will—to actually stand and fight. **All we ever want is a cause worth fighting for, and the cause worth fighting for us is Outrageous Love.**

But if Reality wasn't lined with Outrageous Love, then outrageous pain wouldn't even be an issue. It would just be the way it was. The reason we are outraged, the reason we can call the pain *outrageous*, is because Outrageous Love is the quality of Reality itself.

We live in a world of outrageous pain, and the only response to outrageous pain is Outrageous Love.

2. WE LIVE IN A WORLD OF OUTRAGEOUS BEAUTY

Side by side with the pain, Reality is lined with beauty, goodness, and truth. **Beauty is truth, and truth is beauty; they are completely the same—and out of them comes goodness.** There are billions of acts of goodness and kindness and love that are happening all the time.

On Saturday night, I have a date night with Kristina, my partner, Dr. Kincaid, where we're just going to spend time and hang out and be able to talk to each other. And because it's dark here in Vermont, so KK always falls asleep a little early, so sometimes I come to our date night, and I have to wake her up. Last night, I woke her up and I said: *KK, this is date night. Okay, we'll watch something.* We open up her computer, and we find the show called *New Amsterdam*, which I'm sure a lot of you have seen. I had never seen it before. It's about a hospital in New York. It's based on a novel, *Twelve Patients: Life and Death at Bellevue Hospital.*

We watched four episodes, which are about 30 to 40 minutes each, and I cried through the whole thing. I just couldn't stop crying because **the entire story was about Outrageous Love in response to outrageous pain, and people who are outrageously beautiful, and outrageous acts of beauty**.

If you want a quick spiritual practice, and you want to experience Outrageous Love, take a look at *New Amsterdam*, and you'll see Outrageous Love in action, as a response to outrageous pain and outrageous beauty.

When I looked it up, it was listed number one on Netflix. Why was it number one? Why wasn't there a horror show? Why wasn't there some great crime drama? Why wasn't there a win/lose metrics show that was number one?

Because across the Netflix world, people said, this is what I want to see; this is what I know Reality to be.

There's a resonance, a *knowing* that Reality is Outrageous Love.

- ♦ One: we live in a world of outrageous pain, and the only response is Outrageous Love.

- ◆ Two: we live in a world of outrageous beauty, and outrageous beauty is our response to outrageous pain.

Outrageous beauty is our response, and outrageous beauty evokes in us Outrageous Love.

As you look at the utter beauty of nature, or the utter beauty of doctors in *New Amsterdam*, and all of the billions of acts of kindness in the real life, and you see people performing their lives with outrageous beauty, you are just blown open, and you want to respond with Outrageous Love—because that is the knowledge of Reality's value that lives inside of you. The mysteries are within us.

3. I AM AN OUTRAGEOUS LOVER

What does that mean? What it means is that the response to the question of *who am I, who are you*, is: *I am an Outrageous Lover*. **I am an Outrageous Lover.**

Outrageous Love is not just a *third-person* force.

Eros is not just a third-person force moving through Reality. It is also first person. It's the nature of my I-ness. My I-ness, my interior, is Outrageous Love.

This is what moves you and animates you:

- ◆ All the atoms that create bonds within me, which are bonds of Eros.
- ◆ All the protein strands in me, which are configurations of Eros.
- ◆ All of the cellular structures in me, which are constant

movements of Eros and unique configurations of stunning intimacy.

That's what I am—from protons and electrons, all the way up through my organismic systems that are all working together in non-local love, knowing where each other are, the radical unions and ecstatic movements of unimaginable grace, holding me in every second.

I am—quite literally, physically—Outrageous Love, in my exterior *and* in my interior.

- That's why *New Amsterdam* is number one.
- That's why love songs dominate music in the world. Everywhere in every generation, virtually all music is a love song.

Why? Because the music of Reality, its intrinsic nature, is Outrageous Love.

Outrageous Love moves in me in the first person. Who am I? I am an Outrageous Lover.

This is my actual identity—not my religious identity, not my spiritual identity, not my Human Potential Movement identity, not my New Age identity. The accurate scientific reading, in both interior and exterior sciences, of who I am is: *I am an Outrageous Lover.*

4. OUTRAGEOUS LOVE IS THE HEART OF EXISTENCE ITSELF

What's the difference between Outrageous Love and ordinary love? By ordinary love, we mean love which is understood to be a social construct. You ask GPT-3, the new AI chatbot, if love is real, it is not going to say *yes*. No, GPT-3, **love is not a social construct, it is the intrinsic nature of Reality itself, awake and alive in me.** I am an Outrageous Lover.

Ordinary love is the love that's talked about in GPT-3, love which is understood differently by everyone, and in every generation:

- It doesn't really have any common meaning.
- It's what you decide that it is at a particular time.
- It's a social construct, a fiction.
- It's a lovely emotion, but it's ultimately not intrinsic to Reality. It doesn't bind you.
- It's a particular social construct at a particular moment in time that's always changing, always changing in the sense that you make up what it is in every generation.

No, that's not true. Love evolves, that is true—but love is not merely ordinary love, which is this social construct strategy of the ego to get particular kinds of comfort. It may express that way at particular times, but underneath all of that, there is **the Outrageous Love which is the heart of existence itself**.

Outrageous Love is not ordinary love. It's the Eros that is the very plotline of Reality itself, from muons all the way up the evolutionary chain. **All the way up the evolutionary chain, the entire thing is driven by self-organizing systems animated by Eros, and all of those live between us in the second person, and they live in me in the first person.**

5. THE OUTRAGEOUS LOVER COMMITS OUTRAGEOUS ACTS OF LOVE

What does an Outrageous Lover do?

First, the Outrageous Lover keeps every boundary that should be kept, and breaks every boundary that should be broken.

Outrageous Love is not a license to break inappropriate boundaries. The Outrageous Lover keeps every boundary that should be kept, but breaks every boundary of smallness, contraction, inappropriate and constricting convention, of banality and mediocrity—and calls us to our most gorgeous, our most beautiful, our deepest wonder, and our most radical amazement.

Outrageous Lovers keep every boundary that should be kept, and break every boundary that should be broken.

Okay, but what does an Outrageous Lover do after that? **What does it mean to break every boundary that should be broken?** What does an Outrageous Lover do?

An Outrageous Lover is *outrageous*. To be outrageous is to break the conventions of the pallid and insipid normal, of autopilot, of the unconscious, the automatic, the reflexive, and commit Outrageous Acts of Love. **The Outrageous Lover commits Outrageous Acts of Love.**

This is the core of *One Mountain*: The Outrageous Lover commits Outrageous Acts of Love. Outrageous Acts of Love are our *crimes* of Outrageous Love, because they're outrageous. **They break the boundaries of the conventional, of what is conventionally acceptable in the myth of separation.**

I become an Outrageous Lover, I am filled with that sense of outrage against contraction and outrageous joy—and so, we commit our Outrageous Acts of Love.

6. OUTRAGEOUS ACTS OF LOVE ARE FUNCTION OF UNIQUE SELF

Which Outrageous Acts of Love does the Outrageous Lover commit, when there is so much to be done? **The Outrageous Lover commits the Outrageous Acts of Love that are a function of his or her Unique Self.**

There's something irreducibly unique that lives in you, as you, and through you. It's your unique gift, it's your unique capacity.

The Outrageous Lover commits the Outrageous Acts of Love that can be done—in that particular way, with that particular quality, with that particular taste, with that particular cast, with that particular sense of intimate engagement—*by you and you alone,* and by no one else who ever was, is, or will be, except you.

7. WE NEED TO CLOSE THE GAP BETWEEN OUR ABILITY TO FEEL THE PAIN AND OUR ABILITY TO HEAL THE PAIN

Why isn't everyone committing Outrageous Acts of Love?

Why isn't that welling up from people everywhere?

- Because people are overwhelmed, because it seems so big.
- Because the world seems to be—and *is*—a kind of hyperobject, which is so inordinately complicated, and it seems so impossible to impact it, and the pain seems so overwhelming.
- Because the new structure is based on clickbait, which itself is based on win/lose metrics, and amplifies all that happens that's tragic, and skips the billions of gorgeous, beautiful things happening every day.

We experience this deluge of pain, and we close down. It's too much. We turn away. We look away. It's too hard. We take the low road, we take the easy road. We take the road of least resistance, because we've closed our hearts. **We have closed our hearts, not because we are evil, and not because we are narcissistic—but because it hurts too much.**

So, why don't people commit their Outrageous Acts of Love? Because we don't *know* how to actually affect the world.

We don't know how to heal it, and so we are afraid to feel it. In the gap between our ability to feel the pain and our ability to heal the pain, we close our hearts.

What do we need to do to open our hearts again?

We need to close the gap between our ability to feel the pain and our ability to heal the pain.

8. OUTRAGEOUS ACTS OF LOVE ADDRESS A UNIQUE NEED IN A UNIQUE CIRCLE OF INTIMACY AND INFLUENCE

How do we close the gap? We do that by realizing that it's not on you, and it's not on me, it's not on us to heal the whole thing. **We can't heal the whole thing.**

We close that gap by giving up the narcissistic delusion of the ego that I myself *can* or *must* heal *the whole thing.*

- ◆ It's not mine to *heal* the whole thing.
- ◆ It's mine to *feel* the whole thing.

What's mine to heal is the unique need that can be personally addressed by my capacities and my gifts, in my unique circle of intimacy and influence.

No one person can heal the whole thing.

But what I can do, and what I'm called to do—the very joy and elixir and nectar of my life, the tumescent throbbing grace of my life—is that **I can, in my unique circle of intimacy and influence, address the unique cry and the unique invitation and the unique needs that call me, those that I can see**.

Every single person lives in a unique circle of intimacy and influence, and on the ground, there's what needs to be done. **I can respond directly, as a singular pulsation of Outrageous Love, to the unique pain that's mine to heal in my circle of intimacy and influence.** I can do it myself, or I can join hands with other Unique Selves, and we can come together, each from our unique perspective with our unique qualities of intimacy, and actually begin to heal that pain.

I'm not here by mistake. The Intimate Universe allured me into this place where I am, with these people, in this life, and this situation, and this dynamic. I came here through the allurement of Reality that drew me here. **Addressing my unique circle of intimacy and influence—that's where I commit my Outrageous Acts of Love.**

Let's just feel that, friends. It's so beautiful:

I can heal the pain that's mine to heal,
and that makes me powerful again.

I am powerful because I am actually *living* my Unique Self. I'm addressing the unique pain in my unique circle of intimacy and influence—and that's what's mine to do. When I do that, and I experience my power again, my heart opens again, and I can feel more than I ever did—and when I feel more than I ever did, **it fills me up with even more power, and I can heal wider and wider circles!**

9. PLANETARY AWAKENING IN LOVE THROUGH UNIQUE SELF SYMPHONIES

This is not a top-down vision, but a bottom-up vision of a self-organizing Cosmos: **It is a bottom-up, self-organizing, self-actualizing Cosmos, which generates a Planetary Awakening in Love through Unique Self Symphonies.**

Local, ground, grassroots, self-organizing Unique Self Symphonies, in which people are drawn to each other to create new social technologies and new interior technologies.

They come together to co-create a world that works for everyone, and we do it on the local level through hundreds of thousands of Unique Self Symphonies, taking responsibility to be lived as love, and to play together our unique instruments in that Unique Self Symphony. Wow, that's unimaginable!

My dear evolutionary partner, Barbara Marx Hubbard and I together created a Wheel of Co-Creation 2.0, which says that *each of us* as Unique Selves have something to contribute to the evolution of love in Reality.

We can gather and stand on the edge of the abyss of darkness, in our own unique circle of intimacy and influence, and there, we can heal the pain.

- There is someone we can call.
- There is someone that can be adopted by us there.
- There is a way we can step in.
- There is an endowment we can create.
- There is a gift that we can give.
- There is a piece of our time and our resources that we can give.

This activates the Outrageous Love in us, and heals some dimension of the pain in our unique circle of intimacy and influence.

This closes the gap between our ability to feel the pain and our ability to heal the pain—because it's not our job to heal *all* pain; it's our job to realize that there is no coincidence in Reality.

- I was born where I needed to be born.
- I was gifted with the gifts I was needed to be gifted with.
- I have the unique capacities that I need to heal the pain in my unique circle of intimacy and influence.

10. EVOLUTIONARY FAMILY IS MORE IMPORTANT THAN BIOLOGICAL FAMILY

To do that, I have to break the tyranny of the biological family.

Biological family is wildly important. In my life, I miss my biological family enormously. I left Israel in 2006, and it ruptured my capacity to see my biological family. I've of course gone back to Israel, but for lots of reasons, my commitment to Reality, and the place that I could give gifts, and try and heal suffering, was outside of Israel, where I had lived for almost 20 years.

I don't see my biological family with the kind of regularity that I'd like to. I work too intensely and too insanely, and I miss biological family, and I want to do more and more biological family. I love that. I spoke to all four of my kids in some way this morning—but too briefly, and not enough. I want to really honor the biological family. We are committed to the biological family, because biology is not a coincidence—and that's true and beautiful.

But Evolutionary Family, Evolutionary Love Family, Outrageous Love family is easily as important, and in many ways, exponentially more important than biological family. The people we meet on the path, that become our evolutionary partners—we have to love them and love each other, and be committed to them, and invest in them, and invest our time and our resources and our energy of all kinds, and to actually *be* with them to create new families.

One of the things the world most desperately needs is to break the monopoly on love that ostensibly lives only within the nuclear family. We need Evolutionary Families. We need to take our Evolutionary Families seriously, and we need to find them.

Every day, just personally, in my practice, I reach out to members of my Evolutionary Family, and we send love notes to each other, just like we do to our biological family. *Hey, I love you. Hey, I love you, man.*

We are together in this. We take each other seriously.

In order to create a Planetary Awakening in love as Outrageous Lovers, **Outrageous Love has to break the boundary of nuclear family, which is essentially egocentric.**

- Egocentric means me and my family. That's very important.
- Ethnocentric: me and my country. That's critical but still too small.
- Worldcentric: we are bands of Outrageous Lovers all over the world, and we love each other.
- And cosmocentric: ultimately, we include even beyond the human world.

But let's stick with the human level right now. Let's actually *know* who is in my Evolutionary Family and include more people, and just the right amount—and give them time, and give them attention, and give them love, and take it seriously.

You're not alone. Whatever your biological situation or family context, take it seriously and honor it—and also, **you have to form and find your Evolutionary Family, the people that walk with you on the path, the people you help to grow and who help you to grow.**

LET US BE LIVED AS LOVE

Let's read the code again—and let's feel this, and let's *be* this, and let's do this like we never have before:

> Reality is lined with love. The inside of Reality is LoveIntelligence.
>
> This is not ordinary love, what's usually referred to as *love*. It's what we call Outrageous Love or Evolutionary Love.
>
> Ordinary love is the exile of love to a merely human experience. That experience is often a strategy of the

ego for security or status. Ordinary love is generally a passing emotional state, and most often, the emotion of infatuation, the first level of falling in love.

But Outrageous Love is what Dante called *the love that moves the Sun and other stars, the heart of existence itself.* When human beings participate, when human love participates, when our human love which seems to be ordinary participates in the larger quality of Outrageous Love—it's no longer a passing emotion. It becomes the center of gravity of our life.

We become *lived as love.*

We become radically alive, joy-filled.

We live a purpose-driven and feeling-driven life.

When you and I, when we awaken as Outrageous Love, as Evolutionary Love, we realize our identity as Outrageous Lovers, as Evolutionary Lovers—it's actually who we are.

When you awaken as Outrageous Love, you realize your identity as an Outrageous Lover. You deepen your identity, from *I am Evolution*, to *I am a unique configuration of Evolutionary Love.*

I am Reality's Outrageous Love awake and alive in me.

Oh my God, thank you madly much.

Let's outrageously love each other.

Let us be lived as love.

That's the heartthrob of the revolution. There are massive footnotes to each of these steps, but these steps are clear, they are the center, and they are the heart of the whole thing.

CHAPTER SIXTEEN

SYRIA AND TURKEY EARTHQUAKE: THE ONLY RESPONSE TO OUTRAGEOUS PAIN IS OUTRAGEOUS LOVE

Episode 331 — February 12, 2023

HOW DO WE HOLD THE TRUTH OF A LOVING UNIVERSE AND THE TRUTH OF OUTRAGEOUS PAIN AT THE SAME TIME?

One Mountain, Many Paths is a memory of the future, as we are poised between utopia and dystopia—between existential and catastrophic risk on the one side, and the capacity to manifest the most beautiful world that history has ever manifested, on the other.

Two paths diverge in the woods, and we are here to take the road less traveled by.

- Not the mainstream road.
- Not the road that was painted in the movie *Don't Look Up*.
- Not the road that is non-intimate with the future, and not really intimate with the present, and not even intimate with the past.
- Not the road that lives as a surface structure— the classical separate self, feeling her emptiness,

desiccated, lost in our individual traumas, and

unable to access the Eros of Reality that is awake and alive in us in every moment.

No, our path is the road less traveled by. We are here to be the revolution. We are going to tell the new Story of Value.

The only thing that changes the vector of history is the story from which we generate our Reality.

Telling a new Story of Value, changing the superstructure of Reality, is ultimately infinitely more effective than any other move we can make. **Our ability to heal the suffering comes from a new Story of Value.** In other words, *Homo sapiens* needs to become *Homo amor*; a new human and new humanity needs to emerge. Join the revolution, figure out how you want to step up, and take your seat at the table.

That's how we respond to Aleppo. It's how we respond to Syria. It's how we respond to Turkey.

This is a wildly important week, and I want to go slowly and carefully. We want to talk about the following unbearably agonizing question, which is something like this: *What the fuck?*

- Have you looked at the pain this week?
- How do we dare talk about The Universe: A Love Story in a week in which 33,000 people died, and the expected death toll is 50,000?
- What does that mean?
- What kind of universe is it that allows that kind of event to take place?
- **What does The Universe: A Love Story mean in the face of**

213

immense suffering?

That's our question for today.

We dedicate this question, completely and directly, to our brothers and sisters in Syria, in Turkey, and in Lebanon. We're going to be deep in this, and we're going to transform this. This week's Evolutionary Love Code is short:

> We live in a world of outrageous pain.
>
> The only response is Outrageous Love.

SUFFERING IS REAL AND IT'S OBSCENE TO EXPLAIN IT AWAY

We know we are welcome in Cosmos. But what does it mean to even talk about being welcome in Cosmos when 33,000 people didn't survive last week? **What does it mean to be welcome in Cosmos, when Cosmos is so obviously unfair—in terms of what we understand fairness to be?**

We have to do this for everyone in the world who's now asking this question.

How do we talk about The Universe: A Love Story in the face of outrageous pain?

Last week, we laid down the ten principles of Outrageous Love, and the first principle was: we live in a world of outrageous pain, the only response to outrageous pain is Outrageous Love.

Before we go into this conversation, we need to feel this in the space, and **we need to be willing to not turn away.** Let's take a look at this clip, a holy text of pain. I am going to ask everybody not to look away. It's a short clip, and we have to be willing to take it inside.

Wow. *Allahu Akbar*. Could you see her face? Did you see the smile coming into her eyes? Oh, my God! And of course, there were so many scenes that didn't look that way,

so many scenes where there was just a limb found, or a head severed from a body.

We live in a world of outrageous pain, the only response to outrageous pain is Outrageous Love.

What does that mean?

The response that we cannot give to outrageous pain, the response that's not kosher, is a response that's been given by the religions all through the ages: in some sense, suffering happens because people have sinned, or suffering happens because we've somehow invited that suffering into our life.

I've had conversations with many people who are leading teachers in the Human Potential Movement, and when I would ask them how they dealt with outrageous pain, the response was, in one way or another, *You invited it into your life*. Wow!

I sat with my colleague, Byron Katie, who's a beautiful person, and we were talking about a terrible story of outrageous pain. It was a story about my mother, who was buried alive when she was four years old, during the Holocaust. Byron basically understood suffering as that which you somehow invited into your life, and you tell a story that makes it suffering—it's not about the objective fact, it's about the story you tell about it that creates the suffering.[3]

And I said: *Byron, you actually can't say that. You can only say that from the comfort of your life in the upper-middle class of the United States. What about my mother?*

She said, *Well, your mother could have imagined that she was in a dirt play box, and somehow finding her way out, because after all, she did find her way out.*

---

3 You can listen to the entire dialogue here: https://www.marcgafni.com/dialogues/byron-katie-dialogue.

I said that's obscene. And then I said, *If you want to stop this recording now, we can stop it.*

And she said, *No, no, let's do it.*

She was wonderful, but she wouldn't relent her position because there was a dogmatic orthodoxy, because **she wanted to hold the vision of a loving universe, and the only way she knew how to hold that was to say that suffering is created only by the story that we tell about the suffering.**

That's not correct.

In some sense, there are strains in all mystical traditions that understand suffering as being a created human experience—that at its depth, suffering is *Maya*, an illusion.

In the new Story of Value and CosmoErotic Humanism, which is the story we need to change the trajectory of human history, **we reject categorically those positions.** Suffering is not *Maya*; it's not an illusion.

Suffering is real, and we take suffering seriously.

- We reject the classical position of all the religions, that you are suffering because you sin.
- We reject the position which is suffering is *Maya*, it's an illusion. No, suffering is real. *We live in a world of outrageous pain* means we are not willing to turn away, and when we call suffering an illusion, we are turning away.
- We reject the New Age position, or the Human Potential Movement position, which says you're suffering because you somehow invited it into your life. That's a classical position that appears, for example, at the Avatar seminars, and one version or another of this appears in almost all New Age, Human Potential Movement forms. It's a restatement of the traditional position of the religions. The dogmatic orthodox position was a way of turning away from suffering, and the

new orthodoxy, the new dogmatism, in the New Age and Human Potential Movement, also turns away from suffering.

WE DEMAND ACCOUNTABILITY FROM THE DIVINE

Now, it's not that these were bad people, these were beautiful people—so why did they insist on that position? They wanted to accomplish two things.

- They wanted **to be able to experience Reality as a love story**, and they didn't know how to do it without saying that either you have sinned, or that suffering is an illusion, or that you invited it into your life.

- Even more, they wanted—and understandably so—**to have a measure of control**. Because if I suffer, and I don't know why, then I feel like I've completely lost control.

Nietzsche writes about this very beautifully, and I'm paraphrasing: *I can bear with any suffering if I know why.* The *why* means I have some control: if I'm suffering because I invited it into my life, well, now I won't invite it into my life, I'll change that dynamic that attracts it to me.

I've suffered in my life, and I can't tell you how many well-meaning people have called me and said: *Marc, this is how you've invited this into your life, because there are parts of you that are shadow, that you are now not owning, you are projecting them into the public space, and then they are projected back at you.*

This is one of many versions of *you invited this into your life.* It's really just a New Age statement of sin. The advantage of this position is that you have control, but **it also frees you from the obligation to *respond* to the suffering of others, because in some sense, *that* person invited suffering into their life.**

We categorically reject those positions. That's critical.

In other words, any form of *theo*-logic—any form of New Age, religious, or mystical theology—has to be utterly rejected. **We have to look at the suffering head on and not turn away.**

You just saw that clip. We live in a world of outrageous pain, full stop. *Full stop.*

No *but*, no *if*, no *and*, no theodicy—meaning, no explanation of why God is still good even though God allowed this, or why the world is still a good place even though this happens.

No, we just look at outrageous pain, and we *scream*. We protest. **We are devastated, and we live in the devastation *without attempting to explain it away*.**

Not only do we live in the devastation without attempting to explain it away, but we then turn to Reality itself, to the principle of the Real—the Atman which is Brahman, the *Ma'at*, the Geist, the Implicate Order, the *Ayin*, the *Adonai Elohim*, the Great Spirit, the Great One, God or Goddess, however you want to tell that story of the infinity of value that is Cosmos—**we turn to that principle as it lives in Reality, as it lives *in us*, and we cry out in protest!**

We protest. Prayer itself becomes protest, and we demand accountability from the Divine.

When the divine voice says to Abraham, the great father of Turkey and Syria in the Book of Genesis, *I'm going to destroy the evil of Sodom and Gomorrah, these people are evil, they are corrupt, and they deserve to die,* Abraham doesn't say, *Okay, thank you, God. You're God, and I'm obedient. You're obviously omniscient, all-knowing, and omnipotent, and omni-good. You're infinite goodness. You're God, I'm just Abraham.*

Abraham says, *No!* I participate in the Field of Value. I participate in the Field of Divinity. No! *HaShofet Kol Ha-Aretz Lo Ya'aseh Mishpat* is the text in Genesis: "Will the judge of the whole world not do justice?"

Abraham holds God accountable. Wow!

The divine voice explains to Moses, in the beginning of the Book of Exodus, that he has a plan. God says:

Here's the plan. You're going to go to Pharaoh and you're going to say, *Let my people go.* Pharaoh will then increase their suffering, but then I'll step in, and I'll ultimately liberate them.

Pharaoh does exactly what the God voice said Pharaoh would do. Pharaoh increases the suffering by changing the accountability and the quota of bricks that need to be made. And Moses turns to God and says, *la mah have'ot la'am hazeh*, "Why are you dealing evilly with these people, with these slaves?" Why doesn't Moses say: *Oh, this is the divine plan, this is divine wisdom, this is divine omniscience.* No—**Moses is Moses, and Ibrahim is Ibrahim, because they *challenge* the divine voice and they *demand* justice.**

This gets so deep, so beautiful, and it's so wildly heartbreaking—and so wildly heart-opening.

WE PROTEST BECAUSE WE KNOW THAT LOVE IS REAL

We live in a world of outrageous pain, the only response to outrageous pain is Outrageous Love.

What do we mean by that? There are two meanings.

One meaning is: we can turn to the divine force, the force of love and Eros in Cosmos, **because we have a direct experience of *love.***

- ◆ We know that love is real.

219

- ◆ We stake our lives on love. Every song is a love song.
- ◆ We have direct access to the experience of Eros as the animating force of Reality.

We know it when we see that man in the video taking that girl out from the rubble, and he says, *Allahu Akbar*. You hear the voice of the masculine as he sees the little girl, and the love coming out of his voice.

We all *know* that love is real; we all have this direct experience. We are devastated when someone we love dearly doesn't see us or recognize us, or misunderstands us, or leaves us, or we have to leave them.

Our whole lives are love stories.

The fabric of Reality, the heart of existence itself, is love, and we have direct access to the experience of love being real. It's what we call "Anthro-Ontology": **the mysteries are *within us*, and we know love is real.**

We know that love is real, and that Divinity is not merely omniscient, and not just the Infinity of Power, but what we call **the Infinity of Intimacy—** the actual name of God is the Infinite Intimate. That's the new name of God that we use in CosmoErotic Humanism, this new Story of Value.

Because God/Goddess is the Infinite Intimate, both the God that lives inside of me, the Goddess that incarnates in me, and the Goddess that holds me, that can turn and say, *Will the judge of the whole world not do justice?*

It's only to the God who is the Infinite Intimate that I can scream *zilo*, which means "fair" in Hebrew.

It's not fair. It can't be this way.

I can only protest if I live in a world that I know, in my body and my very being-ness, needs to be fair.

If I don't live in a world of Outrageous Love, then *there's no way of protesting outrageous pain*. What's wrong with it?

- It's ordinary.
- It's just what happens.
- There is nothing we can do about it.
- It's just part of the structure of life.

It's *only* if we know there's a Field of Outrageous Love, which is the intrinsic nature of Reality, that we *realize* this pain is outrageous—it shouldn't be this way, it cannot be that way, and it's not allowed to be that way. Wow.

So we protest. We turn, as Abraham and Moses did, to the divine force, and we say, *We know that you're not just the Infinity of Power, we know you're the Infinity of Intimacy, because we experience that in our own lives. And we say to you, what the fuck!*

When we scream and protest in this way, we're affirming the dignity of life.

When we scream and protest, we are affirming the goodness of Reality, and we hold the uncertainty. We bow before the mystery, even as we seek to change and transform and heal every drop of suffering in Reality, because we are Outrageous Lovers.

And then we step in to create a world that works for everyone. We respond to and anticipate natural disasters in the best way that we can.

FAIRNESS IS A CORE VALUE OF REALITY

We live in a world of outrageous pain, the only response is Outrageous Love.

The simple way of reading it, which is completely right, is: *Oh my God, let's get to Syria, and let's do everything we can in Syria and do everything we can in Turkey.*

221

THE PATH OF OUTRAGEOUS LOVE

And the world has mobilized. This is a moment when worldcentric consciousness has woken up (not sufficiently, but at least at some degree), and is saying: *Oh my God, **the only response to outrageous pain is Outrageous Love, and the response of Outrageous Love has to be to commit Outrageous Acts of Love.***

- There are sixteen countries with rescue teams in Syria on the ground right now. We need to have seventy.
- There are thousands of men and women from international relief organizations combing through rubble.
- There are Outrageous Lovers all over Turkey and Syria, which is unimaginable and beautiful.
- We need to commit Outrageous Acts of Love. That's the first meaning.

The second meaning is that the only way we can *recognize* this is outrageous pain, and that it cannot be and we can't allow for it, is that **we know that Reality demands fairness and integrity**. Reality is a Reality of Eros. **Fairness is one of its core values, rooted in harmony, which is the right relationship between things.**

Therefore, we have to turn to Turkey—before this week—and we have to say:

> Why are you allowing the so-called "amnesties" in your building code, when you know what happened in Turkey in 1939, and you know what happened in Turkey in 1999? Tens of thousands of people were killed. You know very clearly that there are going to be more earthquakes. Most of those buildings should not have collapsed.
>
> **The reason they collapsed was a failure of intimacy— that's why they collapsed.**
>
> They collapsed because there is a corrupt practice in Turkey called "amnesties," which is essentially based on rivalrous conflict governed by win/lose metrics, the success story that governs society. Each independent contractor is able to basically ignore the building code, and they get from

the government these amnesties, fully knowing there are going to be more earthquakes, and that those buildings will probably fall.

The same in Syria. What does it mean in Syria, where Bashar al-Assad is actually not concerned about the refugees. He's only concerned about win/lose metrics, and his politics of brutality and evil. Only if the aid comes through him, and through the areas under his control, will he distribute it—but we know, historically, he won't distribute aid, and he's making a political power play while children are under rubble.

There is only one access road available into the tormented parts of Syria today—when we need at least seven or eight roads.

I want to just track this with you for a second, because it's not *only* about Syria and Turkey.

We live in the first generation in human history in which we have the capacity to respond to a natural disaster *before* it happens. This doesn't mean we can handle *every* disaster.

It doesn't mean natural disasters don't exist—but for the first time in human history, we have the technology and the resources available such that no human being should be left outside the circle.

- We can develop technologies which can, with some degree of accuracy, predict earthquakes.
- We can enforce building codes to ensure that the overwhelming majority of buildings will not collapse on sleeping children and adults.

We can do that when we are intimate with the future, when we're able to *feel* what's coming. We can deploy our technology to support the most vulnerable among us, because no one is left out of the circle. We have that capacity today.

223

We live in a world of outrageous pain, the only response to outrageous pain is Outrageous Love. As Outrageous Lovers, we can respond to natural disasters in a way that no generation in history has ever been able to do.

THE HIDDEN AND THE REVEALED

So why does this continue to happen?

I want to introduce you to one of the First Principles and First Values of Cosmos, which, together with my dear friend and interlocutor, Zak Stein, we just really formalized two weeks ago, although we've been working on this for over a decade.

It is the principle of mystery and gnosis.

- Gnosis means what we know in a deep sense.
- Mystery is what we don't know. The word *mystery* comes from a number of languages, but it ultimately derives from the Hebrew *mistorin seter*, "that which is not known."

Another way to say it: there's the hidden and the revealed. There's a mystery, and there's gnosis. There is knowledge in all areas of Cosmos. When we don't know something, that's not necessarily a systemic failure. No, unknowing is always a quality of Cosmos. There's what we know, and there's what we don't know.

Any attempt to give a definitive answer to the problem of suffering is obscenity. We can never storm the gates of heaven, in this Promethean way, where the nature of the fire that we want to bring down from heaven is that we have an answer for everything.

But our response to that is not blind faith. Our response is:

- First, we protest. We demand answers.
- Second, we commit Outrageous Acts of Love.
- Third, we are willing—because we're mad lovers, because

we're Outrageous Lovers—to live in the uncertainty.

I want to go deep into this because this is where it all happens.

This is what matters. This is everything.

The reason we are willing to live in the uncertainty is not because we're idiots, or because we are faithful fools. It's because we have direct experiences, one after the other, of the intrinsic goodness of Cosmos.

In other words, we have a direct experience that we live in a world of goodness, truth, and beauty, that we live in a world in which Eros animates *everything*.

Aquinas, the great theologian in the Middle Ages, once wrote that his favorite verse in biblical text is, *Taste and see that God is good.* **We have a direct experience of God's goodness.**

When I'm sitting and eating, feeling my body digest the food, I begin to get a sense of the dazzling complexity and beauty of my body functioning in this moment—and I'm blown away by a level of unimaginable awe, radical amazement, and wonder, the dazzling beauty and complexity of my body made up of about thirty-seven trillion cells, and an unimaginable number of molecules and atoms, all in dazzling erotic synchronicity with each other.

- We realize that my body is a love story.
- We realize that the molecular world is a love story.
- We realize that the cellular world, each cell is a love story.
- We realize that Reality is covered with love stories.
- And then sometimes, there's a huge tragedy. We create a boundary of the love story at the human level, and we make it too small. We say the love story is only within this very small

group of people, within this particular tribe or this particular race. That's a tragedy. **We need to evolve with love. We need to move the boundary. There can be no one left out; no one's a stranger.**

We have a direct experience in the world of matter, in the molecular world, in the world of life, the cellular world, and the organismic world, all the way up the evolutionary chain, and in the human world, that:

- What matters to us is taking care of each other.
- What matters to us is our love for each other.
- What matters to us is the depth of our devotion and the depth of our desire.

Our devotion and our desire are two expressions of Reality as a love story.

- We desire each other.
- We desire contact with each other.
- We desire to hug each other and to hold each other.
- We want to touch each other physically, emotionally, existentially, psychologically, and spiritually.

When we feel alone, isolated, or alienated, we are devastated. If we don't have an experience of my interior touching your interior, our entire life is no longer good. We lose.

It's not good for human beings to be lonely, screams one ancient text, because **loneliness—the experience of not knowing that I am in a love story, not being able to touch you, not have you touch me, or have our hearts touch each other—makes my life meaningless.**

That's why every song and every language, across space and time, is a love story.

We know that love is real, and because we know that love is real:

- We look in the face of a baby.

- We look in the face of the beloved.
- We look at the wonder of bees.
- We look at butterflies and their unimaginable beauty.
- We look at the depths of the ocean.

When we do, we see worlds of unimaginable, dazzling, nuanced, and subtle beauty that blows our hearts open again and again.

Then we begin to read, we begin to read the poetry of existence.

We begin to read the poetry of science, and the poetry of the humanities.

We realize that this is actually a love story. There is no other way to explain it. Reality is an Intimate Universe, and the movement of Reality is a progressive deepening of intimacy. Those are certainties: we actually have direct access to those experiences. We can *taste it* directly. Our entire lives are built around it.

Then, when we run into outrageous pain, we don't try to explain it away. We don't try to control it. We respond with Outrageous Love.

IT IS NOT OVER WHEN IT'S OVER

When you think about Reality as a love story, you have to think beyond the boundaries of this dimension. If we think about Reality as a love story, we can't just think about what happens until the moment of death; we have to think beyond. We have to think in a wider Field of Value and Eros. We have to *be* in a wider Field of Value and Eros.

If I die unfairly, as most of my family did in the Holocaust, this is tragic and horrific, and we have no right to use theology to explain it away—neither Buddhist theology, nor New Age theology, nor classical Axial religion theology. That's a given.

But what happens at the moment that I die?

Do I go into eternal nothingness? Game over? Is death the end?

In this case, you cannot talk about Reality as a love story in any way that's ultimately significant. It's made up. We are trying to make it up, but that can't actually be true—because within one lifetime, it's very clear that we *don't* have equitable fairness for every human being. It's just not the way Reality is structured.

Why? Mystery!

Why is that true? Mystery—and we're holding the mystery.

Within one lifetime, if I actually *feel* that no one is a stranger and no one is left out of the circle, I *cannot* experience Reality as being a love story.

Reality is a love story only if I understand that it's not over when it's over, that death itself is a night between two days.

This is not a *faith* claim. It's not a New Age claim or a fundamentalist religious claim. For the first time in human history, we have access to three forms of information, three fields of gnosis, that tell us two things:

- **There is a huge mystery of death.** We don't exactly know what happens. No one has come back, for a long period of time at least, and given us detailed information. No one has come back and said: *Okay, here I am. I've been away for two years, and now I'm back.* We don't have that kind of information, so there's clearly a mystery of death, that it's unknown.
- And yet, there is also the revealed. Opposites are joined at the hip. There is mystery *and* gnosis. **For the first time, in the last 130 or 140 years, we have an enormous amount of knowledge telling us that it's not over when it's over.**

This is a very big topic, and I'm not going into it now. I'll say a few things.

First, we have actual, *empirical* information, which has been very carefully checked.

The British Society for Psychical Research was started in Cambridge, in 1882, by Henry Sidgwick, a brilliant professor at Cambridge. His colleague, William James, started The American Society for Psychical Research at Harvard. So we have now nearly 150 years of carefully vetted research to ferret out the charlatans, the hoaxes, and the sloppy recordings. After we ferreted all that out, we have a huge body of direct information that tells us:

- ◆ Consciousness lives independently of the body.
- ◆ That there is direct communication, at least in some instances, where information is conveyed after a person has died, not explicable by any of what you might think were the explanations (for example, that the relative of a person who's died is holding information, and the medium is reading their mind, and that's telling us something).

There are carefully controlled investigations, real information carefully gathered and vetted for almost 150 years, which show us, beyond the shadow of a doubt, that we actually *have* information from people after they pass, which couldn't be available in any other way than through that person.

A person who has done a very careful analysis of this is one of the greatest Whiteheadian scholars that ever lived, David Ray Griffin, with whom Zak and I communicated before he passed. David was a beautiful man and wrote a book called *Parapsychology, Philosophy, & Spirituality*, in which he examines the evidence very carefully and conservatively. He came to the conclusion that there is definitive and incontrovertible evidence that points to the continuity of consciousness, beyond a shadow of a doubt. It's a very big deal. That's one source of information.

There are other sources of information, which are philosophical in their nature, from the critique of materialism which I'm not going to go into now.

And there are what I would call "anthro-ontological" sources of information, meaning we have **a direct experience within us that it's not over when it's over**:

- We have direct experience that **fairness and justice are real**, that Reality demands fairness.
- We know that **fairness is not accomplished within one lifetime.**

This tells us that the story of Reality cannot exhaust itself in one lifetime.

The empirical approach, the philosophical approach (which I haven't gone into), and the anthro-ontological approach—all three of those come to one conclusion: it's not over when it's over, friends. There's continuity of consciousness, without question. That's a big deal. There is mystery: we don't know exactly how it works. But there is also a new knowing.

REALITY IS A LOVE STORY

However, that doesn't justify suffering in any way.

We are not using this new information in the old way, as a theodicy: *Oh, now we can justify suffering.*

No, our only response to suffering is: We live in a world of outrageous pain, and the only response is Outrageous Love. Outrageous Love means we commit Outrageous Acts of Love, and we protest. We protest because Reality is Outrageous Love. We can therefore turn to the Divine—in ourselves and in the structure of the Field of Value—and *we protest.*

But when we protest, we are not screaming against God. We are also the very voice of the Divine, screaming out and demanding transformation,

230

demanding that Syria and Turkey take themselves seriously and become Outrageous Lovers, which they are not today.

That's why we need a universal grammar of value. We need a shared Story of Value, so we, as an international community, can turn—to the United States, or to Aleppo, or to Turkey—and say: *Hey, we're going to be Outrageous Lovers together, and Outrageous Lovers do everything they can do to respond to natural disasters.*

What if we knew that when a person passes, they don't go into oblivion, and they don't go into a fire-and-brimstone hell set up by a malevolent cruel divinity—but that a person actually is embraced by the Field of the Infinite? They're embraced by *Tachat Kanpah Shekhinah*, by the wings of the Goddess. **There's this sense of integrity and justice, and of coming home, and of welcome.**

There is a welcome sign in this world, but there's also a welcome sign at death's door: *Welcome to the next stage of the journey, welcome to the next stage of your life.* This is not a fanciful claim, but the best empirical understanding we have of Reality today.

In CosmoErotic Humanism, in this new Story of Value, we realize that Reality is a love story.

- Reality is a love story, and we are experiencing that as we see Outrageous Lovers all over Aleppo and Turkey.
- Reality is a love story because we protest any act which violates that love story, and demand it not be that way. We know in our bodies that it's not supposed to be that way because that love story lives *in us.*
- Reality is a love story because there is continuity of consciousness beyond this lifetime.
- Reality is a love story because we experience the Good, the True, and the Beautiful, and we experience the radical certainty. We taste that love story in our bodies, which are

love stories themselves, and in the molecular and atomic world, in all forms and dimensions of the biosphere, and in the human world—love stories every place and everywhere. Every song is a love song.

In all four of those ways, we *know* it's a love story—and in a love story, we hold uncertainty. **We bow before the mystery—not as faithful fools, but as those who have experienced radical trust in Reality.**

We trust Reality, even as we scream out in protest and say, *what the fuck!* In that moment, we only have a question, we only have the agony, and we only have the void. Then we move through the void and find life again. Wow!

To speak of your love in the morning, and to trust you through the night— that's what we say to each other.

- We look at each other's face and say: *To speak of your love in the morning, and to trust you through the night.*
- We turn to the Infinity of Intimacy and say, *To speak of your love in the morning, to trust you through the night.* This week has been a dark night, so we scream and protest. We are furious with you! But we also know, *Taste and see the goodness of Reality*—and so we hold the mystery, we hold the uncertainty, and we hold the agony.

In the original Hebrew, *lehagid baboker chasdecha* is "to speak of your love in the morning," and the divine voice says to us, *ve-emunatcha baleylot*, "and I trust you through the night."

- I trust you to build buildings according to building codes.
- I trust you to be Outrageous Lovers and to create a world in which no one's outside of the circle.

We have the potential today to create the most beautiful world that's ever been created in human history.

That's what we are here to do.

232

CHAPTER SEVENTEEN

SYRIA AND TURKEY EARTHQUAKE—THE ONLY RESPONSE TO OUTRAGEOUS PAIN IS OUTRAGEOUS LOVE, PART 2: A DEEPER DIVE INTO THE MYSTERY OF SUFFERING, PLUS QUESTIONS & ANSWERS

Episode 332 — February 19, 2023

EVEN AS WE FACE OUTRAGEOUS PAIN, WE NEED TO BE IN OUTRAGEOUS LOVE

We have to be in the fullness of joy, the fullness of celebration, and the fullness of the garden, even when we are dealing with the most intense and painful suffering in the world. In the fullness of the suffering, we need to be in the garden.

This is one of the themes that we return to time and time again:

What happens to a dream deferred?

Does it dry up like a raisin in the sun?

That's the great poem of Langston Hughes. You can't defer the dream. You can't wait. There is a book behind me on the shelf called *Laughter in Hell*. Very few people bought the

book; people didn't quite know what to make of it. It is about jokes, laughter, and celebration in the concentration camps.

In order not to become bitter and lose our connection to the fullness of Reality, even as we face outrageous pain, we need to be in Outrageous Love.

We need to live in the truth of laughter, which embraces all paradoxes, even as we deny easy, feel-good answers—be they New Age, contemporary, or ancient—to outrageous pain.

Let's start with a little story.

There was a moment when I had just run into a brick wall. You know what happens when you run into a brick wall? There is no way to move forward.

It was this moment where I felt like there was just nothing left to say.

It was 2012. We were doing the beginning of what we call *dharma* Circles, and there were about, I don't know, 50 to 60 people on the line. I was supposed to start talking, and I just couldn't say anything. I was so incredibly disappointed and pained by Reality—and I just couldn't say anything at all.

People were respectful, thinking that I was going through some profound experience of deep silence. I wasn't. I just had nothing to say. I really thought: *Okay, I'm done teaching. There's nothing I can actually say now in the face of this suffering.*

I don't even know what happened next—this is what happens when Spirit seizes you. It's a genuine experience that is empirically verifiable, where you experience that **something takes you over**. But you have to clarify your experience to know that it's a *daemon* and not a *demon*—both daemons and demons can take us over, so you've got to make sure who's who.

That time, it was daemonic, meaning it felt *clarified*. And then I said this line, and I had no idea where it came from:

We live in a world of outrageous pain, and the only response to outrageous pain is Outrageous Love.

I then talked for about an hour, and when it was over, I had no memory of what was said. We still have the recording of it. Sally Kempton was there, and she started taking notes because she felt this whole new world open up. That's where the Outrageous Love teaching was born.

Right around that time, I shared that teaching with Sally Rainey, who was on the way to see the Pope the next day. She goes to see the Pope and she says, the only thing I could say to the Pope was: *We live in a world of outrageous pain, and the only response to outrageous pain is Outrageous Love.* And the Pope got it.

There's something you get in your body even before explanations. You get it in this embodied sense: We live in a world of outrageous pain. The only response to outrageous pain is Outrageous Love.

We are confronted with outrageous pain, the pain of hell. Samantha Powers, who was a key adviser to the Obama administration on the issue of suffering, wrote a book called *A Problem from Hell*, where she talked about the seven genocides of the twentieth century, and how world governments did or did not respond to them. She maps out the seven possible responses to a genocide—from boots on the ground to some sort of significant protest—and points out that in all seven genocides, essentially, *nothing happened*. No genuine response emerged from the civilized world.

What does that mean?

These are problems from hell. What's happening in Turkey and Syria is a problem from hell.

So how do you respond to a problem from hell?

THE MYSTERY OF SUFFERING

The primary reason why people reject living in a system of value, why we reject being part of a larger order of Spirit that guides us, is because of this enormous problem of pain, this problem of evil. If our notion of Spirit, or of God/Goddess, is that She is omnipotent (all powerful), omniscient (all knowing), and omni-benevolent (all good), then **suffering doesn't seem to work with that**.

If you trace back through the history of religious thought, you'll see that different schools rejected one of these three:

- **God is all-knowing, but not all-powerful**, so *She* is stuck. God is as powerless as you are. One famous expression of that position was a hugely popular book in the United States and Europe by a guy named Harold Kushner, *When Bad Things Happen to Good People*. I wrote my first public article rejecting that book, called "Is Religion for the Happy-Minded?" Basically, what he was saying is, *God has the same problem you do*. God/Goddess can't handle this: no power. She may be all knowing, and may be all good—but clearly not all powerful.

- Other thinkers made another move, which is to say that **God is really powerful but not really tracking everything**. God is not reading the news. In other words, Divinity is not all knowing.

- Finally, others say that **Divinity is not good** but merely a neutral force of Cosmos. God is an unleashed creative force but with no sense of goodness. **Therefore, there is no inherent moral arc to the Cosmos.**

All three of those positions are a mistake. In other words, all of them refuse another possibility.

The other possibility is *the mystery*.

We have a direct experience of a force that *inheres* in Cosmos, and it's a force that knows everything. If you want to get a sense of that, read John Stuart Bell, who talks about the non-locality of the quantum universe. The entire quantum universe is entangled with all the rest of the quantum universe, and once one quantum particle touches another particle, they know everything about each other forever. And since Divinity as a Field of Creativity is touching everything, there is constant knowing throughout the system.

Or if you want to check it in another way, you have somewhere around thirty-seven trillion cells in your body. But here's the deal: **They all know each other**. They all know everything that's going on in each other. That's wild! Isn't that a beautiful image for omniscience? Every cell knows what every other cell is doing. This gives you a sense of omniscience, this sense of all knowing.

Now, there's this notion that this force of divine creativity has the power to initiate the Big Bang, the power to set up the laws of mathematics, the power to develop photosynthesis, mitosis and meiosis—but completely lost power once human beings came on board. What happened? It just makes no sense. That power actually disappears? Divinity is suddenly emptied of power?

When we say "divine power," we don't mean some all-powerful *fairy* God. We mean that the power of the universe is all-knowing.

It has a *personal* dimension and a *systems* dimension. (Notice the words we're using: I'm not saying "personal" and "impersonal," but a personal and systems dimension. It's a much better way to say it.) **There is a personal dimension of Divinity, and a systems dimension of Divinity, and those are all-powerful.**

We have a direct experience of goodness. It's why we call God good. We have robust scientific information, based on extensive developmental research, showing that the experience that the world should be fair is one that all children have, cross-culturally, from the earliest ages. Meaning, you can't say that it's a culture-specific notion. There is an enormous developmental literature demonstrating that the notion of fairness is inborn.

What does that mean? It means that **we have to hold the mystery—it means that we actually *don't understand*.**

DON'T RELY ON GOD IN THE FACE OF OUTRAGEOUS PAIN

We don't really understand suffering.

- Yes, we understand that suffering makes us more noble.
- Yes, we understand that human beings freely choose, and that much suffering ascribed to God is actually human beings making choices.
- Yes, we understand that there is a larger play than just this lifetime, and that if you look across lifetimes, suffering would be understood completely differently.
- Yes, we understand that when you die, however you die, you are entering into an entirely new world of Reality and beauty and goodness. If you have that experience, then obviously you're going to experience death differently.

All four of those things are true.

Nonetheless, **we cannot use any of them to deny the tragedy of suffering *in any way whatsoever*.** We live in a world of outrageous pain, and the response is *not* what the religions called *theodicy*, meaning an explanation of *why* it happens.

The four possible explanations I just listed are given in different ways by the great traditions, and they are true but insufficient, meaning you *cannot* use them to avoid the tragedy.

No theodicy works in the face of burning children, or in the face of children buried for days, suffocating under rubble.

No theodicy holds. There is no theodicy that's kosher in the face of crushed human bodies and agonizing pain.

If anyone sells you a theodicy, stop the conversation, it's over.

- Whether it's a New Age theodicy (you attracted it into your life),
- Or a religious theodicy, some form of sin and punishment,
- Or it's some form of a broader afterlife system,
- Or it's some form of what's called a "soul-making" theodicy.

It is not that they're *wrong*—there is validity to each one of them—but the only response to outrageous pain has to be Outrageous Love.

What does this mean in practice?

One, we commit Outrageous Acts of Love. Nachman of Breslov, one of my lineage masters, says atheism was created for meeting with outrageous pain. When you meet outrageous pain, you become an atheist. Meaning, **don't rely on God, don't rely on a theodicy, don't rely on the next lifetime. Don't rely on any explanation at all.**

If you meet outrageous pain, commit Outrageous Acts of Love.

There is no God, it's just you. It's your response. The only response to outrageous pain is Outrageous Love.

But there is the second meaning of that statement, and this is critical. It changes everything.

- You cannot demand a fair world,
- you can't be motivated to heal the world,

- you can't be motivated to commit Outrageous Acts of Love,
- you can't be motivated to demand, with your activism and with your protest, that there *not* be outrageous pain—

—unless **outrageous pain is a violation of *something***. Unless you know it shouldn't be that way.

If the world is happenstance, if the world is an accident, if the world is random, if the world is meaningless, well, then it's a dog-eat-dog world. So people in Turkey are certainly going to try to make a little money, and they won't comply with the building codes, and buildings will fall down and children will be buried for days. That's just the way it goes, we should be used to that.

It's been that way throughout all of history. It's just what happens, whatever.

If that were true, it shouldn't even move us.

But we *are* moved. **We're not just moved—we are outraged**. We call that pain outrageous. It's a violation of the way Reality should be. Why?

- Because the universe is a love story.
- Because Reality is an Intimate Universe.
- Because Eros is the quality of Reality itself, the quality of the self-organizing Cosmos.

EVIL IS A FAILURE OF PLEASURE

I want to add one thing. What is the interior experience of Eros? What does Eros feel like on the inside? Isn't that wonderful?

What Eros feels like on the inside is pleasure.

Now, by pleasure, I don't mean ice cream. (Although what's not to like about ice cream? I remember there were two or three flavors when I was a kid, vanilla, chocolate, and strawberry. And then I remember the first Baskin Robbins, which had 31 flavors. I was ten years old, and it was an ecstatic moment of my childhood! So I don't want to knock ice cream for pleasure. Ice cream matters, and the world would clearly be a worse place without ice cream.)

But when I say *pleasure*, I'm saying something much deeper. Pleasure is a far more nuanced thing.

Pleasure is the source of all ethics.

Clarifying your pleasure, knowing your *true* pleasure is everything. Pleasure is much deeper than ice cream.

I want to put these things together, so we really get this:

1. We live in a world of outrageous pain, and the only response is Outrageous Love.
2. Outrageous Love means not *ordinary* love, but love that's the heart of existence itself.
3. Outrageous Love is what we call *Eros*.
4. The interior feeling of Eros is pleasure, clarified pleasure, the deepest sense of pleasure.
5. Pleasure is the source of all ethics.

Now this next piece is a crazy beautiful sentence: **Evil is a failure of pleasure. Specifically, evil is a failure of clarified pleasure.**

Pleasure is also a birthright. It's not an entitlement or a privilege. It's a birthright.

- That's why we have food. We don't have little pills, we have *food*.
- We have colors.
- We have skin. We have nerve receptors on skin.
- We have natural beauty.
- We have taste.
- We have touch.

241

These are all forms of pleasure. In other words, pleasure is an inherent structure of Reality, and the evolution of Reality is also the evolution of pleasure, so that we have deeper and wider forms of pleasure, and a deeper capacity to receive pleasure.

For example, an enlightened person can get ecstatic pleasure from drinking a glass of water. In Zen, in the Japanese tea ceremony, they get ecstatic pleasure from drinking a cup of tea.

The deeper and the more clarified you are, the more pleasure you get from ordinary activities.

Addiction simply means I can't get pleasure from ordinary life activities. Addiction is the inability to derive pleasure from ordinary life activity. Enlightenment is the opposite of addiction; it's the capacity to derive unimaginable depths of pleasure from ordinary life activity. Wow.

Suffering is a violation of the birthright to pleasure, which is the inherent nature of Reality.

In the experience of atoms and subatomic particles that are attracted to each other, they are experiencing a kind of *quantum hedonism*, and I'm using that word precisely. (It's used by Kathy Kauffman in a formal academic article.) The experience of pleasure exists all the way down and all the way up.

If you want to know what drives evolution, I want to give you a big sentence. And this is a second simplicity sentence—not a first simplicity sentence, not a casual sentence, this is integrating an enormous amount of information. **Evolution evolves because it feels good.**

That's a very important sentence. Evolution evolves because it feels good. It's not a casual sentence or a cute sentence. And when we say *feels good*, we've got to clarify *feeling good*.

An addict only has a *surface* experience of feeling good, which leaves a terrible aftertaste. This is *not* feeling good—it has to feel good over long periods of time. It has to be sustainable across time. It's not just an instantaneous good. It's a good that *sustains itself.*

Evolution evolves because it feels good. If you get that, then you get it that **evil is a failure of pleasure**. Suffering is a failure of pleasure, and pleasure is an inherent birthright.

THE WHOLE THING DEPENDS ON US

When we respond to Turkey, we say: Oh my God, evil is a failure of pleasure. In other words, evil is a failure of Outrageous Love, and the reason we scream and protest—to the Turkish and Syrian governments, to the failures of international aid agencies, and to the Divine—is because **it shouldn't be this way, and we *know* it shouldn't be this way**. We are absolutely sure that we live in an Intimate Universe.

- Suffering doesn't cause me to *lose* connection to the goodness of the universe.
- Suffering *connects* me to the goodness of the universe.

One of the reasons I went deeper into spirit in my twenties is that I realized **I couldn't formulate the sentence "Evil is wrong"** *without* **spirit.**

When I say *wrong*, it doesn't mean "technically" wrong or "functionally" wrong—but it is **a violation of the order of Reality**. You cannot say that without spirit. And when I say *spirit*, I mean "a ground of intrinsic value." Let me use the word Tao, if that works better for you. The Tao means a Field of Intrinsic Value.

If good is not real, and truth is not real, and beauty is not real, then evil is not a violation of anything real.

By the way, the guy who really got this was Bertrand Russell, who said something like, *The only problem with my atheism is that I can't believe that the only problem with wanton cruelty is that I don't like it.* Isn't that a great sentence?

But it's not just a preference. It's a violation of Reality, and **it's only this sense that we have violated the Field of Value that arouses our political will and arouses our moral will.**

To sum up:

- We live in a world of outrageous pain, and the only response is Outrageous Love.
- The response of Outrageous Love is the affirmation of the Intimate Universe.
- Evil is a failure of intimacy, a failure of Eros, and a failure of clarified pleasure.
- We commit Outrageous Acts of Love. In response to outrageous suffering, we are atheists; we don't just say this was God's will. No, it's just us—**the whole thing depends on us.** We have to step in and commit our Outrageous Acts of Love in every possible way that we can.

QUESTIONS AND ANSWERS

IS IT MINE TO HEAL THE WHOLE THING?

David: You just said that "the whole thing depends on us." However, a few weeks ago, in the ninth principle of Outrageous Love, you said that in order **to close the gap between our ability to heal and feel the pain, we have to realize that it's *not* all up to us to heal the whole thing.** Rather, we address our unique need in our unique circle of intimacy and influence.

But now you said it all depends on us. Sometimes you say it all hangs in the balance, fifty-fifty, and in the next moment, that it all depends on us.

Also, when you have talked about pleasure before, you have said that the highest level of pleasure is that **my personal transformation transforms the whole thing. This is the pleasure of power**. It can seem contradictory on the surface.

So I'm curious to see how you want to reconcile those two statements.

Marc: That's great. Thank you, David.

David is referring to three things:

- One, as we just said, it's all up to you. As atheists, it's only you. It's yours to do.
- Two, there is a general experience of *Homo amor* that we've talked about—the new human and the new humanity, the fulfillment of *Homo sapiens*, what we call the Fourth Big Bang. One of the characteristics of *Homo amor*, and this is what David was referring to, is that *Homo amor* **experiences all of Reality as fifty-fifty in the balance, and my next action tips the scale**. That's part of the evolutionary experience of *Homo amor*.

The third thing David refers to is that in the six levels of pleasure, the highest level is the experience of pleasure, of what we call *Evolutionary Unique Self*.

- First there is your separate self, which is just ordinary me: separate self, ego self.
- Then I realize, no, I'm True Self. I'm part of The One. I am inextricable and inseparable from the Field of Value.
- But then I realize I am Unique Self, a unique expression of the Field of Value.
- Finally, I realize that I'm a unique expression *living in an evolutionary context*. **Evolution is moving through me. I am Evolutionary Unique Self.**

Those are the four selves. The experience of Evolutionary Unique Self is: **I am omni-considerate for the sake of the whole.** Every move I make is not just me. I don't just have integrity, but I have *evolutionary* integrity, which means that I consider everything. Every move I make, it's not just me, but how does it affect the whole? I can feel the whole living inside of me.

That's the experience of the sixth level of pleasure, which is the pleasure of power, where I *know*, I have a lived direct experience:

- That my next action affects the whole.
- That the whole actually lives in me, and I live in the whole.
- That I am part of the fabric of existence, and therefore I have the power to take an action which will ripple through the whole system.

Think about the butterfly effect in physics. A butterfly flaps its wings in Tokyo, and something happens here in Vermont.

David says, *You've got all of that on one side.* But then on the other side, in the principles of Outrageous Love, we ask the question, *Why isn't everyone committing their act of Outrageous Love?*

If we are Unique Selves, and we are supposed to commit the Outrageous Acts of Love that are a function of our Unique Self, the question is, why isn't everyone doing it? If it's the most ecstatic, beautiful experience, **why isn't everyone out there committing their Outrageous Acts of Love, and healing the whole?**

The answer is that it's because people are overwhelmed. Not because we are bad people. Not because our ego hijacked us, and we are lost in narcissistic selfishness. No, that's not why. When we look at it, it's just too big. There is too much, we are just overwhelmed. How can we even step in? How can we take our seat at the table? It just seems impossible.

Our response to that, in the ten steps of Outrageous Love and the *dharma* of Outrageous Love, is that it's actually an egoic trap to say *you've got to do the whole thing.* The answer is, you don't have to do the whole thing. It's not yours to do. Let it all go. However, **there is a unique set of Outrageous Acts of Love that *are* yours to do in your unique circle of intimacy and influence**.

In other words, the reason we don't step in and commit Outrageous Acts of Love is because we feel like we won't have any impact. We feel the pain— but the gap between our ability to feel the pain and heal the pain is too great, so we close our hearts. Our response to that is: *No, you don't have to heal the whole thing. Just do what's yours to do, your Outrageous Acts of Love that are a function of your Unique Self.*

As David points out here, and it is a very sharp discernment on his part, there are these two different strains in the story of CosmoErotic Humanism.

- One says, you heal the whole thing, it's yours to do.
- The other says, well, actually, no, that's an egoic movement. You have to step back and realize it's not all *yours* to heal, and instead you commit your Outrageous Acts of Love.

Which is right? You all remember the old Jewish story about the two people who come to the rabbi, and the wife overhears the conversation. The rabbi says to one, *You're right.* Then the other person offers with a completely contradictory claim, and the rabbi says, *You're right.* And then his wife comes in and says, *How can you do that? They're contradicting each other.* And then the rabbi says to his wife, *You're also right.*

There is a sense of paradox here. Both positions are holding something that's right. On the one hand, I have a real lived experience that it's all mine to heal, a direct experience that I'm not separate from the Field of Value, and that what I do enters the Field of Value.

It is quite literal. I do an action, and that action is not a separate-self action in my domain. If you can just imagine it as a virus, that action is a virus. It's a positive virus, and it enters the Field, and it literally affects the entire

Field. In that sense, **my next action directly affects the entire Field, and has the capacity to transform the whole thing**, which is why my experience of *Homo amor* is that my transformation is the transformation of the whole.

Because my transformation participates in the whole, because CosmoErotic Humanism is what we might call a "participatory" spirituality, I participate in the whole, and the whole participates in me. There is a mutual participatory experience.

When I do something, it's *not* a separate self doing something in this very limited domain.

Imagine that I'm a cell. Just like all cells in the body know each other and impact each other, imagine that every being in Reality is a cell. **All of Reality is organismic, and we are all cells in that Reality**. What I do directly impacts the whole. In other words, you actually understand Reality as being this great body.

Remember da Vinci's famous image of the body, with the hands out, and there's this meridian grid. That image comes from the interior sciences, which envisions all of Reality as a human body, and in this human body, all the cells know each other.

That image went from Luria to da Vinci and to the Renaissance, and it was the basis of modern humanism—humanity actually *is* the body of Reality. We left out animals, so we need to include animals—but **there's this body of living being in which everything affects each other**.

The human being is obviously a quantum leap. That's why dogs don't build hospitals. I love dogs, all the dogs—but I've never seen a dog build a hospital. It doesn't happen. Now, dogs also don't make atomic bombs, I understand. In other words, human beings have the capacity for exponential destruction, and for exponential creativity and care. But human beings and animals, we are all cells in this larger piece.

When I awaken to my own self-realization, I realize that I am a cell in the whole.

We don't have any information that a cell *realizes* that it's part of the whole. It's just inherent. We don't know the interior experience of a cell, but there are lots of reasons to believe that cells don't have that realization the way we do. But once we realize that we are part of the whole, then my transformation transforms the whole.

At the same time, **from an egoic, separate-self perspective, I can't take on the sense that I have to heal the whole**. From a separate-self perspective, what I have to do is to say:

- Okay, let me first fix myself, let me transform myself from separate self to Unique Self.
- Number two, now as Unique Self, what are the unique, Outrageous Acts of Love that I can commit in my unique circle of intimacy and influence?

We say that because **that's the methodology that liberates us from the experience of impotence**. When I am impotent, I close my heart, because the gap between my ability to feel the pain and heal the pain is too great—so I need to re-potentiate, to become potent again.

How do I become potent again? By realizing it's not mine to heal the whole thing in a *direct* way. I'm talking about direct healing, not that my virus or my cell knows all the other cells. It's not that experience of realization, **but in a direct way, I know I cannot take all that on, but I can take on what's mine to do.**

Does everyone get that? You have to hold both. It's paradoxical. Beautiful, right?

David, that's a fantastic question.

DO WE CREATE OUR OWN SUFFERING?

Terry: I'm sitting here in California, I look over my back and I can see where the San Andreas Fault is. And all the scientists have said that the big one is coming. Now I want to say that I'm hoping, should the big one come to where I am now, that people will be attentive to my suffering and not say: *You dummy, you shouldn't have done that! You chose to live where there are earthquakes, so you don't deserve my compassion. You allured it. You brought it on yourself.*

Now, in regard to *we invited our own suffering*, my question is, if I go through—or if anybody goes through—life with a "Kick Me" sign over their head, literally or figuratively, and they get kicked, it looks to me like they bring that suffering on themselves. I find myself challenged to be compassionate for that kind of suffering. Maybe I'll be compassionate that they weren't loved well when they were younger, and now they go through life with a sense that *I deserve to be kicked*, and maybe my approach to that suffering would be to help them see the sign, or maybe help them author a different sign.

But I'm challenged when I see people going through life with a "Kick Me" sign, because when most people see and experience somebody with a "Kick Me" sign, it's really hard not to kick them. In that case, it seems like we invite our suffering.

Marc: Terry is a dear friend and partner, and I am going to respond super gently. Terry also has been a major trainer in the Human Potential world. Both the Human Potential world and the New Age world adopt a modern version of the medieval religious position (and Terry's question is evidence for this). The medieval religious position was, *You create your own suffering through sinning.* The Human Potential version of it is, *You create your own suffering by wearing a "Kick Me" sign.*

There is a certain truth to both of these positions. If I go and punch someone, and they punch me back, well, I probably had something to do with

250

that circuit. If I don't take responsibility to fix my life, then there is some responsibility—that's obviously true.

However, **there's a certain dimension of suffering to which that doesn't apply**. I am going to make two points.

First, it doesn't apply to Rwanda.

Let's go a little deeper here. What Terry is saying is a version of Dennis Prager's position. He runs something called Prager University, which is very popular and is now the center of the conservative response to "woke" on the United States political scene. Dennis' basic position is, *don't get mad at Reality you **chose**. It was your choice.* It's human choice that creates suffering, so take responsibility for your choice.

We had a debate in 2005, and I said to him: **Yes, there is a dimension of human choice that creates suffering,** *and* **there's also this huge dimension that you cannot attribute to human choice.** There is this quality of Reality which allows for suffering, and you *cannot* attribute that quality of Reality to choice alone, certainly not within one lifetime.

You cannot say to the mother of a Tutsi child in Rwanda, who sees her child being ripped apart by Hutu swords, that she invited that suffering into her life, nor can you say it to that baby. You just cannot do it.

Now, of course, there is this religious position that says, *Oh, it's a reincarnation, so it's payback from a previous life.* That's where we move into obscenity—and **it's obscene even if it's true.**

In other words, when you we live in a world of outrageous pain, the only response is Outrageous Love. That's the *only* possible response you can give. **Any appeal to theodicy is obscene.** You have to respond with Outrageous Love. Once you've rejected all theodicies, then you can consider them again *on the other side.*

But here is the second point. **Why do some people have the capacity to turn their suffering into transformation, while others don't?** We work

251

with some people, and they have the capacity to transform it, and others for some reason don't. In other words, people can have the same experience of suffering. For example, I went through an enormous life tragedy in 2006, a false accusation. That should have crushed me and killed me, and I did everything I could to move through it and to come out more joyous and more alive. I can explain to you all the good things that I did to transform myself—but my capacity to do that, where did I get *that* capacity from? Oh, because I trained myself earlier? Where did I get *that* capacity from? In other words, **any capacity that we have is, in the end, not fully ours. Why some have the capacity to do the work and others don't is a mystery.**

Yes, we should push people to do the work.

Yes, we should invite people to change the sign on their life from a "Kick Me" sign to a beautiful sign.

But in the end, **we have to be devotional to people and love people madly, and know that we don't fully understand why some people get shattered, while other people manage to turn fate into destiny**. That's a mystery.

Part of the arrogance of religion, and the arrogance of the Human Potential religion, is the capacity to stand in front of the room and tell everyone: *One size fits all, you can transform this.* That's not true—not everyone in that room can. It's cruel to do that—and so we need to both help people towards transformation and be in devotion to them regardless, at the same time.

That's what *Homo amor* needs to be.

HOW CAN PLEASURE BE THE SOURCE OF ALL ETHICS?

Vashti Cherun: It's really good to be here. You said today that **pleasure is the source of all ethic**s, which reminded me that in many places in the *dharma*, both written and spoken, you say that **the source of all ethics is**

in the sexual. I don't understand that, so I would like examples of how that happened.

Marc: That's a fantastic inquiry, Vashti, and I'll go through it here briefly.

First, we don't exactly say that .What we say is that the sexual *models* the erotic, and part of the experience of the sexual is pleasure. Let me answer that just in a few sentences.

1. Eros and sex are not the same. Eros is the movement of radical aliveness desiring ever deeper contact and ever greater wholeness. That's the Eros equation.

2. There were about 12 billion years of Eros before there was any sex in the world.

3. Eros always seeks to create new wholes, so when Eros ran out of its ability to create new wholes, it said, *let's make love*. Meaning, let's create this new form of Eros, sexual reproduction, in which we create new originalities. What sexual reproduction means is that, through the chromosomal process, we create radical new original expressions. When Reality started sexuality, it made a commitment to Unique Self, meaning a commitment to radical uniqueness. Sexuality is a new form of Eros that generates radical uniqueness. It takes half of mom and half of dad and creates something new.

4. Once the sexual becomes a model for the erotic, you can look at the sexual and realize that in the sexual is all ethics. That's true. In the sexual, for example, giving and receiving are one, there's no split between giving and receiving. And there's a whole list of the twelve qualities of the sexual that model Eros, in a book called *A Return to Eros*.

Now, one of the qualities of the sexual is pleasure. That's one of the qualities of the sexual, on a good day. What that means is that **pleasure itself is a value of Reality**. Sexuality and pleasure actually go together, they're not separate.

You can't actually split the sexual and pleasure. They are completely entwined experiences. When I say *pleasure*, I don't mean the pleasure of orgasm. I'm talking about sexuality in its broadest sense, in the sense of being touched, and felt, and the pleasure of embodied contact. **The sexual and the pleasure of embodied contact are one.**

Through the sexual, you can get to all of ethics. But you'll have to *raise* the sexual, and understand the sexual is not merely physical—**the sexual is the beauty and depth of Eros in embodied contact between human beings.** In that sense, the sexual is the source of all ethics.

However, it's also true that if you understand the sexual on its deepest level, the sexual is happening not only on the physical level—but Reality is sex all the way up and all the way down.

The way Isaac Luria said it, *Reality is lines and circles interpenetrating each other in every second.* Or the way many in the great interior sciences said it: **Reality is *hieros gamos*, the marriage of God and Goddess happening all across the Field of Reality every second.**

Reality itself is Eros, or Reality itself is sexing. In other words, Reality is always sexing. Every encounter is an encounter in which:

- We are either loving the moment open, or allowing the moment to love us open.
- We are touching the moment, or the moment is touching us.
- We are arousing the moment, or the moment is arousing us.

In that deep inner penetration of contact, something new is born.

When we say the sexual models all ethics, we don't mean just the sexual—we mean the sexual at all levels of Reality. We mean *hieros gamos* at all levels of Reality. We actually live in an Amorous Cosmos, a Sexual Cosmos—it's sexuality all the way up and all the way down.

In every learning experience, and in every creative experience, there is a penetration and there is a receiving. Every exchange and every moment is a sexual interaction. We have exiled the sexual to what we call *sex*—but actually, the sexual is Eros. It's Eros all the way up and all the way down.

- The way we *start* the *dharma* is that we split and we say: **there's sex, but sex is a model of Eros.**
- But then on the other side of the *dharma*, once we realize that the sexual is an expression of the erotic, of Eros, then we go deeper and we realize that **sex and Eros come back together**.

It's sexual Eros and erotic sexuality at the physical, spiritual, emotional, psychological, intellectual, existential, and even at the technological levels of Reality.

I apologize for saying it this way, but it captures something: it's Fuck all the way down, and Fuck all the way up. But by Fuck, we mean love plus Eros; we don't mean it in its degraded sense. It's Eros all the way up and all the way down.

There is that quality all the way up and all the way down.

Thank you, Vashti. That's a beautiful inquiry.

Let's end with prayer, the holy and the broken *Hallelujah*. It matters to pray together, and we ask for everything when we pray.

Prayer itself is considered, in the interior sciences, an act of sexing with the Divine.

We are penetrating divine consciousness with prayer. When I really pray, I become what's called in the lineage by the Vilna Gaon in the eighteenth century:

- *Ever chai*, which is **a fully alive throbbing**—that's the masculine expression of it.
- *Hit'orut mayim nukvin*, **the arousal of the feminine waters**—that's the feminine expression of it.

That's real prayer: you are fully alive, fully throbbing, fully tumescent, and therefore, you are penetrating divine Reality.

Then Reality, Divinity is aroused and penetrates us back, opening up the space of new possibility.

In this way, prayer itself becomes a form of sexing, a form of Eros.

CHAPTER EIGHTEEN

OUTRAGEOUS LOVE BEGINS WITH RAGE: THE HOLY OUTRAGE OF THE PROPHET

Episode 333 — February 26, 2023

EVOLUTIONARY LOVE CODE: WHY DO WE CALL OUTRAGEOUS LOVE *OUTRAGEOUS*?

What is the character of the Outrageous Lover?

Why do we call it Outrageous Love and not Unlimited Love?

Because Outrageous Love is animated by both outrage and love. Outrage and love come together in a higher synergy of sacred activism.

The Outrageous Lover is filled with pure joy, and yet the purity of the Outrageous Lover is always tinged with paradox. It is joy and paradox that merge outrage and love into the higher union of Outrageous Love.

Welcome, everyone, to One Mountain, Many Paths, which is the heart of the revolution. Revolution is a quality of evolution, and the revolution of today means telling a new Story of Value, a New Story of *Homo sapiens* becoming *Homo amor*, becoming a new human, because this is the only way we can respond to the meta-crisis.

I want to focus today on one dimension of this new Story of Value, which is encoded in the sentence that we've been looking at recently:

We live in the world of outrageous pain, and the only response is Outrageous Love. We are in the conversation around Outrageous Love.

Outrageous Love is not just human love. Human love is very beautiful, but in its contracted form:

- Human love is an expression of cultural mores.
- Human love is a drive to get some security or status, to avoid what we feel as the emptiness.
- Human love is this narrow human trait in which I love one person, and that's the end of my love list. I want that person to give me everything, and I want to give them everything, and if that relationship doesn't work, I'm shattered.

This is *ordinary love*, which is a strategy of the ego.

Outrageous Love is human love participating in the very current of Cosmos, in what is called Eros.

That's Outrageous Love. We live in a world of outrageous pain, and the only response to outrageous pain is Outrageous Love.

What I want to do now is to focus on the word *outrageous*.

What is this thing we're calling *Outrageous Love*? Why is it *outrageous*?

My friend John Mackey (who was our Board Chair at the Center for a time, and who started a company called Whole Foods, which he has since left) once wrote to me:

> Marc, *outrageous* is troublesome. We can't call it *outrageous*, let's call it maybe *unlimited* love, so we don't have that notion of *outrage* which has some *anger* and *rage* in it. It's just a little bit outrageous, so let's go for "unlimited love."

I wrote John a funny response, and we had a long talk about it. I want to just share with you why it is *Outrageous* Love, because this a very important piece of the new Story of Value we are telling.

First off, just check in with your body, and do a little experiment. What happens, what do you feel, when I say:

- We live in a world of outrageous pain, and the only response is Outrageous Love.
- We live in a world of unlimited pain, and the only response is unlimited love?

Does it do the same thing?

No it doesn't. The words outrageous and unlimited are different words, and they evoke something different in our bodies.

Our bodies are wise. The book of Job, Chapter 19, from the classical Hebrew texts, says, *mibesari echeza Eloha*, "from my body, I vision Spirit." The body has profound wisdom, and it holds a kind of cellular wisdom.

There is something about the word *outrageous* which is itself outrageous. In the original lineage text of the Song of Solomon, the text reads *azah ki'mavet ahava*, "love is as outrageous as death." Wow! Feel the word *azah* in your body. *Azah* means "outrageous" **Love is as outrageous as death.**

Again: We live in a world of outrageous pain, the only response is Outrageous Love.

OUTRAGEOUS LOVE HAS TO INCLUDE HOLY OUTRAGE

In the word *outrageous*, there's this dimension of *rage*, and John said to me, *I don't like this dimension of rage.* **But we *need* the dimension of rage. The dimension of rage *matters*.** It's not all outrageous, but it's a crucial dimension.

259

- You have to be willing to get mad.
- You have to be willing to get angry, because anger is a form of arousal.

Of course, there is a form of anger that is egoic, self-absorbed, narcissistic, and superficial. This is the form of anger which is pseudo-eros, where I can't find the fullness of who I am. So I get angry to give myself a quick hit of pseudo-eros, which is like taking a quick hit of cocaine, or too many shots of whiskey, or engaging in sexing that I don't really want to be doing, or eating that fourth Baby Ruth chocolate bar.

There's a dimension of anger which is an addictive form of acting out, a form of pseudo-eros, but there is *another* form of anger: *sacred* outrage, *holy* outrage.

Can everyone feel that?

There is a form of anger which is the anger of the Prophet.

One Aramaic text from the third century talks about *retikha da'oraita*: the holy outrage of the prophet. **The holy outrage of the prophet doesn't lead me to kill or to massacre; instead, it leads me to transform Reality.**

It leads me to stand on the abyss of darkness and say:

- It's got to be more, and it's got to be better.
- I take responsibility for the transformation of Reality.
- I take responsibility for making the world a different place than it is now.

But I cannot feel that unless I'm willing to be outraged.

If I'm not willing to be outraged, then I can't begin to take action. *Oh right, yeah, something happened in Turkey?* You don't even have time to be outraged. You watch the news quickly, but you're not willing to *sit in the outrage*.

Now let's see a clip from the 1970s movie *Network*, where a television commentator is fired. They give him one more talk on the air—and for the first time, he speaks the truth. It's a prophetic moment. That notion of prophecy—*retikha da'oraita*, "the holy outrage"—is captured in this clip. **Outrageous Love has to include holy outrage.**

It doesn't capture all of the word *outrageous*, but it's a crucial dimension. Let's watch this clip carefully and notice that this is a scene of prophecy. Sometimes, the prophet doesn't even know that they're prophesying. As this man begins to speak, all over the world, everyone stops what they're doing, and they begin to listen to him—because real prophecy evokes our hearts and our mind and our body.

I'm mad as hell, and I'm not going to take it anymore— that's the practice. That's the first practice of Outrageous Love: I'm actually willing to get mad. Who's willing to do it? Not so easy to do, is it? It's not polite. It's not New Age, not sweet.

It's not all sweetness and light, writes Rudolf Otto in his great book, *The Idea of the Holy*. **The numinous must include outrage.**

I am mad as hell!—who's willing to say it? Let go of the ego. Let go of the smallness.

I am the prophet. I'm mad as hell, and I'm not going to take it anymore. I'm mad as hell. I am the prophet. I'm looking at what is, and it can't be this way. I'm mad as hell and I'm not going to take it anymore!

Your rage is the beginning of Outrageous Love—but you've got to first *access* the rage. It's not the end, but you can't skip the step. And it takes something to say it. **If you're not willing to be mad as hell, you're not going to change anything.**

I'm mad as hell. My rage matters, and it counts.

It's not *unlimited* love. Unlimited love is tepid, flaccid, boring, and ordinary—it's just talking about something, and we don't even know what it is. It doesn't jump out of our body.

I'm mad as hell, and I'm not going to take this anymore.

OUTRAGE AND LOVE ARE THE SAME WORD

The scene is an incredible scene. What's it about?

The announcer Howard Beale has been fired, and he is devolving psychologically. He's going through an episode, which psychology has defined as a psychotic episode, because psychology doesn't know what to do with *mad as hell*. You go to the therapist and they prescribe you a set of drugs, which can often destroy you, because **psychology doesn't know how to hold the root of the sacred that's at the core of a lot of psychotic episodes.**

There is no great virtue in being well-adjusted in a maladjusted society. If you think you're perfectly sane and perfectly normal in an insane society, well, then there's something wrong with you. There's something wrong with all of us if we don't get as mad as hell:

- "I've got to stay in control, and I've got to be doing the win/ lose metrics game."
- "I have to show up in a particular way, and everyone has to think about me in a particular way."
- "I'm at a cocktail party, and I need people to like me, and I need to have a certain kind of social circle."
- "I have to stay appropriate here, or else I won't survive. I'll be cast out by the tribe."

No, it's *insane*—so get mad! The beginning of Outrageous Love is the willing heart that says, *I'm willing to be mad as hell.*

- It is not *surface* anger.
- It's not the anger of *losing your temper*, some show of narcissism.
- It's not *destructive* anger.
- It's not *abusive* anger.

That's not what we are talking about. Abusive anger, destructive anger, narcissistic anger—that's all pseudo-eros.

But there is an *Eros* anger.

The original lineage word for anger is *chemah*, which is derived from the two-letter roots in the original Hebrew, *chom* in Aramaic. *Chom* means "love," and *chemah* means "outrageous anger." So *outrage* and *love* are in fact the same word. And the Song of Solomon writes, *azah ki'mavat ahavah:* "Love is as outrageous as death."

Feel that sense of outrage that comes from knowing that it's not *supposed* to be this way. It can't be this way. It's not okay.

If you noticed in the clip, they give him the microphone at this last moment in order to usher him out. He starts talking, and all of a sudden people start listening. And the woman, a tragic figure in the movie who represents win/lose metrics, senses an opportunity. She wants to commodify his rage and use it to get more ratings. It's a cynical moment: *Let's grab his rage, and let's commodify it.* That happens a lot to spirituality—it's seized and commodified and sold. We are not trying to commodify anything here.

Outrageous Love is rooted in outrage, and that outrage has to be pure.

WE CANNOT STOP AT OUTRAGE

Of course, you can't live in outrage all the time.

That's not *the end* of the story; it's *the beginning* of the story.

You cannot walk around outraged in a way that burns your gut and ulcerates your soul—but you do have to *begin* in outrage.

The prophet begins in outrage—and we have to be prophets. We have to speak prophecy. We have to be willing to not just see around the corner, speak truth to power, and turn over the money carts in the temple. That's not enough.

We have to articulate a cogent, coherent, and compelling vision of what the new possibility is.

What is the new possible human? If we cannot articulate, in our body and in ourselves, the new possible human, what the fulfillment of *Homo sapiens* looks like—the fulfillment of *Homo sapiens,* which is *Homo Amor*—then the outrage will destroy us.

I *begin* with outrage.

It's not okay.

- I refuse to look away. (Robert Jay Lifton wrote a book called *Facing Apocalypse.*)
- I refuse to be anesthetized.
- I refuse to be dead.
- I refuse to become, as Pink Floyd said some forty years ago, "comfortably numb."
- I want the pleasure of outrage.

I get a certain amount of critique for getting too excited. Why am I not doing this kind of dispassionate podcast, where you are talking like this and explaining? Why is Gafni getting so excited? That's evangelical.

Really? I mean, **are we not aroused by outrageous pain?**

Can we really be dispassionate in talking about outrageous pain?

Has passion become the ultimate sin?

Do we only associate passion with its pathologies and not with its potency?

We live in a passionate universe. When we say *the Universe is a Love Story*, we mean it's a passionate universe. I need to be willing to reclaim my passion—and my passion involves my outrage. I have to begin with outrage. I'm outraged by the way it is, unwilling to be anesthetized by what Aldous Huxley called *soma*.

- So much of religion, whether it's the New Age version or the old version, is *soma*. It anesthetizes us.
- Conspiracy theories can also be *soma*: I'm anesthetized by my screaming all the time about what's wrong, but I don't take myself seriously enough to take my seat at the table to get involved in making it right.

Let's take our seat at the table.

This is a phrase that I've been using for the last few years, but I forgot about it. And then I started a beautiful set of conversations with a dear friend, and that phrase came back in my mind. We've been talking about what it means *to take your seat at the table*.

It means that **we are willing to be outraged, but we don't stop there.** If you stop at outrage, it destroys you. **I have to then be willing to step into love**—and not just ordinary love, but Outrageous Love.

Outrageous Love feels different, looks different, and tastes different.

Outrageous Love means:

- I'm willing to put it all on the line.
- I'm willing to stop thinking through the lens of my trauma patterns.
- I'm willing to stop thinking only according to obsessive self-involvement (even though I should be self-involved, and I should be working on my transformation). I should be doing everything for my family, my son, my brother, my daughter,

my sister, but my family has got to get bigger. Our love lists are too short.

I have to become an Outrageous Lover. I have to love myself outrageously.

- ◆ When you love yourself outrageously, you can break through trauma patterns.
- ◆ When I love you outrageously, I can help *you* break through trauma patterns, if we are willing to stay in.

Stay in, and don't leave the table. I'm willing to stay in, no matter what happens. I'm here at the table. We're going to work it through, we're going to hold hands, and we are going to love outrageously—**beyond our love lists, in a deeper and wider way, willing to give all of ourselves**.

TO LOVE OUTRAGEOUSLY IS TO PUT IT ALL ON THE LINE

I want to read you something, a story from January 2007. Wesley Autrey is a fifty-year-old American Black man, a construction worker, and a Navy veteran. He's waiting for a subway train in Manhattan with his two daughters. It's about 12:45pm, and he notices a young man. The man's name turns out to be Cameron Hollopeter. He's about twenty, and he's having a seizure. He gets to his feet, but stumbles from the platform and onto the tracks between the two rail lines.

Autrey sees the light of an approaching train, and he makes an instantaneous decision in Outrageous Love: he jumps onto the tracks, thinking he'd have time to drag Hollopeter away. He then realizes in an instant that it's impossible, so he covers Hollopeter's body with his own, and he presses Hollopeter and himself down into a drainage ditch that's about a foot deep in the tracks. The train operator tries to stop, the brakes screech, but by the time he could stop the train, five cars had passed over the two men.

It was the closest of close calls. The cars were so close to Autrey that they smudged grease on his blue knit cap. Autrey hears onlookers screaming, and he yells back: *We're okay down here, but I got two daughters up there on the platform, let them know their father is okay.* And then he hears cries of wonder and applause from the bystanders.

Hollopeter, who was a student at the New York Film Academy, is taken to the hospital, but he just had bumps and bruises. Autrey didn't need medical help, and when interviewed by *The New York Times* he said: *I don't think I did something spectacular, I just saw someone who needed help and I did what I felt was right. I used to be a construction worker, so I'm good at working in confined spaces, and I had a sense that this might work.*

Of course, he became a celebrity overnight, and gifts poured in: scholarships, offers of college tuition for his kids, and season tickets to the New Jersey Nets. He was named a CNN hero, and all of that. He was a guest in Congress in the United States and given a standing ovation.

But why? Because he *knew* something. He was *outrageous*. He knew in that moment that there was something to be done. It didn't make sense. He didn't know the man. He didn't have time to think. But he embodied something that lives in all of us, something that's true: **we are all actually** *connected*:

- We are part of the one heart.
- We are part of the one Eros.
- We are part of the one mind.

We are unique, distinct, individuated, and wildly valuable. We are irreducibly unique parts of the whole—but we are not *separate*. Separateness is an "optical delusion of consciousness," as Albert Einstein correctly wrote.

Autrey knew that in that moment that jumping in to try to save this person was true, and it was good, and it was beautiful. He was named a hero because he spoke the truth that everyone knew—but he lived into it.

We often think our Outrageous Love is only for our family—for my son or my daughter, for my brother or my sister. No, Outrageous Love is outrageous. I am willing to put it all on the line.

For most of us, Outrageous Love doesn't mean jumping on the subway tracks—but it always means showing up beyond our comfort zone.

WRITE A CHECK OF YOUR OPEN HEART

I'm going to give you another example. There's something in the Hebrew wisdom lineage called *phylacteries*. They are these black leather instruments that you wrap on your hand. They are also called *teffilin*. They've been passed down the lineage for like 3,200 years, and part of my personal practice for the last few decades is that I wear them every day. It's my private practice. In my public life, I'm a global citizen—and, I hope, a galactic citizen—and I think that's what we need to be. But in private, I also practice in the lineage of the original masters in my life. Now, I'm not wealthy. As a matter of fact, I'm probably poor by any definition of funding. I once bought this pair of phylacteries—they are called a pair because there are two sets, one you wear on your head and one you wear on your arm—that was $1,500, and I was really excited to have them.

Not too long afterwards, I was giving a talk at an event called *Meta-Mind*, run by a colleague of mine at the time. There was a brilliant musician there, we were talking, and he says: *I was born into that same lineage you were, I lost connection to it, and I have this desire to connect to it.*

I said to him, literally, without missing a beat, but it was just obvious to me: *Wow, I just bought this beautiful pair of phylacteries, leather straps. It's a beautiful ritual. And I'm sure that I bought them for you, so let me show you how they work.*

I gave them to him, and he took them, he received them, and he put them on. They've been with him since then, though I never saw him again. I think someone might have sent me online someplace where he told the story. But those were his, it was clear as day to me.

That's what Outrageous Love means.

Outrageous Love means we step up for each other, we show up for each other, and we show up full on, outrageously.

It's not ordinary. It's a willingness to show up with Outrageous Love. And sometimes it has to do with finances. There was a time in my life where I was making a lot of money when I was in Israel, because I was just doing a lot of speeches. I had a friend who needed $60,000, and at that time in my life, I happened to have about $60,000 in the bank. He needed it more than I did, so I wrote him a check for $60,000, end of story.

That's how you have to live.

You have to live outrageously. Not irresponsibly, but outrageously.

And it doesn't need to be an actual check.

You can:

- Write a check of your smile.
- Write a check of your open heart.
- Write a check of your love.
- Write a check of your attention.
- Write a check of the way you show up.

But there is a check that you need to write every day. That check has your signature on it, and that check is your Outrageous Act of Love. Because that's what an Outrageous Lover does:

An Outrageous Lover commits Outrageous Acts of Love.

EVOLUTION IS LOVE IN ACTION

Here's the crazy thing: it is the most healing thing you can do. The most healing transformative act you can do in your life is to commit Outrageous Acts of Love.

It's not a one-time event, but part of the fabric of your life. I am an Outrageous Lover.

Most of those acts may be symbolic. You can't give different people $60,000 every day, because you'd quickly be out of money (at least that was true for me). But **your life becomes part of a fabric of the Outrageous Love of the universe that's moving uniquely through you**—and the way you listen is outrageous, the way you forgive is outrageous, the way you take a stand is outrageous. You live in that outrageous place.

In other words, you access the energy of the rage, but then you transmute it into love.

The outrage stops being outrageous *anger*—but that rejection of the status quo which lives in the prophetic rage then becomes *love*.

The prophets are described as the erotic maiden, who is the mad lover of Song of Songs. The prophet in the lineage is also called the *Bat Me'lech*, the daughter of the king, the mad lover. The prophet is the one who—in her body, in his body—loves madly.

- She gives her radiance.
- She shows up.
- She walks into a room and asks not, *What can I get out of this room?*
- She asks, *What can I pour into this room?*

We sometimes walk into situations thinking, *What can I get out of this?* What did I *get out* of this broadcast?

But what would it mean to *pour my energy* into this broadcast? Oh my God, we can actually feel it exploding in the space.

To be an Outrageous Lover is to commit Outrageous Acts of Love.

Next week, we're going to talk all about what it means to commit Outrageous Acts of Love. But for now, let me just close with this:

Evolution is love in action, and my hands are the hands of evolution.

My hands are the hands of God, and my feet are the feet of God, and my embodiment is the embodiment of the Divine. I live to be Outrageous Love, and I live to commit Outrageous Acts of Love—not those that take down my life, but those that expand my life, those that make me alive.

Every single day, I want to weave together a tapestry of Outrageous Love.

And you have to do it uniquely. There is a way to do it in your life.

When we do that, we become healthier, stronger, more alive, more filled with joy, more aligned with your true nature—and we begin to play our instrument in the Unique Self Symphony.

This is not *Homo sapiens*, who's trying to figure out what I can get out of this? Have I gotten enough from this person that they deserve my love?

I become an Outrageous Lover. I'm going to show up *just because*.

Sometimes you meet someone—every once in a long while, you can't do it often, for everyone—you meet someone and you say, *I'm going to show up just because*. I'm in. **Outrageous Love—it's the only truth.**

We live in a world of outrageous pain, the only response to outrageous pain is Outrageous Love.

271

Our Outrageous Love includes all of our holy and broken *Hallelujahs*. Our ultimate prayer, Leonard Cohen's song, "Hallelujah," is the prayer we do every week.

Our only prayer is: **Can I turn all of my holy and broken *Hallelujahs* into poetry, into Outrageous Love, into the poetry of Outrageous Love?**

CHAPTER NINETEEN

THERE IS ONLY ONE SIDE, THE SIDE OF LOVE: TEN PRINCIPLES

Episode 378 — January 20, 2024

THE MALAISE OF POLARIZATION

I want to address the malaise that lives so deep in the current culture: It's the malaise of **polarization**, where sides are drawn. When we draw these sides, the assumption is that this side is all true, and that side's all false. This side is all right, and that side is all wrong.

The sides are drawn:

- Based on boundaries that shouldn't be boundaries
- Based on superficial distinctions that shouldn't be distinctions
- Based on levels of ignorance that violate love's knowledge

Such polarizations are drawn in order to give us comfort and to salve our sense of unmoored identity.

That's the way *Homo sapiens* have always been. *Homo sapiens* have always been—in one way or the other—driven by rivalrous conflict governed by win/lose metrics, in which ideas are deployed as part of the arsenal of conflict.

Ideas are part of what forms my sense of peoplehood or my personhood. Polarized ideas become part of my identity, and then I fight to defend my identity, whether that's my national identity, my ethnic identity, or my

273

racial identity. Old systems of discrimination, which were a horror, were based on these false divisions, this false taking of sides. Part of the post-modern response to the old systems of oppression is identity politics and critical race theory, which themselves are a false drawing of lines and forms of discrimination.

Instead, we need to come together in order to move from *Homo sapiens* to *Homo amor*, and say, boldly, audaciously, dramatically: **There is only one side. We stand on the side of love.**

So that's what we are here to do today.

Are we ready, my friends?

Are we ready to move from *Homo sapiens*, the old human, to *Homo amor*, the new human and the new humanity?

Are we ready to cross to the other side?

This is the moment of the Crossing.

We are in a meta-crisis, and it cannot be sufficiently addressed by evolutions of infrastructure (new technology), as important as those are, or by evolutions of social structure (new laws, new communal models, new economic models, new government models), as important as those are. They are all necessary but insufficient.

We need new *superstructure*, which means, in our language, a new Story of Value.

This is not just a new story, but a new Story of Value rooted in First Principles and First Values that can *generate* a new human and a new humanity. Only a new human and a new humanity—the movement from *Homo sapiens* to *Homo amor*—can address the outrageous pain and generate Outrageous Love.

WE ALL STAND TOGETHER ON THE SIDE OF LOVE

A dear friend of mine left me a text on Friday where he said that a friend of his—a teacher, an old woman I knew back in the day—said to herself that Buddha's First Noble Truth, *life is suffering*, speaks to her so resonantly these days. Although I was coming from a very different place, back in 2011, I tried to ground the movement from *Homo sapiens* to *Homo amor* in a couple of sentences:

- **We live in a world of outrageous pain**. Full stop. No explanation, no theodicy, no theological justification, no reductive materialistic acceptance, no spiritual dismissal such as saying *it's all an illusion*. No. We don't turn away. We acknowledge and look at the pain.
- **We live in a world of outrageous beauty.** That's absolutely true. Full stop.
- **The only response to outrageous pain is Outrageous Love.**
- **The only response to outrageous beauty is Outrageous Love.**

In order to move from *Homo sapiens* to *Homo amor*, to generate a new superstructure, a new Story of Value that births a new human and a new humanity, *we have to become the new human*. That's *the Crossing*. We cross over to the other side.

To become the new human, we have to move away from superficial boundaries, superficial distinctions, and from dominator hierarchies—we have to stand on the side of love.

But to stand on the side of love is not an intellectual, cognitive move. As we practice together at the symposium on world religion, we need to be able to look in each other's eyes and say, "Behold, you're beautiful, beloved. Behold. Behold." I need to evoke and *feel* the love rising in me, even for people whom I disagree with profoundly, even for people who I think are on the wrong side of things.

We are both on the side of love now.

I'll give you an example. Say you have a couple, and they have this huge set of conflicts. These conflicts are real, but each one has become an attorney. They're collecting evidence against the other side—the other side just happens to be their beloved. This means we're clearly not on the side of love anymore.

The beginning, the pivoting point, the shift, the transformation, the opening into love and joy is when both sides of the couple—whatever kind of couple, a romantic couple, a teacher-student couple, two friends, a brother-sister couple—realize: "No, we're *not* against each other."

The two sides literally step onto the same side. Sometimes, when I work deeply with a couple, we'll actually do that: they'll actually both stand. They'll start standing facing each other, seemingly against each other, and then I'll have them move to the same side and face in the same direction.

There's only one force we're against. **We are against the force of un-love.** We're against un-love. We are on the side of love. Can you feel that?

We are not against each other. We both step onto the same side. There's only one side, the side of love. **We all stand together on the side of love.**

LOVE DOESN'T ERASE DISTINCTIONS

Let me just first say what that *doesn't* mean.

It doesn't mean that there are no distinctions. Of course it doesn't mean that.

Love is not only an emotion. Love is a perception. **Love is a capacity *to see*.** Implicit in the capacity to see is the capacity to make distinctions. Either we live in a Cosmos that has an *ought*—and I *ought* to do something— or we don't. If there is an *ought* in Cosmos, then there are distinctions. Love is always about perception, and perception is always about seeing clearly. I can see clearly now. It's perception—and when I perceive, I make distinctions.

Love doesn't mean a leveling of differences. That's not what love means. **Love is the capacity to deepen and make distinctions.** And as long as there's an *ought*, there's that which ought be done, and there's that which ought *not* be done—there are distinctions.

Love is not about effacing distinctions.

Love is not about a leveling of differences.

Love is about seeing clearly and realizing that, in the end, we all stand together on the side of love.

EVOLUTIONARY LOVE CODE: THERE IS ONLY ONE SIDE, THE SIDE OF LOVE

There is only one side, the side of love.

What that means about what should be done is a question of impossible complexity, pain, and uncertainty. We stand for a culture of Eros against a culture of death. We stand for intimacy against alienation. This requires us to be both tender and fierce, to stand for love against all forms of un-love.

Distinctions around value are an expression of love. Love and un-love are real. But love and un-love are not an inherent split along racial, or national, or ethnic, or religious grounds. That kind of thinking itself is an expression of un-love and anti-value. That, in and of itself, is the cause of so much horror

There is only one side, the side of love. We all stand together on the side of love.

In our formulation, good and evil is discerned simply: to be good is to stand for love. No one is outside of the circle of love. To be on the side of love requires the cultivation of radical discernment within a broken information ecology.

There is only one side, the side of love. We all stand together on the side of love.

So let's go deep into that. Let's take it from a *dharmic meme theme*, if you will, and let's go deep inside. I would like to go through ten distinct principles. Each one should be the subject of an entire One Mountain broadcast. But let's go through each one, so we get the general vision.

What are the ten principles *of*?

There are no sides. We all stand together on the side of love. The only side that exists is the side of love.

I was talking to a dear friend of mine on Thursday, and we had a beautiful conversation. There was a moment of conflict in the conversation. It got hard for a moment, and then the sentence came down to us: *There's only one side, the side of love.* We all stand together on the side of love. And then our hearts relaxed, and we realized, "No, of course. Of course, we're on the side of love."

It wasn't about content. It was about where I locate myself. I locate myself on the side of love, and we're together on the side of love. We stand against un-love.

PRINCIPLE ONE: YOU CAN'T LOVE UNLESS YOU CAN LAUGH TOGETHER

Principle one: laughter. The principle of laughter. You can't love unless you can laugh together.

Laughter is the move from polarization to paradox.

To be on the side of love means I move from contradiction to paradox. I move:

- From *contradiction*, which creates polarization,
- To *paradox*, which creates new poignancy and new potency, which allows me to say the promise will be kept. It creates a new promise.

Paradox means that I'm standing *against* Aristotle's law of the excluded middle, which states that it's either this side or that side. It's either this way or that way.

You know, in the lineage of Solomon, this is a very strong idea. The master is issuing decisions, and a person comes to the master and says, "This is what happened."

And the master says, "You're right. I totally understand what you're saying. You're totally right."

And then the second person comes, who's the litigant against the first person, and explains to the master what happens. The master says, "Hey, well, I totally understand. You're totally right."

And then his beloved, his wife, storms in and says, "I was listening to all of that. You told the first person they're right and the second person they're right. And how could you do that?"

And he looks at his beloved, and he says, "You're also right."

Paradox and laughter increase our ability to hold a larger view. That's what laughter does.

Laughter cuts through the illusion of polarization.

Laughter cuts through the pomposity of superficiality, through surface identities, where my position is not emerging from my love—it's coming only from my identity, or from superficial outrage without gnosis, without deep knowing.

Laughter punctures easy certainties and opens the space to hold paradox, to hold the impossibility of paradox.

279

To be on the side of love, I require the capacity to hold paradox. To hold paradox, I require the capacity to laugh. One of the most important dimensions of peacemaking is to be in a room and laugh together.

PRINCIPLE TWO: LOVE IS THE MOVEMENT BETWEEN CERTAINTY AND UNCERTAINTY

Principle two is related to principle one, but it's not quite the same: love is related to the dialectic, to the movement between certainty and uncertainty.

To love, I need to see you clearly, with a kind of certainty—I need clarity. I also need to hold a deep clarity about my identity and about my vision. I need *revelation* in order to love. So, love is certainty because love is not merely an emotion. Love is a perception, and it has to be a perception that gives me some dimension of certainty.

Yet, along with my certainty, I also hold uncertainty. I'm not sure. I don't know. I am able to bracket my certainty and step into uncertainty.

Let me say it a different way:

Love is the movement between revelation and mystery.

Love always holds the certainty of revelation and the uncertainty of mystery.

In love, I'm at the edge of mystery.

PRINCIPLE THREE: FEEL ME FEELING YOU

Love requires the capacity to be intimate.

The capacity to be intimate has a number of dimensions, the first of which is *feel me feeling you.*

Feel me feeling you. You've got to be able to feel me feeling you, and I've got to be able to see your face. To love means we look at each other, *pa-nim-el-panim*, face-to-face.

I often mention Sam Keen's book called *The Face of the Enemy*. He talks about propaganda posters, where the face of the enemy is always effaced. The enemy never has a face.

The enemy is not a monster. The beauty sees through the beast and sees a prince.

Love is a perception that opens my capacity to see your face and to feel you. Intimacy means I feel you, and you feel me. That's the first level of intimacy in this principle.

But there is a second level of intimacy, when I feel you feeling me. Imagine, in the midst of a war, you not only feel the other side, but you feel the other side feeling you back. War is over. **Intimacy is the exact opposite of the structure of war.** The structure of war is to deface the enemy and to shatter intimacy.

PRINCIPLE FOUR: LOVE EXTENDS TIME AND HOLDS THE PRESENT, PAST, AND FUTURE

Love is connected to the capacity to hold *deep* time, not just *surface* time.

Deep time means I don't only see what's in front of me in this moment. I can *extend* the sense of time.

An animal has, based on what we know, a large collective memory, but a significantly shorter personal memory. There is the memory of the herd, which is relatively extensive in its general parameters, but not detailed. And there is personal memory, which is relatively limited.

So love is the capacity to extend time—to be out of the moment and hold past, present, and future. I'm not just looking at this moment. I am holding the past and I'm holding the future.

This quality of love is related to the capacity to hold deep time. I'm not holding the past only from *my* perspective, only from the way *I* feel it. I feel the way *you* feel the past, and you feel the way I feel the past. We meet in the present—and then we have this vision of the future.

> *Love is the depth of the present in which the deep memory of the past and the deep memory of the future are merged.*

When I see something in front of me, when I'm a mad lover, I'm drawn into the present—but then I extend beyond the present, and I begin to see a larger vision. Another way to say that is that love has the capacity to simultaneously place attention on past, present, and future—or **love has the capacity to place attention on a storyline.**

We need to actually *feel* each other's storylines.

PRINCIPLE FIVE: TO LOVE IS TO KNOW

Love is connected to *gnosis*, to knowledge. To love is to know, which is why *to know* is always to know *intimately*, to know *carnally*. (*And Adam knew his wife, Eve.*)

Carnal knowledge is: I know you *sensually*.

- It means I can do sensemaking.
- It means I have *gnosis*, I have knowledge.
- It means I can touch you, I can feel you, and I know about you.

Love can never come from ignorance. **Love always has to come from the deepest capacity for knowing. Love and knowledge are intimately related.**

Love can't be dissociated from the basis of facts. Facts are always important. And facts are not merely subjective. It's not just *everybody has their facts*. That's not true. There has to be a way to bring the facts together and get this larger perspective.

Let me say it a little bit differently: Love is connected to gnosis. And *gnosis* means I want to know. To know, I have to be open. I am open to new information. I am prepared to be moved by you. I am prepared to be moved by new gnosis, by new feeling, by new possibility, by new vision, by new facts.

If people enter into a conversation and neither is moved by each other's adducing of new information, and new facts, and new gnosis, then they are haters, not lovers.

Lovers are moved by each other.

They affect each other, and they impact each other.

PRINCIPLE SIX: LOVE IS A BRACKETING OF THE EGO

Love is a bracketing of the ego in devotion to the full emergence of the beloved.

Love is a bracketing of the ego self. I bracket my ego self, and I open myself in devotion to the fullest emergence of my beloved.

- ♦ I am interested in my beloved.
- ♦ I am curious about my beloved.
- ♦ I want to know how they feel.
- ♦ I want to know everything about them.
- ♦ I want to collect all the facts and feelings I can, both interior qualities and objective information.

That matters. In other words, love can never emerge in a postmodern world in which the 2016 Word of the Year in the Oxford Dictionary is *post-truth*.

If we are post-truth, we are also post-love.

Love is a perception. It emerges not from ignorance, but from *gnosis*. Love unmoored from fact, unmoored from storyline, cannot be love.

Now, we can have two different perspectives that we need to look at. We can have two different sets of feelings that we need to feel together, but we need to be open because we've bracketed our ego self. **We are in devotion to each other's fullness, to each other's emergence.**

Love's knowledge is the opposite of propaganda. Propaganda means each side propagandizes, or accuses the other of propagandizing. Differences are leveled, neither side impacts each other, and no one ever changes their position—because everyone is locked in a position which is not about love but about identity.

My position is my identity. I can't compromise my identity. I'm insanely filled with terror of not existing because I've lost my identity. My identity is my particular position. In that moment, I'm not a lover but a narcissist. **To be a lover means to bracket myself, so that I'm in devotion to your emergence.**

Therefore, I'm open to you, and I'm open to be impacted by your information. Your information in-forms you, and I'm willing to let your information in-form me. *I'm informed by your information.*

PRINCIPLE SEVEN: LOVE IS A PERCEPTION

We have already mentioned this, but this is a distinct principle in its own right: **love is not merely a feeling, love is a perception.** *Perception* means *I'm placing my attention.*

To love is to place attention. That's why sexuality is love in the body—because in sex, in its ultimate beautiful sense, I place my attention on you. I bracket myself and I place my attention on you. And by placing my attention on you, I become more fully and more dramatically myself because I've dramatically bracketed myself in devotion to you. That's the perception of loving.

When I perceive, I make distinctions—so love makes distinctions. Love perceives distinctions because there's an *ought* in Cosmos. If there's an ought in Cosmos, it means something ought to be one way, that it's better for it to be one way than another way. There's a *better* and *worse*. Love implies that something's better than something else because love means I see distinction. I perceive an *ought*.

This is one of the great mistakes of the way that people talk about "unconditional" love. Unconditional love means I level all distinctions, and that nothing matters. No, that's not what love means. **Love means the capacity to make distinctions. To love you means I see you.**

I see you means I see *beneath the surface.*

- I see your essence.
- I see your infinite specialness.
- I see your irreducible uniqueness.
- I don't get caught only on the surface expressions of you.

I'm able to see deeply. I can see clearly. But remember, it's a clarity that also holds the mystery (Principle Two).

PRINCIPLE EIGHT: LOVE IS THE ENERGY OF TRANSFORMATION

This is a big one. Love means I stand for my transformation—and for your transformation. Love is the energy of transformation.

Love means that I'm not tyrannized by yesterday. That is unimaginably beautiful and unimaginably important, but **love is the Possibility of Possibility**. Love is the possibility of a new tomorrow. Love means we can transform.

I'm going to give you an example. For those of us who think that we can't move beyond atrocity, we *have* to move beyond atrocity. Not easily, not glibly, not with instant forgiveness. That would be absurd.

But ultimately, we don't, today, demonize every German in Germany, even though Germany, not that many decades ago, affected a true genocide—the intention to kill every last Jewish person on the planet, if possible. That's what *genocide* means—the desire to eradicate an entire people to every last person, period, for its own sake. That word is thrown around a little bit insanely these days, but that's what genocide means, and that was a clear intention of the German government. And as Daniel Goldhagen wrote in a book called *Hitler's Willing Executioners*, it enjoyed enormous popular support.

It was an enormous tragedy, beyond imagination. It killed most of my family. But that doesn't mean that today we demonize every German, or even Germany as a nation. We can recognize that Germany went through a process of transformation, and we can ally ourselves with Germany some seventy-eighty years later.

How is that even possible? It's only possible because of the transformative power of love.

Love always creates the possibility of a new tomorrow.

PRINCIPLE NINE: LOVE DEMANDS A POST-TRAGIC EMBRACE

Love demands that we shift into a post-tragic mode of consciousness.

- *Pre-tragic* seems like loving before the tragedy strikes.
- *Tragic*: the tragedy strikes, and there is no room for love.
- *Post-tragic* is when we love *after* the tragic. **We love after unbearable pain.**

Love requires post-tragic consciousness. It requires a radical embrace of the post-tragic.

PRINCIPLE TEN: TRACE EVERY STORY BACK TO ITS ROOTS

Love requires a realization that **that which unites us is far greater than that which divides us.** To be in a culture of love, a culture of Eros, means we need a set of shared First Principles and First Values that allow us to stand together on the side of love.

- It doesn't mean that we need to have the same full worldview.
- It doesn't mean we can't radically disagree on dimensions of reality—we can.
- But there needs to be **a core grammar of value that we share.**

We need a shared grammar of value, a shared language of love, a shared recognition that every human being is worthy of love, in order to stand together on the side of love.

Here's where it gets very subtle, my friends. In order to articulate, to formulate, and to tell that new Story of Value in which we all participate in a musical score (which is Eros), in the shared grammar of value, we need *vision* and *imagination*.

Now I want to say something here that's impossible. Sometimes, there's a necessity of what we might call *a just war*. For example, the war against Nazism, many people would think was a just, a necessary war. I think it was.

But even when I participate in a just war, I cannot demonize the person who in this moment is my enemy. Because if we do that, if we basically say that my enemy is inherently demonic forever, then we have war forever.

Then we can't have transformation.

Then we can't have Nazi Germany transform into postwar democratic Germany that—rightly or wrongly—absorbed more refugees than any other European country. We have to allow for the possibility of transformation. **To allow for the possibility of transformation is to stand against demonization.**

In order to do that, I need to trace every story back to its roots.

Even if my enemy has a story that's in violation of *everything* I believe in, I have to try and find the root of that story. I have to trace the surface of the story back to the root. I need to locate the spark of the sacred at the root, and then help my enemy tell a new story that emerges from their vision of value.

What I just said is subtle, so let me try and state it clearly.

I cannot demonize the other in a way that they become subhuman. Even if they behave in a way that's a violation of all of humanity, and I need to respond fiercely in the moment to protect myself, I nonetheless need to be able to engage in what I would call *the Tantra principle of non-rejection*, which says that I've got to trace everything back to its root. **I have to find the spark of the sacred even in what seems to be the most broken vessel in order to hold the possibility that that vessel can become whole again.**

There's a text in *Talmud Sanhedrin*, from the third century, that says when I take out a person to be executed, I'm still under the command of *love your neighbor as yourself*. I still have to love the person, even at that most painful moment.

We all stand together on the side of love.

It doesn't mean that there are no distinctions. It doesn't mean we level differences. It means that the music of love ultimately lives in every human being.

We are all notes in the symphony of loving.

When an ideology goes wrong, it's because it's a failed love story. But it *is* a love story. The fact that it's a love story means that if I can find its roots, I can rewrite that story.

- ◆ Together, we can evolve that story.
- ◆ Together, we can write that symphony.
- ◆ Together, we can all stand on the side of love.

There's only one side, the side of love.

We all stand together on the side of love.

CHAPTER TWENTY

LOVE DEMANDS TRANSFORMATION: CROSSING OVER TO THE SIDE OF LOVE

Episode 379 — January 27, 2024

THE CROSSING

I want to open up, if we can, this very deep gate today: the gate of *The Crossing*.

What does it mean, to cross over to the other side?

It is to know that, ultimately, there are no two sides. **The only place to stand is on the side of love.**

I woke up this morning after a long and difficult night. I couldn't get to sleep last night. I was still up at three in the morning, which I don't usually do. I try to go to sleep by nine and get up at five or six. But I was up very late, studying, and writing, and thinking.

I woke up in the morning, and the first thought that went through my head was, "What do I truly want? I want to serve *She*. I'm in devotion to *She*." *I knew it was true, and I was ecstatic, and I was so wildly grateful.* Of course, that doesn't mean I get everything right, but I had this very clear sense of my own interiority, which is this mad devotion to *She*—and I was so grateful for it.

- Thank you for not degrading my heart.

- ◆ Thank you for not making me bitter.
- ◆ Thank you for breaking my heart time and again. Each time my heart breaks, I realize that there's nothing more whole than a broken heart.

I felt mad gratitude to be outraged, mad gratitude to taste, mad gratitude *to feel*, whether I'm feeling the agony or the ecstasy.

As one master writes, "What can I say? I'm alive." It's the mad joy of being alive.

That's the context for our conversation today.

We have the same Code as last week. We're going to go in deeper into what *is* this notion—that wherever I stand, I'm standing on the side of love. What does it mean?

There are no two sides, there is only a side of love. We looked at ten dimensions of it last week, and we're going to go deeper into it this week. We're going to talk about what it means to be in this moment of The Crossing, **this realization that I can only respond to the crisis through The Crossing.**

What is The Crossing? The Crossing, at its core, is a crossing *over*:

- ◆ From *one* side—and on that side, there are always two sides fighting each other
- ◆ To the other side—and on the other side, there's only one side, the side of love

That's The Crossing.

We are about to do a big event in Europe called The Crossing. It's enormously exciting. It emerges out of the Mystery Schools of the last decade and out of the important work and facilitation that's been done in Belgium under my dear friend James Bampfield's leadership. I called James about a year and a half ago, and we had this deep-dive conversation, and together we birthed The Crossing.

The Crossing is unlike the Mystery School, which is on the edge of culture. It's the leading edge of the edge in order to influence, change, and evolve the whole source code. It's the edge of the edge of the edge.

The Crossing is an event that we want to place in the very center of culture. Our vision, our dream is there'd be Crossing events all over the world.

We're going to be talking today about what it means to cross over to the side of love.

And what does that mean in the context of One Mountain, Many Paths?

Why is that the heart and the seat of the revolution?

THE BATTLE BETWEEN GOOD AND EVIL INVITES ME TO THE CROSSING

In this world of intense pain, the idea that we all need to be on the side of love is everything. As we said last week, that doesn't mean there is no discernment.

- ♦ It doesn't mean that all positions are equal.
- ♦ It doesn't mean there's no battle between good and evil.

Those are real. There *is* a battle between good and evil that lives inside of every one of us. There actually *is* a jihad. A jihad—in the deepest interpretation of the leading edges of the truth, at the heart of Islam—is not a battle where you place other people on the other side and you kill them. **It's a battle that takes place inside of every human being.**

It's the battle which invites me to *The Crossing*.

Can I cross over, inside of me, and move beyond arbitrary *us* and *them*, beyond racist *us* and *them*, jihadi *us* and *them*—beyond any form of *us* and *them* that says, "We are the chosen ones, and you are inferior?"

Can we actually realize that that which unites us is so much greater than that which divides us, and that we are all together on the side of love?

Of course:

- We can still have distinctions.
- We can be unique instruments in the Unique Self Symphony.
- We can experience unique qualities of intimacy.
- We can embody unique expressions of our divinity.
- We can have unique stories that we tell.

We can have unique religions and unique histories—as we should, because we need diversity. Diversity is one of the fundamental intentions of Cosmos. Cosmos intends diversity. Evolution intends diversity. **We never want a monochrome oneness, which effaces diversity**. That's called totalitarianism; it's called depression. But we do need to know that there is a shared Story of Value, which is a *context* for our diversity—and that we're all living in the mad joy of the God house. We're all living in the mad joy of Cosmo-Erotic Humanism, the CosmoErotic Universe, in whose heart pulses and beats Eros and love.

It's about kindness.

It's about caring.

It's about discernment.

It's about feeling each other.

There is more *Hallelujah* to come. *Hallelujah* is both drunken intoxication—in Hebrew, we say *holelut*—and pristine praise, *hallel* in Hebrew. *Hallelujah* is the unique thread of my life, where my moments of utter brokenness, of my drunken intoxication come together with my moments of clarity, of pristine and gorgeous praise. Together they form the unique wholeness of my life, which is a unique expression of the Godhead.

There is a mad joy of being at home in the world, of being welcomed in the Cosmos. There is more God to come in the mystery of the *Hallelujah*.

That is my life. *And even though it all went wrong, I'll stand before the Lord of Song with nothing on my lips but Hallelujah.* It's the joy of my unique intimacy, of my life, my religion, and my people, as I play my instrument in the Unique Self Symphony, and we all realize that we're all playing the same music, and that the music is Eros, that the music is love.

That's our intention this week.

Welcome to One Mountain, Many Paths. We are at this time between worlds, this time between stories, and this is the heart of the revolution. We understand that to respond to the meta-crisis, we need a new Story of Value. We need to invoke the new human and the new humanity, and tell that new story, which is the only thing that can respond to the meta-crisis.

EVOLUTIONARY LOVE CODE: THERE IS ONLY ONE SIDE, THE SIDE OF LOVE.

There is only one side, the side of love.

What that means about what should be done is a question of impossible complexity, pain, and uncertainty.

We stand for a culture of Eros against a culture of death.

We stand for intimacy against alienation.

This requires us to be both tender and fierce, to stand for love against all forms of un-love.

Distinctions around value are an expression of love. Love and un-love are real.

But love and un-love are not an inherent split on racial, or national, or ethnic, or religious grounds. That kind of thinking itself is an expression of un-love and anti-value, that in and of itself is the cause of so much horror.

There is only one side, the side of love. We all stand together on the side of love.

In our formulation, good and evil are discerned simply: to be good is to stand for love. No one is outside of the circle of love. To be on the side of love requires the cultivation of radical discernment within a broken information ecology.

There is only one side, the side of love. We all stand together on the side of love.

EVEN AS LOVE CROWNS YOU, SHALL HE CRUCIFY YOU

I want to read for you a piece that was written in 1923 by Kahlil Gibran, eight years before he died. It is a famous piece that's been wildly misinterpreted. I want to bring it to bear.

A dear student and friend sent me this three or four days ago, and I wrote her back that Gibran misses the larger context. We need to put Gibran in context. He's actually referring to something very specific, but he doesn't quite name it.

First, let me read the piece. We are talking about being on the side of love: what does it mean that there's not two sides, that there is only the side of love?

Here's what Gibran, this Lebanese mystic, writes:

> Then, said Almitra, speak to us of love.
>
> And he raised his head and looked upon the people. He raised his head, and he looked upon the people, and there fell a stillness upon them.
>
> And with a great voice, he said:
>
> "When love beckons to you, follow her, though her ways are hard and steep.

He said *his* ways, but I'm making some changes as we go.

> And when his wings enfold you, yield to him, though the sword hidden among his pinions may wound you.
>
> And when he speaks to you, believe in him, though his voice may shadow your dreams as the north wind lays

295

waste the garden.

For even as love crowns you, shall he crucify you. Even as he is for your growth, so is he for your pruning.

Here we can say that *pruning* also means *clarification*.

Even as he ascends to your height and caresses your tenderest branches that quiver in the sun, so shall he descend to your roots and shake them in their clinging to the earth.

Like sheaves of corn, love gathers you onto himself.

He threshes you to make you naked.

He sifts you.

He sifts you to free you from your husks.

He grinds you to whiteness.

He kneads you until you are pliant.

And then he assigns you to his sacred fire, that you may become sacred bread for God's sacred feast.

He's talking about love as the process of kneading dough into bread, with all of the agony and the ecstasy.

And these things shall love do unto you, that you may know the secrets of your heart, and in that knowledge become a fragment of life's heart.

Hear it again:

And these things shall love do unto you that you may know the secrets of your heart, and in that knowledge become a fragment of life's heart.

But if in your heart you would seek only love's peace and love's pleasure, then it is better for you that you cover your nakedness and pass out of love's threshing-floor, into the seasonless world where you shall laugh, but not all of your laughter, and weep, but not all of your tears.

Love gives naught but itself and takes naught but from itself.

Love possesses not nor would it be possessed; for love is

sufficient unto love.

When you love, you should not say, "God is in my heart," but rather, "I am in the heart of God."

And think not you can direct the course of love, for love, if it finds you worthy, directs your course.

Love has no other desire but to fulfill itself.

But if you love and must needs have desires, but if you love and you're going to have desires, let these be your desires:

To melt and be like a running brook that sings its melody to the night.

To know the pain of too much tenderness.

To be wounded by your own understanding of love, and to bleed willingly and joyfully.

To wake at dawn with a winged heart and give thanks for another day of loving.

To rest at the noon hour and meditate love's ecstasy.

To return home at eventide with gratitude.

And then to sleep with a prayer for the beloved in your heart and a song of praise upon your lips."

Can you feel that my friends? Feel that with me. Wow.

LOVE MOVES US TOWARDS TRANSFORMATION

What Gibran is talking about is what we call Outrageous Love or Evolutionary Love.

This is not ordinary love. This is not love that is the panacea. This is not the easy sweetness-and-light love, where everything works out easily and everyone feels good. They've taken the perfect medicine, and it's good MDMA, and we're all holding each other lovingly.

Yes, that's a piece of love. But oh my God, it's so much deeper.

When we say, *There are no two sides, there is only the side of love*, we're not talking about love that's all sweetness and light. We're not talking about ordinary love, which is the psychological love between human beings, who are deluded and think they're separate selves and use a particular social construction of love to give themselves a little bit of comfort, peace, and security before the inevitable darkness of death (as they understand it) that engulfs them.

- They use love as a shield to avoid truly looking at their situation.
- They use love as a way to obscure the clouds and the thunder that live so deep inside.
- They use love as a path of *a-void-dance*—of dancing around the void.

That's not the love we're talking about, my friends. That kind of love always has two sides, because that's the love of separate selves, and the separate selves are always fighting. That kind of love becomes just another idolatry of the separate self: *Oh, I love God in my way, and my separate self has my separate God, and my separate God is better than your separate God. My separate self is my separate religion. My separate religion is better than your separate religion.*

This kind of love is just a poor, dull sword, which cuts brutally without precision, without potency and without poignancy.

That's not the love we're looking for, my friends. **When we say there's only one side, the side of love, and we stand together on the side of love, we are talking about Evolutionary Love.**

- We are talking about Outrageous Love.
- We are talking about love that's not merely a contrived, human, separate-self crutch or socially constructed sentiment.
- We are talking about love that is the heart of existence itself.
- We are talking about the love that Solomon described when he said in the *Song of Songs*: *Its insides are lined with love.*

What's the nature of Outrageous Love?

What's the nature of this love, which is the only side that there is?

The first quality of this love, which is only one side—this love that is the only side that exists—is that **love moves us towards transformation**.

Love is not only *being*. Love is not only sweetness and light. Love is not only the cuddling that we do where we just want to stay in the exact right position and rest deeply in this place where we're loving each other—there's no place to go, and there's nothing to do, so let's just be on our journey.

That is *a* quality of love. That is one face of love. It's beautiful, this love that's a quality of *being*, but love is much more than that. The first quality of love is being—not separate-self being, but True-Self being.

When I cuddle with my beloved, I'm not just cuddling with them—I'm cuddling with the field of True Self, the field of Being. I'm at home and I'm welcome in the universe. That's the first quality of love.

It's not separate-self cuddling. Separate-self cuddling leads to war: Why are you cuddling with them and not with me? And why is it happening this way and not that way?

True-Self cuddling is resting and being. That's one dimension, one quality of love. It's beautiful.

The second quality of love is that it moves us towards transformation. Love rips us open, demands that we get naked, and that we strip away all that's impure, all that's posturing, and all that's impostor-ing. **Love demands authenticity.** This is why Kali is one of the faces of love in Kashmir Shaivism.

Love has a quality of fire. Love is outrageous. It has a quality of passion, and passion is a flame. Passion *drives* us. It *moves* us.

Love not only is *being*, it's *telerotic*. It has radical *telos*. My beloved whole mate, Barbara Marx Hubbard, loved the word *telerotic*.

It's *telos* and Eros together. It's going somewhere. There is no love without the evolution of love, and the evolution of love is the journey of love itself.

- Love's journey is evolutionary.
- Love's journey is transformational.

If I'm in love, but I'm not being transformed, then I'm using the name *love* in vain, and I've taken the name in vain. Then I'm talking about pseudo-eros, or a pseudo-love, or a separate-self illusion of being.

But when I'm talking about Outrageous Love, about Evolutionary Love, then it has two qualities.

One is, yes, I cuddle into an infinity. There's no place to go, and no place to change, and nothing to move. **But from that place of deep being wells up this urge towards becoming, towards transformation, this urge not just to *merge* in *being*, but to *emerge* into *becoming*.**

Love demands transformation. That's its nature. Love that doesn't transform you isn't love. Love must:

- Rip you apart
- Burn your heart
- Make you face inside and see yourself in the mirror
- Pull you kicking and screaming towards your own deepest transfiguration

Love loves you so insanely much that She wants you to be all that you are. Love is so madly in love with you that She won't settle for anything less than the best version of yourself.

WE HAVE TO FEEL EACH OTHER, ACROSS ANY BOUNDARIES

If love is splitting me from you for superficial reasons—not based on the content of your character, but based on the color of your skin, not based on the depth of your deepest heart's desire, but on a degraded version of discrimination, on a degraded depiction of dogma—if love divides degrades, and discriminates based not on depth, but on that which is superficial— then love is actually *not* love. It's pseudo-love.

It's love that's not real.

It's love that's masquerading.

It's love that has stolen love's crown. It is a pretender to the throne, a usurper. It's anti-love in the guise of love. **True love moves towards transformation, and transformation is the movement of separate parts towards a larger whole. Transformation is the desire for ever deeper contact and ever deeper love.**

I want to go into this so deeply, my friends. It's so deep.

If you are a mad lover in the tradition of Islam, if love moves in you in any way, you *cannot* cross the border on October 7th, and walk into houses, and rape, and pound nails into people as you rape them, and murder them, and butcher them—that's not love. No matter what you call it, it's not love.

Love means I feel you so deeply that I know that we are already part of a prior union. We are part of a larger field, part of a larger fabric of desire.

Love also means that there may be a necessity to respond to something as egregious and as horrible as the October 7 Hamas attack on the kibbutzim in Israel that were filled with people who were peace activists.

If Israel is forced to respond, Israel has to respond wisely. **It's not easy to respond wisely.**

Here is the impossible minimum. I want to feel that with you, and this is impossible. What I'm about to say is impossible.

If I'm looking every day at the faces of Israeli boys that are killed, I also have to look every day at the faces of innocent Palestinian civilians that are also killed, as always happens in war, as a result of bombing. **I cannot make those other faces invisible.**

What is a wise response?

The beginning of a wise response is a response that feels.

You have to feel. You cannot look at a list of your own dead, and not look at the list of the dead on the other side. And when you look at the list of the dead on the other side, you have to look at the list of all of the innocent women, and children, and men who are killed. **If I cut them off, if I cut off *from* them, if I can't *feel* them, then I cannot be on the side of love.**

I know that that's impossible.

Meaning, it's impossible for an ordinary human being to do—if love is separate self, and someone in my family has been brutalized and killed, and babies have been killed and were beheaded on October 7th.

Babies were beheaded. I want you to get what we're talking about. *Babies were beheaded.* What does that even mean? Intentionally! Not the unavoidable tragedy of a bombing in order to target vicious murderers who plant their centers in the middle of the most populated places. We're talking about intentionally taking a baby in your hand and cutting the baby's head off.

How do you respond to that?

Let's get real here.

How do you respond? How do you not become crazed?

You have to become completely crazed, and have your heart ripped out a thousand times—and then you have to have the capacity to feel the baby who is innocent, and who is in a building that maybe needed to be bombed.

Let's start with the bare minimum.

The bare minimum is we have to feel each other.

We have to feel each other. I cannot make the innocent deaths on any side irrelevant.

That's why I'm so insanely proud that, in Israel, there are demonstrations today against the government as it fights a war. As they participate appropriately in the war as necessary to respond to October 7, at the same time people are demonstrating and saying, "Oh my God, we have to feel the pain of the babies, and the pain of the women, and the pain of the men that are killed that are innocent civilians." In Israel today, there are protests, and columns being written against the way the government fights this war.

I want you to feel that it's a big deal.

And I want the same protests to break out in Gaza—the protests that *feel* the Israelis. When in Gaza we break out with protests that feel Israel, just like in Israel we break out with protests that feel Gaza, then something happens.

We have to feel each other.

NO ONE IS OUTSIDE THE CIRCLE

The love that Gibran is describing in 1923 is what we would call Evolutionary Love. It's the love that is the very heart of evolution. It's the evolutionary Eros that drives Cosmos itself. That's what love is.

Love has *integrity*. Integrity means that love *integrates*, that it draws together distinct parts into larger wholes. This is the love that realizes that what unites all human beings at this precise moment in time is far greater than anything that divides us. Love creates a world that works for every human being alive today. Love asks, how will my action or policy affect not only my country or my region, but every human being on the face of the planet? And when love expands, it encompasses not only every human being, but all of life, and the entire substrate that births and sustains life. So, **to stand on the side of love is to know that no human beings are outside the circle**.

But love has not only integrity, but also *evolutionary* integrity. That means that love stands not only for every human being alive *today*, but that **love—in charting its course of action—takes into account every human being alive, *past, present, and future*.** Love asks, how will my actions, my policies, affect all the generations? Love is the strange attractor in the covenant between generations. Evolutionary Love is filled with evolutionary integrity which spans generations. So, to stand on the side of love is to stand on the side of all the generations—which means **to stand on the side of the evolution of consciousness itself.**

I have a practice, and it's a hard practice. Every single day, I look on my phone—I look at who's been killed in Israel, and the names of the boys, and who they are—and then I have another thread, and I look at who are the people who have been killed on the other side, and I try and find as many of the names as I can, to see their faces, to look into their eyes.

No one is outside the circle.

That's the beginning.

Start small, my friends, but small is so big. Can you feel what I'm saying?

I have to transform myself.

Love moves towards transformation, and transformation means that even when I'm ripped apart and in pain, and even when I need to take fierce action, I don't demonize and dehumanize the other. **I can see the face of the enemy, and I can see the face of innocent civilians, and I feel them.**

Their body is my body, and their heart is my heart, and their breath is my breath.

We are one breath, we're one love, we're one heart, and we live in the same Field of ErosDesire. All of us stand together on the side of love.

- We refuse to demonize each other.
- We refuse to make the other "other," even when we're in the midst of a war.
- We plant the seeds of love, and we let love rip our hearts apart and demand that we hold paradox, that we don't make easy walls, and that we don't make easy discriminations.

That's the first transformation. Love has to transform me.

And for love to transform me, I need to become a human being.

To become a human being means:

- I can feel you even when you're not my family.
- I can feel you even when you're not of my tribe.
- I can feel you and your pain even when your people have stood against me and hurt me brutally.

When you are innocent and hurt brutally, whatever I feel of what the necessities of war were or weren't, I begin with *I feel you.* I feel you.

I *refuse* not to feel you. And even if you can't feel me, I'm going to feel you. That's just the minimum.

This is not about policy. It's not what Israel should or shouldn't do. **I refuse not to feel you.**

And I know that your life is a holy and broken *Hallelujah.*

And I know that there's a blaze of light in every word, it doesn't matter what you heard.

It's all the holy and the broken *Hallelujah.*

PRACTICE: I BRACKET MYSELF, AND I CROSS OVER TO THE OTHER SIDE

We start by feeling each other. Feeling each other, it's for real. **It is an actual practice: I bracket myself, I take myself out. I feel you.**

It's a very deep practice.

I bracket myself, I look at you, but I don't love you as a shiny object. I don't love you as an erotic object, even though it's beautiful to love a person as an erotic object. Erotic objectification is a sacred process when it's done in the context of sensitivity and holiness. There is deep literature on our desire to be beautiful to the other. We want to be erotic objects for each other.

That's beautiful, but I am talking about a different level of love.

This different level of love is: I actually bracket myself.

I bracket myself, and I cross over to the other side. When I cross over to the other side, I feel you.

That's what it means to cross over to the other side. *The Crossing* is: I have the capacity to bracket myself, to cross over to the other side, and to feel you in your depth.

I don't exist now—I just feel *you*. I am *actually* feeling you. I'm effaced. I don't exist. I just feel you. That's what it means to be a great lover—**for a moment, I disappear, and I just feel you.**

That's the Christ quality.

It's the God quality.

It's the great lover quality.

And that's The Crossing. I have the ability, for a moment, to set myself aside and be completely in devotion to feeling you. And then I come back—and when I come back after setting myself aside, I realize that we've both *always* been on the same side.

When I set myself aside, and I turn to you, and I cross over to your side and I feel you:

- With my full heart
- With my full body
- With all my nerve endings
- With all of my existential sensitivity
- With the simplicity of the raw naked soul that's me when I feel you

When I open my eyes again and reappear, I realize we've always been on the same side. **We've never *not* been on the same side.**

That's the practice of love. That's the transformation. That's The Crossing.

Paradoxically, when you cross over to the other side, you don't lose yourself.

People are afraid, *if I cross over to the other side, if I become a saint, I'll lose myself.*

You don't lose yourself.

Actually, we need to democratize being a saint. The saints are filled with joy, *Ashrei Yoshvei Veitecha*, mad joy, sitting in the God house.

When I cross over and feel you so radically, it's not that I disappear—it's that when I come back, when I reappear, I am more *me*, more present, more full, and I am less lonely and isolated than I've ever been.

- I'm with you in the field.
- We are together in the field.

Most people never even really get to do that with one beloved. We love our beloved as a shiny object. To love my beloved means *I feel you, I cross over, and I feel your side*. I know I feel you. And then I realize, "Oh my God, there's only one side. It's the side of love."

That's the transformation. That's what we've been heading towards. That's what this whole conversation has been about today.

BEING ON THE SIDE OF LOVE DOESN'T MEAN MORAL EQUIVALENCE

Here is where we start. Here is where we cross over to the side of love. There's only one side, the side of love. It's this mad commitment to cross over from my side to yours, and to feel you.

Even if I'm devastated, even if I've seen the worst horrors that could be seen, I still can cross over and feel the suffering of the innocent. The innocent cannot remain a metaphor or a generalization. **I've got to be willing to look in the faces of the other and feel them. Every baby, every woman, every man.**

I am so proud of the people who, in this moment of intense pain and agony, in the pluralistic democracy in the Middle East called Israel, are protesting and saying, "We have to feel the pain of women and children in Gaza." I want demonstrations to also break out all over Gaza and all over the Arab world that would say, "Oh my God, we have to feel the pain of the brutality that happened in Israel."

Being on the side of love doesn't make a moral equivalence. We're not making a moral equivalence. We're going so much deeper.

Part of what we do on the side of love is we battle against evil. That's part of what love requires. In some sense, although he didn't name it—he didn't take it into evolution or politics but kept it in the personal realm—that's exactly the point that Gibran was intuitively making.

In other words, there is a *fierceness* to love, and that we're all on the side of love means:

- Step one: There's a battle against evil.
- Step two: Can I then find the spark of the sacred in evil, and transform it into light?

There are two steps, and everyone wants to skip steps.

Step one is: There is light and darkness. It's actually true. There is a battle between good and evil in the world, unquestionably. And step two is: Greater is the light that comes from the darkness. But it's hard.

Even in jihad, there's a spark of the sacred, and I need to battle against Hamas.

The minimal way I can hold this polarity is to hold the other side and feel their pain, even as I do battle, which is impossibly hard. I mean, can you imagine if someone came in and ripped and cut our babies' heads off—which is what happened to Israeli children.

Nevertheless, there are still protests in Israel today for innocent people being killed in Gaza, even though it's a byproduct of the very structure of collateral damage in war, and it's exponentially increased by Hamas placing its terror centers in schools and hospitals. I'm so proud of Israel for protesting anyway. I am so proud. It's so impossible. And they are protesting anyway.

And I am desperate to hear of protests in Gaza, by Gazans, against the brutality of Hamas. That is impossible, you might say, because Hamas will kill the protesters. But to be on the side of love we have to at least notice that distinction.

But I would be delighted as well—and so proud of the people—to hear of protests exploding around the Islamic world, in western countries against the deliberate beheading of babies, against the raping of women as they are being mutilated and then murdered afterwards.

I long to hear about those protests. And when we can hear those protests, then we will all be standing together on the side of love.

And that is a great beginning.

That is the beginning of the true road to peace.

CHAPTER TWENTY-ONE

SALLY KEMPTON MEMORIAL: THE ONLY SANITY IS TO LOVE INSANELY

Episode 406 — July 21, 2024

EULOGY IS LIBERATION FROM LONELINESS

Can you believe, my friends, that it's been a year since Sally Kempton died?

We are here to have a memorial service for Sally. (The words *Sally* and *memorial service* don't go together well. Sally is alive.)

What is the nature of a memorial service? It's to recover memory. We want to recover the memory of the past—not in a mechanical way, but in the sense of history—*his* story, *her* story. We want to capture something of her story.

The job of memorial is eulogy. The job of the eulogist is not to whitewash, not to paint in pretty costumes, not to parade the soul of the one who has passed in politically correct forms.

The job of the eulogist is to liberate the person who has passed, the beloved, from loneliness.

The job of the eulogist is to ask forgiveness. We ask forgiveness for not having recognized you when you were here.

There is a beautiful text in Jeremiah, which points to this truth: *me'rahoq Adonai nir'ah li*, "God has appeared to me from afar," from a distance. That is to say, when She is right in front of me, I can't see Her. It's only when She is far away that we begin to see Her. When She is right in front of me, then we exchange words, and it's sweet, and it's good, but we don't quite see Her. And now, we would give everything to be able to exchange words one more time, to speak together one more time, to feel our Sally one more time.

We just had the board conclave. Sally participated in every single board conclave we did since 2009. She was one of the co-founders of the Center in its originating vision as the Center for World Spirituality, and she was with us as we became the Center for Integral Wisdom (because we wanted to incorporate *wisdom* in the title). We gradually evolved into the Center for World Philosophy and Religion, but it's the same vision—**articulating a world religion as a context for our diversity**.

Sally was a profoundly religious person even as she was of this world entirely, and even as she wanted desperately to transcend the world and to merge ecstatically into the utter delight and erotic truth of Reality. Sally's password was *blissfreak*. That was her password to that which was most important, whether it was the internet at her house, or her computer. Sally was interested in bliss.

We want to recover our memory of Sally. Sally, we want to turn to you today, not as your students, because our relationship—yours and mine—was of the most beloved and dear friends, a brother and sister in the *dharma*, beloved whole mates in the *dharma*, if you will (although that wasn't a term we used)—deep, profound, on the Inside of the Inside, *hadi ona ha-pnimi she-b'fnim*, *peti*, my beloved sister.

I turn to you, Sally, as beloved—beloved visioning partner, beloved study partner—the many and beautiful meanings of beloved, and we should all be beloved to each other.

I turn to you as a friend, as a dear and wondrous friend.

We turn to you here, not as your student community, but as the spiritual community of the Center—the think tank with a vision of changing the source code of culture—One Mountain, Many Paths, the Great Library, the mystery schools, standing in this time between worlds and time between stories.

You have a very important student community that your books, and your writings, and your meditations speak to, and I'm sure they did some form of memorial, which is beautiful. We are bowing to that world, recognizing the beauty of the thousands of students you have around the world.

That's not what this conversation is about. This is about our friend Sally, who was part of the very fabric of the Center. She was, in some sense, part of the space in which the Center arose. All of us know it.

Sally was our friend—and we are turning to you, Sally, to liberate you from loneliness, to recognize you, to share you. We are coming to liberate something of your essence from loneliness, and to liberate something of your teaching from loneliness, to share some dimension of you that is radical, and potent, and needed, and gorgeous. This is so wildly important, because Sally was the ground of so much that was revealed and disclosed, and so much that was in the holy, esoteric places that were the very weave of the fabric, the air, the oxygen, the breath that we all breathed together in this mystical society, in this revolution, in this think tank, as this band of Outrageous Lovers.

I would like to do this in two stages.

First, I want to share with everyone a video that Chahatie made about Sally, which we played last year at the memorial. And then I want to do a short eulogy, but in the eulogy, I am not going to use my words. I am going to use Sally's words.

I am going to pick one dimension of Sally's teaching, the teaching of Krishna and Radha. The great Krishna and Radha teaching first takes root

313

in the early Vedas of Hinduism, and then around the 1300s becomes far more prominent, at the exact same time that *The Zohar* emerges in Hebrew wisdom. The teaching flowers for over 300 years, and then really explodes in the sixteenth century, much like *The Zohar* in the Hebrew wisdom side of things explodes in the teachings of Luria.

It's a teaching about Eros. It's a teaching about what it means to be a lover—not in the narrow sense, but in what I would call the *Outrageous Love* sense. I was often at Sally's house when these chapters were written, in a series of essays called *Awakening Shakti*, and we went back and forth on these essays. Many of our conversations will be clear in the writing.

I would like to liberate from loneliness a dimension of her teaching that's not quite fully grasped or understood; a teaching that lived in the space between us, but moves through Sally's writing, in her own unique structures. Sally and I engaged this teaching for five years at Esalen, where we taught five years in a row. My entire eulogy today will be Sally's words; to weave together her teaching—to transmit it, but also to share Sally, to share this dimension, this glimpse into what moved her heart, and what was this being named *Sally-ness*.

Hi, Sally. I apologize if I'm not getting this exactly right. I'm doing my best, and we miss you, all of us, we miss you insanely. You were—you *are*—beyond precious. About two weeks ago, they sprinkled your ashes. I don't even know what that means that you have ashes. I can see you in front of me.

Can you feel her?

Can you feel this just utter delight in being alive?

That's bliss freak. Just feel the joy—the utter joy, the moment of bliss.

We are going to feel something of Sally's life, and then we're going to go into Sally's words. The fabric of the feminine teacher, of a feminine power. The feminine quality of *Shakti*—of Radical Aliveness—is in Kashmir Shaivism, Sally's root tradition.

- ◆ *Shiva* is pure consciousness; the masculine, or the line quality.
- ◆ *Shakti* is energy, but it's also power.

Pure consciousness and power—Shiva and *Shakti*, the line and the circle—meet, and then they become something new. **The line and the circle become the spiral.** Something new emerges. There is a *hieros gamos*, there is a new emergent.

Sally was very much the power of bliss merged with a profound consciousness. Sally meditated generally several hours a day, deep on the Inside of the Inside, for forty years.

V'eynaynu et merachoq: "let our eyes see our beloveds." We are here in this brother-sister place just filled with that joy.

We can be Outrageous Lovers—we can love each other outrageously—beyond the classical structures. We get to love each other madly.

- ◆ Our love lists are too short.
- ◆ Let's love each other madly.
- ◆ Let's love each other outrageously.
- ◆ Let's love each other in this holiest way.

It's all rooted. It's all held by the love of Krishna and Radha.

Let's take a look at this clip, this beautiful clip that Chahatie prepared about Sally.

ALL OF REALITY IS GREAT SEDUCTION

I introduced Sally to one of my dearest friends, Fred Jealous, and they had wonderful, nuanced conversations about politics, and subtlety, and art, and human nature, and psychology. Sally knew all the kings and queens of England, and all of the subtle political plays. Fred knew Sally's nuance, her depth, and many people did. She could talk to you about the currency fluctuations in China, and how they would affect American politics, et cetera, et cetera.

But at her very core, Sally was what I would call an erotic mystic. She was a mad lover of Reality. It was hard-won; it wasn't cheap grace. It wasn't, as she said in the story, in the film, "oh, haven't you ever taken acid before?" And Sally said, "No, no, but it wasn't acid, I actually realized that love (or what we would call *Eros*) was the true nature of Reality." She says, I was to be a novelist of pain, but how can I be a novelist of pain when I realized the truth is ecstasy? And it was a long, hard-won path.

In the Dick Cavett clip where Sally and Susan Brownmiller are debating Hugh Hefner, the founder of *Playboy*—one of the epic moments of second wave feminism in 1972—Sally says we shouldn't have seduction in the world. There should be no necessity for seduction in the world. She says, the good thing we can say about Helen Gurley Brown is that she legitimized women not getting married into their 40s, into their 50s. And, of course, other than a short marriage, Sally lived most of her life alone.

Sally chose that path, but it wasn't a loveless path. It was a path in which the love of any one single person, as beautiful as that was and needed to be, wasn't enough. Sally shifted to a place in which she realized that **the problem with the seducing in the world was not that there should be a world without seduction, but that seduction had become too limited**. It had lost its radiance, it had lost its beauty. Seduction became unholy seduction, meaning: the world is really materialist, and seduction is basically a form of manipulation, where I get someone to break their appropriate boundary for the sake of my greed.

That's the exile of seduction.

But what Sally was going to come to realize—that's her very core, and at the very heart of her teaching—is that **all of Reality is a great seduction**. All of Reality is a great seduction, but it's a *holy* seduction, where people are invited—where *She* invites us—to break the boundary of our contraction for the sake of our own deepest need.

Our own deepest need is the experience of radical aliveness, the experience of radical loving. Not just self-love, although self-love is critical. But self-love exists in this larger matrix of a world whose *insides are lined with love,* in the language of Solomon. It's all about seduction. We are always seducing each other. We are always falling in love with each other.

There is a chapter about it in one of her books, but it was the essence of her teaching that she almost never talked about. She usually talked about the divine Mother. But there was another teaching, and it's that teaching I want to share with you, and I want to share it in Sally's words. It is the teaching of holy seduction, the teaching of becoming insane with love. **The teaching of love that's not held by the conventional categories of loving, but actually points to a deeper truth and a deeper Reality.**

I want to just introduce one principle of tantra, and then I want to look at Sally's texts.

A principle of tantra is the principle of non-rejection.

Tantra is non-rejection. Tantra is a particular path. It's a path that exists as deep in Hinduism, but there is also a Kabbalistic Tantra, there is also a kind of Christian Tantra, there is a Buddhist Tantra. What all of the tantric traditions share in common is: *tantra* means to expand, *tantra* means to liberate. The word *tan* means to expand, *tra* means to liberate. *Tantra* also means *to weave.* I am expanding, taking God out of the temple, out of the conventional. I am taking God and Goddess out of the conventional—out of the temple, out of the appropriate, out of the politically correct, so that I can actually experience liberation.

Liberation is when I can actually trust myself, I can trust my body, I can trust my desire, I can trust my passion. **I know that this desire is expressing— when I clarify it—the deepest truth that emerges.** I clarify my desire, I clarify my passion—not my politically correct desire and passion, but my lovesickness. I am sick with love. The great *Vidagdhamadhava* says, "Who could cease to tell of that quintessence of erotic mood, save one speechless utterly with ecstasy."

That's the verse that Sally decided to translate, and it's about Radha.

RADHA'S ENERGY

So, from now on, it's going to be Sally doing most of the talking:

> Have you ever been so wildly in love that you could think of nothing but your lover? Has your heart ever ached with longing for another person, or even for an unknown beloved? Has separation from your lover felt like being torn apart from your own soul? Have you felt ecstatic with your lover's arms around you, in despair when she doesn't call for a day? Has your lover sometimes appeared so numinously beautiful—even when he leaves his towel on the bathroom floor—that you felt an almost worshipful adoration for him? Have you ever had passionate feelings for the divine or for the unknown beloved who can, perhaps, only meet you in your soul?
>
> Then you know what it is to love like Radha.
>
> Radha is the goddess of lovers and desperate romantics. The beloved mistress of the youthful god Krishna, Radha's passionate, erotic drama is one of the world's great myths of love and separation.

Radha is the beloved mistress of the youthful God, Krishna. Radha's passionate erotic drama is at the core of divine worship. The Radha energy is present whenever there is a passionate love and the wish to become one with the beloved. Sometimes she manifests—you get glimmerings of Radha—(and again, this is all Sally talking) in a teenager's romantic fantasies, or in the delicious experience of erotic truth and delight (which we're told by psychologists should be pathologized), when you actually want to be just simply immersed in a beloved other. And she might show up as a reckless compulsion, which sometimes you should follow and sometimes you shouldn't, to follow your erotic impulse in its clarified truth.

I'm not talking about being irresponsible in the superficial sense. The word that I added here is *clarified*—when you clarify and you identify your erotic impulse and you follow it, despite, as Sally says, "all reason and practicality."

Radha is a divine force. She's deeper than any of these human stirrings, but these human strings *point* to this divine force.

> As a divine archetype, however, Radha's *Shakti* goes far deeper than the human impulse toward romantic passion. Tuning into the Radha *Shakti* can uncover the burning heart of universal Eros—the radically impersonal life-force energy that creates life's sweetness—within your desire for a human lover.

Radha uncovers the burning heart of universal Eros, the radical life-force energy that creates life's sweetness that lives as the inside of your desire for a human lover. The desire for a human lover is an incarnation of this deeper erotic yearning.

> When Radha's energy awakens within you, she can transform a mild interest in inner practice into a wildly personal love affair with the inner beloved. She is one of the secret *Shaktis* who transmutes ordinary desire into longing and passion into fuel for the spiritual journey.

This is the Radha energy. Teresa of Ávila held it, and St. John of the Cross, and Therese of Lisieux, and Mirabai, and all the Sufi mystics, and Shimon bar Yochai. The Radha energy is imprinted in our heart and in our soul.

THE STORY OF KRISHNA AND RADHA

> In the original stories of Krishna's early life, Radha appears only as a nameless cowherd girl, one of the group of the young God Krishna's teenage companions and lovers known as the *gopis* (the cowgirls).

319

She only emerges as a full-fledged Goddess in the thirteenth century.

Let's talk a little bit about the story of Radha, who is in love with Krishna. **The key insight is that any human emotion, if you follow it to its root, is turned in an expression of the mad love for the Divine.** The way I would say it would be something like: whenever you are on your knees in mad love, you are always on your knees before She. This is one of Sally's favorite ways of expressing this.

Radha and Krishna's lives imply a radical possibility that **any human being can be approached as a form of the Divine and can be loved with mad devotion.** We bring it into our relationship. I can have a Krishna-Radha relationship with a teacher. I can have a Krishna-Radha relationship with myself. I can have a Krishna-Radha relationship with a very close friend in which there is nothing that can't be spoken. It's not like: Oh, this is appropriate to speak, this is not—no, we speak everything. We whisper sweet nothings into each other's ears. We are passionately in love, and we are madly in love.

Love mad!

Anyone who's been drawn to this circle of Outrageous Lovers, this think tank that we are, knows what we mean when we say, *let's love madly*. KK and I started using the word, *love mad*, when we wrote Outrageous Love Letters, and Sally was ecstatic, because, she said, Outrageous Love Letters, that's the energy of Radha.

If you don't love madly someone other than yourself, you're not a mad lover. You'll be lost and wallowing in your own experience, and how you were hurt, and how you were offended, and how you are feeling. All you can think about is how you feel, because you've got no place to put it.

This is a very subtle moment. I can't even put words to it. It's very deep. This is who we are. Let's love madly, unreasonably. Give to each other madly, unreasonably. Stand for each other madly, unreasonably.

Truth is, it's the only way to be at home in the universe. **If we don't love in that way, we are not at home. Everything else is boring and uninteresting, because God loves madly.** That's the point. God wouldn't manifest reality without mad love. God loves insanely, madly. God is madly loving, desiring to be in us. That's the nature of reality.

> Chandidas, a poet who practiced the most radical form of *bhakti*, wrote exquisite devotional verses to a teenage prostitute whom he worshipped as the Goddess. He described his Tantric approach to communing with the divine through human love as "the natural (*sahaja*) path." Ramakrishna taught a more conventional version of this principle of natural devotion. He once asked a woman devotee who complained that she couldn't feel love for God, "Who do you love?" When she told him that she adored her baby nephew, Ramakrishna said, "Love him as Krishna."

In other words, love Krishna in whatever way comes naturally—as a child, a youth, a friend, or a teacher. Any form of radical love of this devotional, wild, ecstatic, erotic nature, can trigger the flow of bliss, which, if you cultivate the flow, will melt you into the highest form of realization, of *blissfuck* realization. It's the realization of the *blissfuck* of Reality, the bliss-Eros of Reality.

It's what Meister Eckhart means when he says, *Reality is kissing in every moment.* It's the Eros that animates everything, all the way up and all the way down. I am mixing my words with Sally. This was the path. This is Sally speaking of the erotic romantic lover, the path that's called, *parakriya bhakti.*

> Like the troubadours of medieval Europe, the bhakti writers believed that the obsession a woman feels for her paramour can transform the heart in a way that no ordinary, respectable love can ever do. It's the greatest form of love, they argued, both because it's dangerous and because it can never be taken for granted. Love outside of marriage, especially in those premodern days, could ruin your life. Your love could be discovered,

and you could be ostracized for it—or, in a traditional society, killed. At the very least, you risked heartbreak at the hands of a lover who had no legal obligation to go on loving you. To direct such love toward the divine was to court ego dissolution and risk your life (as happened to the poet-queen Mirabai). It also opened you to the highest form of sweetness. Real love risks everything.

Sally's voice continues:

> Radha is a young woman, growing up in the cowherd village of Vraja. Her lover, Krishna, had been sent there as a baby to escape death at the hands of his uncle, who had sworn to kill him. So Krishna was raised among the village children. He and Radha are childhood playmates, but as they grow, Radha falls helplessly in love with Krishna.

According to Indian myth, Krishna is the masculine incarnation of the Divine's irresistible beauty, allure, and love. **Krishna embodies the power of Divine Allurement, the radical bliss that turns a lover's heart towards mystical union.**

Krishna is distracting to the point of addiction. The Krishna energy is a cosmic intoxicant, which draws your attention away from your work, your duties, your very survival. This is the energy of Krishna.

> In later life, Krishna would become a king, a statesman, and a world teacher. But at this stage, when he is just past childhood, he is simply, cosmically adorable.

He's pure divine allure. Everyone in the town of Vraja adores Krishna. Everyone has a unique relationship with Krishna. Krishna is this energy of allurement, and everyone loves Krishna. Everyone loves Krishna, his mother, and the older woman of the village, they love him as a son, and they dote on his baby mischief.

> The cowherd boys love him as a friend and as a ringleader. Their sisters, the cowherd girls, the gopis are erotically and intensely in love with him.

> In another situation, this would be scandalous. But

because everyone in the village of Vraja is part of a mythic conspiracy to adore this incarnate deity, the conventional rules don't apply. One of Krishna's incarnational tasks, in fact, is to exemplify the secret truth that true devotion to God allows you to bypass normal social and religious boundaries.

The town of Vraja is a band of Outrageous Lovers. The conventional rules don't apply.

I just want to be clear, the energy of Krishna can live in both man and woman. Krishna and Radha live in each one of us. Krishna and Radha, the line and circle that are the *hieros gamos* that create the spiral that spirals all galaxies, the love that moves the Sun and other stars, lives in each one of us. We each of us have the capacity to be Krishna and to be Radha. But Krishna represents the mad distraction of insane love that fills me, and at the root of that insanity, writes Sally, is the ultimate sanity, the ultimate realization, the ultimate knowing.

> So, in the magical world of Vraja, Krishna's lovers spend their days in ecstasy. Their god is no invisible figure to be reached in prayer, but a living, breathing person. He is audacious, sweet, mischievous—and he also happens to be invincible. (All through his childhood, Krishna keeps casually disposing of the demons sent by his wicked uncle to assassinate him.) In paintings of Krishna, you see him playing his flute for the long-horned cows, surrounded by boys. You see him dancing with the cowherd girls. And you see him with one particular girl, the two of them entwined, embracing, gazing into each other's eyes.
>
> That is Radha. Radha stands out among this village of Krishna lovers because she is his feminine counterpart— his *Shakti*—and because she loves Krishna to the point of losing all self-consciousness.

See, when it comes to loving the Divine, the devotional traditions tell us that the conventional affection isn't enough. You need a radical pathway into the deep heart of Reality, which comes only from wild, erotic love, in which I become literally lovesick, so that I am healed and whole. **It's only through becoming lovesick that I become healed.**

That's the story of Krishna and Radha.

RADHA'S WOUND

Chandidas, the poet who we cited earlier, has Radha saying:

> And now I know
> That love adheres wholly
> To its own laws.

And:

> I took no thought for what would be said of me.
> I abandoned everything.

"He takes my clothes away," the Bengali poet writes. "I lose my body at his touch." Sally writes:

> But Radha's passionate attachment to Krishna contains its own wound, which is as much a part of her love as the ecstasy. She cannot ever hold Krishna, who will never be tied down to one lover.

Krishna will never be tied down to one lover. He loves Radha, but he loves all the cowgirls. Krishna incarnates the personal face of God, and God is polyamorous. **God loves every nation and every person. That's the Divine nature.**

The Divine is connected inside and out to every heart. The Krishna being is to share love, and never to confine it just to one person.

> With Krishna, opportunities for heartbreak and jealousy are endless. When he's with her, Radha is lost in bliss. When he's away, she wants to throw herself in the river. Radha lives in the midst of an emotional earthquake. Her state is the very reverse of yogic equanimity, but it affects everyone who meets her with a similar ecstasy.

The most famous of the erotic Krishna stories begins when the cowherd girls beg Krishna to dance with them in the forest at night. Smiling his mischievous smile, Krishna tells them, "Yes, we'll dance when the moon is right. But when you hear the sound of my flute, you have to drop everything and come. Whatever you're doing—feeding your child, cooking, serving dinner to your husband—you must come!" He's voicing the ultimate demand that the divine makes of a devotional lover. Call yourself a lover? Then prove it. Don't make love something that you save for your leisure time. Go for it. Throw yourself away for the sake of love!

One August night, as the moon rises over the river, the *gopis* hear the notes of Krishna's flute lilting through the trees around the village. True to their promise, they put down their babies. They leave their cooking untended on the fire. Half-dressed, they run to the woods where he waits in a clearing by the river.

There, they begin to dance together. The dance is known in Indian myth as the *raslila*, or flavorful game, the sport of delight. One of the most famous images in Indian art shows Krishna dancing in the midst of the circle of young women. He plays his flute, the women sway and bend, so lost in ecstasy that their clothes are falling off their bodies. In another image, Krishna has multiplied himself so that each of the girls has Krishna in her arms. God belongs to everyone who loves Him as long as you don't hold back. He won't hold back Himself.

And yet, Krishna cannot resist Radha. At one point in the evening he disappears from the circle and when the *gopis* look for him, they find him embracing Radha, the two of them lying in a bed of flowers by the river. Radha's love for Krishna kindles his love for her, and it gives her as much power over him as he has over her. And Radha knows it. Sometimes, disgusted by his infidelity, she will refuse to speak to him. Then Krishna follows her, begging her to relent and embrace him. He demands her full attention. She weeps because she can never have his.

Can you feel that?

THE BLISS OF THE PAIN OF SEPARATION

Krishna and Radha never marry, their time together is heightened by its shortness, tumbled hair, entwined limbs, long kisses, passion, arguments, passionate reconciliation. In the end, Krishna always leaves Radha. And yet, Krishna always comes back, and he never forgets. Radha is a peasant girl married to another man. She stays behind, and yet, as the chariot carries him away, Krishna looks back longingly at Radha.

> Radha, for her part, goes mad with grief. Krishna, too, is devastated. The *bhakti* poets describe how—at least for a while—he sees her everywhere he goes. "How is it," he asks, "that for me, the three worlds have become Radha?"

> Radha never forgets. For the rest of her life she spends her days meditating on Krishna. But in her obsession and grief at being separated from her beloved, something amazing happens. She begins to see Krishna everywhere.

The whole world becomes her beloved, even as she loves Krishna himself most personally.

> Every leaf in the forest, the cows, the household butter churn, everything becomes for her, the form of Krishna. In the Indian devotional tradition, her state is called "the bliss of the pain of separation" and it is considered one of the highest of all spiritual experiences. When Radha weeps for Krishna, her tears wash away all veils from the heart and everything becomes the form of her beloved.

> One day, Krishna, who never stops thinking about the people who love him, calls his friend Uddhava and asks him to go to Vraja and see how everyone is doing. "Especially," he asks Uddhava, "find out how Radha is. She above all others holds my heart."

> When Uddhava gets to the village, he is shocked to find Radha and her friends walking around like crazy women. They are beautifully adorned, it is true. They are taking care of themselves physically. But it turns out that they are doing all this because they live in a fantasy. They walk around caressing the trees, embracing the cows,

saying, "Krishna! Krishna!" When they walk from house to house to sell their milk and butter, they call out "Buy Krishna! Buy Gopala!"

Uddhava is a great yogi, a master of asana and meditation. He cannot believe his eyes. "These women have gone insane," he reasons. "I have to do something for them."

So he calls the cowgirl maidens together and gives them a lecture on yoga. "Krishna loves you all," he says, in the tone that reasonable people use when talking to children. "He sent me to comfort you. Now, you should take that great love you have and turn it inside. Sit for meditation. Close your eyes and imagine Krishna in the heart. Do some breath control. Try to still those wandering minds!"

And Radha and the girls look at Uddhava indulgently because they see he doesn't understand.

"Oh, Uddhava," says Radha, "you just don't get it! Why should we close our eyes when Krishna is all we see? You might have to close your eyes and meditate in order to find God in your dry heart. But we see him with our eyes wide open. Everywhere we look, we see Krishna."

Can you feel that, my friend? It's the path of the wound. **But all wounds become the wounds of love.** That's the way I would summarize this whole teaching.

THE PATH OF OUTRAGEOUS LOVE

Some of you might notice that the path of the Outrageous Lover is the path of Krishna and Radha. It's not reasonable, it's outrageous, it's an unreasonable path. John of the Cross felt and understood this path. He writes,

Oh, living flame of love that tenderly wounds my soul in its deepest center!

Oh, delightful wound, oh gentle hand, oh delicate touch that tastes of eternal life and pays every debt, in killing you change death to life!

The path of Krishna and Radha.

Feel the insanity of it all. It's what we need when we talk of mad love. There is a reason why in our community, we look at each other and we say, *I love you madly*. It's Outrageous Love, because we're talking about the path of Krishna and Radha. It's the liberation of insanity. It's the holy spark at the center of insanity.

Do you think that we can address the meta-crisis from a dry and desiccated sanity, which dissects the world into materialist forms of causation?

No, **we can only address the meta-crisis as a waiting lover, feeling the pulsing, throb and tumescence of Reality, and feel Her own urgencies in the Fields of Value that animate Her, and find our way into the very impulse of Reality itself, identify Her plotlines, and tell Her true story, and let that New Story of Value be the strange attractor, which begins to allow us to find a way home.** That's what Ficino did in the Florentine Platonic Academy in the Renaissance, in that time between worlds and time between stories.

We can only do it as Krishna and Radha.

We can only do it when we actually realize that we live in a CosmoErotic Universe.

Not as a mythopoetic statement. Krishna and Radha is the very fabric of Reality itself. It's the heart of existence itself.

It's what we always mean when we say, citing the Bengali mystics of Krishna-Radha:

Love is not mere human sentiment.
Love is not merely a social construction.
Love is the heart of existence itself.

It's radical. *Radical* means it goes to the root.

Of course, in the deepest place, **the radical and the responsible live together,** because there is nothing more responsible and more responsive to Reality. It capacitates us to respond to the deepest yearnings of our own holy self, to claim the only true sanity which lives in the depths of insane love.

Insane love is the only true sanity.

We love each other insanely in that unique way that Krishna loves Radha, in those unique personal bonds that are intimate, and irreplaceable, and irreducible, that live only between two people. And yet, that Outrageous Love that lives between two people must participate in the Field of Outrageous Love, and then we have to fall in love outrageously, each time in the most right way.

Every Outrageous Love has its own parameters, its own invitation, its own plotline.

Sometimes we fall in love outrageously with animals. And sometimes we fall in love outrageously with a tree. And sometimes we fall in love outrageously with a friend, a true friend, even if we haven't talked to them for a long time.

We love each other outrageously.

We break convention, but not to become pre-conventional. It's not a surface abandonment of responsibility. It's not an abandonment of goodness or of integrity. It's the ultimate integrity. It's the highest integrity. There is room for everyone in the circle of Outrageous Love.

Our love lists are too short.

We are not going to save our world through mere analysis, although analysis is necessary. **We are going to save our world by being outrageously in love with our world.**

We are going to save the environment by being outrageously in love with the rivers, with the trees, with every species.

329

And ultimately, we are going to save our world by being outrageously in love with each other. We turn the entire world into the Field of Krishna and Radha.

Now, friends, does everyone understand why Sally was so much at the core and fabric of the Center, and how her own Krishna and Radha teaching was the very core of her being, was the very core of her aliveness. She was madly in love with a new outfit and with new upholstery, and madly in love with the sacred texts. Madly in love. That's where she lived.

She went from appearing on *The Dick Cavett Show*, where she said there is no place for seduction in the world, to realizing that she was rejecting unholy seduction, that the only way is the way of holy seduction.

- We seduce our split-off selves into romantic union with ourselves.
- We seduce each other into the holy union of radical responsibility and radical bliss, where we feel each other and we live alive.

And as we live that, we pour it back into you, Sally. We pour it back into you, and tears were streaming down my cheeks at the very end of the film about you.

Thank you, Sally Kempton, for walking among us. We need your help.

We need your blissfreak.

We need your wisdom.

We need your laughter.

We need your joy, and we need your willingness to wrestle with loneliness, to wrestle with the traumas, to wrestle with the demons, because you wrestled with the demons even into the last years, especially in the last four or five years. You wrestled with the demons, and you always came out on the side of love.

POSTSCRIPT: FROM PRE-TRAGIC TO POST-TRAGIC SEDUCTION

As the day ended yesterday, which was a very heart-rending, heart-opening, and beautiful day, when we did the first Sally Kempton memorial Dharma talk, Kristina and I wanted to do something to feel Sally and her era, her life journey, the transformations that it went through.

We decided to find a movie from that era, from the 1960s. It a biopic from Australia, 2019, about Helen Reddy, who sang the "I Am Woman" song.

I recommend the biopic just because the actress who plays Helen is phenomenal. And you just feel, as Helen Reddy finds that space of *I Am Woman*, and sings the song and brings it into culture. I just broke down crying. I've always been privileged to be in devotion, in devotion to She, in devotion to the Goddess. That was Sally's time. They were in New York at the same time. They were part of the same circle. It was part of the same unimaginable emergence of the feminine, what Luria calls *Aliyat HaNukva*, or "the ascent of the feminine."

Since then, I have gone through many stages of thinking and holding and feeling into what that ascent means. Of course, the feminine lives in the embodied She, but it also lives in all of us. The circle quality—the feminine quality, the *Shakti* quality—lives in the body of a woman in a particular way, but it also lives in the body of a man. We are all line and circle, *Shiva* and *Shakti*, or *Shekinah* and *Kudsha Berich Hu* in the language of the tree of life of Kabbalah.

I was feeling into "I Am Woman" in a haze of tears, at the ways in which we've lost the feminine, the ways in which the feminine has been hurt, degraded, and defaced over thousands of years, and the ways that she's been honored and held. I was thinking particularly about Sally's journey, so I wanted just to add a thought.

If you notice, when Dick Cavett asks Sally, "Can I light your cigarette?" and she says no, and they have this funny exchange. And then, Sally says in a very, very serious way, *I want to live in a world where there is no necessity for seduction. There is no need for seducing.*

That was the beginning. The more subtle play between men and women, the autonomy and the allurement, the surrender and the individuation—that play hadn't been well articulated. The funny line in that interview is when Susan Brownmiller says, *You have conversations with very, very smart and powerful women.*

And Cavett says, *That's just because I like to be dominated.*

The whole place erupts in laughter because he is pointing to this subtle play in the space between men and women that hasn't been articulated clearly. And then we did a eulogy, in Sally's words, on the teaching of Krishna and Radha.

We noticed yesterday that the Krishna and Radha teaching is all about seduction being a fundamental quality of Cosmos, the experience of being so deeply in love that all I want is to have my beloved cross the boundary of her contraction and open to me. Of course, we distinguished between what we call *unholy seduction* and *holy seduction*. When I attempt to seduce the beloved in order to break their appropriate boundary, for the sake of my greed, that's unholy seduction. That's what Sally was talking about in the Dick Cavett Show.

But then, as she went deep into the world of profound study with a profound teacher in a deep lineage of Kashmir Shaivism, she began to realize (and I'll use my language) that **we have exiled seduction to its unholy form**, and we need to *liberate seduction*. Not seduction in its unholy form, but we always want to seduce each other to our highest: we seduce each other in mad love to break the inappropriate boundary of our contraction, the boundary of our smallness, and we call each other to our greatness.

There is that great poem by Hafiz:

> *You are a divine elephant with amnesia*
> *Trying to live in an ant*

Hole.
Sweetheart, O sweetheart
You are God in
Drag!

This calling from our holy amnesia, this recovering of the memory of our true nature, is what holy seduction is: I love you so much that I call you to your gorgeousness. And then, when you step out of your narrowed boundary and into your fullness, into your beauty, then perhaps you'll open that beauty to me, and you'll invite me to open that beauty to you.

Something happens in the depth of devotion that is the very intention of Reality's manifestation. It's so intensely beautiful.

In some sense, the pre-tragic, level-one seduction is exactly the kind of seduction that Sally was saying we don't need in the world, when the woman is forced to seduce for the sake of her survival. We need to move beyond this. *To seduce* doesn't necessarily mean sexually. *To seduce* means: I got to put on the right makeup, and look the right way, and play the right part in order to survive. That was an evolutionary mechanism for a very long time. I submit to my role as a woman, and I have to seduce you. And that's the expectation, in all of its distressing disguises. Sally was saying, "Enough, enough, we need to move beyond that first level, that level one of loving to level two."

Level two is: *now we are partners.* We are equal partners, we are engaged intellectually, and we are in an appropriate, 50-50 exchange. We've removed that element of Eros and seduction in all those forms. We are meeting in this fullness of our mutuality, which is necessary and sacred and important. It's the next stage.

We moved from the pre-tragic to this next stage, but this next stage has something tragic in it. **The tragic is the loss of the living, breathing Eros of the heartbreak and heart opening, of the heart ecstasy, and the heart explosion of great love**—not in its narrow form, but in its widest, most stunning form. Mad devotion, Outrageous Love, awake and aflame as the beloveds turn towards each other, is the very intention of Reality.

Then Sally moved from the tragic, the utter rejection of that flame of Eros (it doesn't have a place because it's been too abused and too misappropriated; there is no place for that in the world) to level three, which is **the post-tragic**. In the frame of the Baal Shem Tov, the master of the Hasidic movement, we can say:

- The first level is *hachna'ah*, submission: "I submit to my role. That's what I have to do. I'm the seducer. That's how I survive." Then the feminine becomes furious with that role. She becomes angry.

- Next we get to the second role, and it's balanced, and it's appropriate, and it's mutual, but there is a bitterness on both the male and the female side, because we can't live in the world when we are not madly in love. To live in a world and *not* be madly in love—the suffering becomes unbearable. **The world is filled with unbearable suffering, and it's only the experience of being madly in love which clarifies my vision.** It's the tears of mad love which purify my heart and allow me to live, and to see, and to act, and to create. The Baal Shem Tov calls the second level of the tragic *Havdalah*, or "separation." We are still in the relationship, we are still in mutuality, we are still whatever the relationship is, but there is a separation: I am separated from myself, my true nature. I am separated from Reality, the inner nature of Reality. I am separated from the beloved.

- Finally, we move from the tragic to the post-tragic, which is *hamtakah*, which means radical sweetness, but not of the saccharine kind. It's not a saccharine, superficial sweetness. It is the experience that, every moment, Reality is seducing me. Every moment, Reality is waiting for me to seduce Reality.

In every conversation, we are seducing each other to our highest, to our most beautiful, so that desire and devotion merge.

We are talking about desire in all of its levels—desire to create, desire to give, desire to be in radical amazement, desire for precision, desire for insight, desire for gifting, desire for tenderness, desire for quivering aliveness, all of it. **Desire and devotion merge. I am at this higher level, where I am committed to always seducing you, like She, the Goddess, is committed to always seducing us.**

She sends us the depth of the color blue. We look into the blue and see that She is seducing us.

We look out the window here and see the dance of the tree, and the blue, and the green, and the brightness and the clarity of the day. We are just dazzled by the sunlight, and see that She is seducing us.

She is seducing us in every second—every taste, water in my mouth, an orange as I peel it. The ability to feel the ripple of communion that moves between people. An idea that clarifies in our mind.

She is seducing us in every second.

That's the true experience of Reality.

She is reaching for us.

Hakadosh Baruch Hu Mit'Aveh de-Shekhinah Mit'Aveh La'asot Dirato, Batachtonim: "She, the Goddess, lusts to seduce us into mad desire and devotion," as we emerge and explode into our irreducibly gorgeous uniqueness, and then unfold the vector of our unique seductions.

We seduce Reality to our highest. We create. We are the entrepreneurial expressions of the Universe's seductions. We seduce Reality, each other, ourselves, to our highest. **All creativity, all science, all entrepreneurship, all invention, all activism, all intellectual work, all teaching, all studying,**

all studenting—it's all seduction. In its most holy and most beautiful sense, it's alive.

That's the post-tragic.

We have to allow ourselves to be heartbroken because our hearts get broken again and again.

We have to be able to live in the unbearable suffering of Reality, but the unbearable suffering becomes, in and of itself, unbearably sweet when we step out of the narrow contraction of our self-boundary, where we wallow in sense of being perpetually hurt, and perpetually offended, and perpetually hypersensitive expressions of victimization and hyper recursive loops, reviewing the places where we've been injured and offended again and again, even forty years later.

We get lost in that way. We are not seduced beyond that. **The only way to engage the outrageous pain of my life is to love madly.** That's the Krishna-Radha realization. Ordinary love doesn't do it. It's only Outrageous Love. It's only this mad, wild love where I step out of myself and I love you, She, the Goddess.

She, the color blue.

She, the dazzling sunlight.

She, the animal that moves across my path that looks me in the eyes.

She, my many beloveds—from the mailman, to the clerk, to the waiter, to the waitress, all of it.

If I'm not madly in love, I'm insane. I cannot bear Reality. I am out of alignment with Reality. **The only sanity, which is the only alignment with the Reality, in which I feel welcome and at home in the universe, is when I love insanely.**

That's Krishna-Radha.

That's a world that's filled with seduction.

As we said yesterday, "We can only step into a meta-crisis, into the outrageous pain of it, through Krishna and Radha, through Outrageous Love, through all of the heartbreak and all the pain that opens up. My heart breaks and then my heart opens."

That's the tantric principle of non-rejection.

That experience, that feeling is not a mistake of evolutionary psychology. It's not that evolutionary psychology developed this human notion of love. Evolutionary psychology says that love is this uniquely human invention that's a social construction of a materialist universe.

No, no, no. **Outrageous Love is the very nature of Reality itself.** It's those lines from Yeats that Sally loved so much:

> *When such as I cast out remorse,*
> *So great a sweetness fills my breast.*
> *We can dance and we can sing.*
> *We are blest by everything.*

That's level three.

That's the post-tragic.

That's the nondual incarnation, my unique life of wild, Krishna-Radha ecstatic, Outrageous Love.

And only from there we can respond to the meta-crisis.

It's the energy of revolution.

It's the energy of possibility.

It's the energy of radical activism—evolution as love in action.

That's the sense we wanted to convey for Sally at her memorial.

HOPE AT THE EDGE OF THE TRAGIC: POST-TRAGIC KRISHNA-AND-RADHA

Here's a little postscript on the postscript.

It's beautiful to clarify love. **To clarify love is to participate in the evolution of love**.

In some sense, what we are understanding is that there's:

+ A pre-tragic Krishna and Radha
+ A tragic Krishna and Radha
+ A post-tragic Krishna and Radha

The pre-tragic Krishna and Radha is when we turn to love in all of its impossibilities, and we try and love anyways. We somehow think that it's going to work out in a particular way, and it's going to feel a particular way, and it's going to look a particular way. We reach for impossibilities, and we break all the rules, thinking that somehow it's going to come together exactly in the way thought it would be.

We are in the pre-tragic, and we think that within this lifetime, our picture-perfect dream we have as the fulfillment of our fantasy of loving will inevitably be fulfilled. That's the pre-tragic moment. It's rooted in the field of what we would call ordinary love that lives between human beings, which of course is not ordinary at all. It's unique, spectacular, and beautiful—but it's ordinary in the sense that, as in the classical forms of evolutionary psychology, it's a particular emergent, or a social construction, of the human world. It's filled with pathos and beauty, and it's essentially a pre-tragic form.

But of course, Krishna and Radha very rapidly becomes tragic. We dream of a possibility that can't be fulfilled. Our hearts are shattered. We open our hearts so wide in expectation of a particular result, and when that result doesn't happen, then our hearts hurt so achingly. We are so devastated by the tragic that our hearts close, and very often a person's heart never opens again. We opened our hearts so wide, it's so insanely painful so that we have to contract, we have to close.

We have met the tragic.

Krishna and Radha hasn't fulfilled itself.

The white picket fence didn't reveal itself, and we are dashed against the sharp, angular, painful embankments of the tragic. We feel shattered, and we somehow try to piece our lives and our hearts back together. But we never quite succeed, and our hearts close, and we never experience that sense of aliveness, that sense of yearning, that sense of sweetness, that sense of possibility, that sense of unimaginable, unutterable, unbearable joy.

That's the tragic.

That's where most people live.

That's the tragic of ordinary love.

And then, there is a place, there is a possibility, there is a portal, there is a poignancy, there is a potency, there is a promise that lives at the edges of the tragic, which is elicited by this deepening of love itself, where I begin to realize that love is not a coincidence of evolutionary psychology generating a social construction.

I realize that love is not only a human sentiment. It's the sentience of Cosmos itself.

Love is not a mere human sentiment. Love is the sentience, the nature, of Reality itself.

Love is the heart of existence itself. It is the animating force of all of Reality. It's not ordinary love. It's the Eros Value of Reality. It's Reality experiencing its own radical aliveness, Reality desiring ever deeper contact, Reality desiring new wholeness.

That quality of Eros is Outrageous Love.

When I love outrageously, my heart breaks again and again. But when my heart breaks, it breaks open. It doesn't break closed. It breaks good. It doesn't break bad.

Shever is the word for the shattering, the breaking. It's the breaking of the vessels that opens up Reality to a possibility that was unimaginable before.

The crisis of the broken heart becomes a driver of new love.

Our crisis births a new heart, a new possibility, a new poignancy, a new depth, and a new sweetness.

We've moved into Outrageous Love in which I am—in which I become, in which I embody—the generous radiance of Reality living uniquely through me. It's most personal, most intimate—and yet, it's also the personal of all of Reality flowing through me. There is a depth to that, a goodness to that, a truth to that, a beauty to that, which opens me into the post-tragic.

Now I am Krishna and Radha at the post-tragic.

Now the personal shattering and the personal heart opening participate in the larger field. My personal desire participates in the Field of Desire.

I realize there is no local desire.

I realize that the pulse of desire and devotion living in me are the pulse of desire and devotion, which is *She*—reaching, yearning for me in every second. It's the post-tragic Krishna and Radha.

That move, that evolution of consciousness that takes place through the Krishna and Radha archetype, the Krishna and Radha incarnation, is the evolution of She.

- ◆ It's the Evolution of Love.
- ◆ It's the Evolution of Eros.

- ◆ That's what we're reaching for.
- ◆ That's what we know to be true.

That's what we're pointing towards, and what Sally was pointing towards in her teaching on Krishna and Radha.

OUTRAGEOUS LOVE IS THE ULTIMATE PATH OF SELF-REALIZATION

What Sally is saying in her chapter on Krishna and Radha, what we are saying in the teaching of Outrageous Love, is that **this is the ultimate path of self-realization**.

This is the path to awakening.

This is the path to maturity.

This is the path to my full humanity, which is my full divinity.

The tantric principle of non-rejection is pointing to something. It's saying, "This is the most searing, the most radically amazing, the most ecstatic, erotic, the most radically alive human experience."

That's not a mere coincidence of evolutionary psychology. It's what the lineage would call *it'aruta dila'eila*, "arousal from above." It courses through me. That sense of the gift of it coursing through me is what the Greeks were talking about when they portrayed Cupid's arrow hitting you.

But it wasn't the arbitrary arrow of some cherubic god who was bored. **It is the radical gift of She.** It's arousal from above. It's this gift that courses through me, that dashes me against the rocks, and yet holds me closer than close in every second; there's no distance.

That experience, which lies at the very core of human existence, is of course the hidden path. I go from tragic to post-tragic when I realize that that radical, heart-rending, heart-agonizing, heart-ecstatic bliss is the path itself.

The tradition says, stay away from all that; it's dangerous. And we *should* stay away from the obsessive versions and the shadow versions, of course. But Chuang Tzu wasn't wrong when he said, *I come to speak dangerous words, I ask only that you listen dangerously.* It's the realization that to go the whole way in this lifetime is to risk it all.

To risk it all means risking my heart again and again, which I can't do from the place of ordinary love. Why would I risk my heart again and again? I'll fall. I'll be killed. I'll die. I can't bear it.

But in the Field of Outrageous Love—in the *chakal tapuchin kadishi*, "the field of holy apples"—in the Field of Eros Value, the only thing to do is to open my heart again and again and again, and keep receiving that gift of arousal from above.

When I'm willing to open my heart again and again, *She* opens her heart again and again, and pours into me unimaginable power. *Shakti* is power in Kashmir Shaivism. Sally always taught that.

She pours into me unimaginable *Shakti*, unimaginable power.

It's that power which transforms my essence. It's that power that's the only true one heart of the political that transforms Reality.

It's only by not turning away from the Krishna and Radha depths of my own life, only by not turning away from the heartbreak and heart opening of the Krishna and Radha in my life that I find my way.

That arousal from above is an invitation to my Unique Self, to my irreducible uniqueness, to my unique *tikkun.* The word *tikkun* means the unique way in which I make love to the Divine, in which I evolve God, in which I give my gift, and live a life that's mine to live.

Every place you've been, you needed to be.

My Krishna and Radha dynamic, my Krishna and Radha aliveness is not a coincidence of cosmos.

It's the intimate communion of *She*.

It's the invitation to my life.

It's not the place where I should *turn away*—it's the place where I *turn towards*.

INDEX

INDEX

VOLUME 20 — *The Path of Outrageous Love*

LIST OF EPISODES